A CONCISE HISTORY OF GLASS

A CONCISE HISTORY OF GLASS

Represented in
The Chrysler Museum Glass Collection

Nancy O. Merrill

THE CHRYSLER MUSEUM
1989

This publication was funded in part by a grant from The National Endowment for the Arts, a federal agency.

LCCN 88-63529
ISBN 0-940744-58-9
Copyright 1989 The Chrysler Museum
Olney Road and Mowbray Arch
Norfolk, Virginia 23510
(804) 622-1211
All Rights Reserved

Designed by Mary Lou Littrell
Color photography by Raymond Errett; black and white photography by Scott Wolff and Karen Twiddy.
Objects are not reproduced actual size.

Typeset in Bembo and Sabon by
Village Craftsmen/Princeton Polychrome Press,
Rosemont, New Jersey
Printed on Lustro Gloss stock by
Village Craftsmen/Princeton Polychrome Press,
Princeton, New Jersey

COVER: Compote
The New England Glass Company
Cambridge, Massachusetts. c. 1855

Contributions in support of this handbook were generously donated by:

John S. Cohen Foundation
Mr. and Mrs. Arthur Diamonstein
Janine R. Face
Constance W. Gregg
Dr. Gladstone Hill
Lenore Laibstain
Harriet N. Martin
Donna Dearth Morrison
Dr. and Mrs. Harry Pariser
Kathryn K. Porter
Dr. and Mrs. Arthur Siegel
Betty Harper Wyatt

TABLE OF CONTENTS

Introduction		9
Ancient Glass:	500 B.C. to 1000 A.D	13
Venetian Glass:	1500–1800	23
German Glass: Blown and Enameled	1500–1750	27
European Glass:	1700–1880	30
European Art Nouveau Glass:	1878–1920	47
European *Pâte de Verre* Glass:	1890–1970	76
European Glass:	1920 to the Present Day	86
American Blown and Mold-Blown Glass:	1790–1840	96
American Early Pressed and Lacy Glass:	1827–1860	106
American Pattern (Pressed) Glass:	1850–1875	120
American Cut, Engraved, and Enameled Glass:	1850–1880	128
American Art Glass:	1878–1900	137
American Glass of the Art Nouveau Period:	1895–1920	154
American Glass of the Art Deco Period:	1920–1939	177
American Studio Glass:	1960 to the Present Day	180
Catalogue Information		185
Bibliography		225

INTRODUCTION

The two most frequently asked questions about The Chrysler Museum are "who was Mr. Chrysler?" and "how did the Chrysler collection come to Norfolk?" The answers to both go back to the early years of this century.

Walter P. Chrysler, Jr. was born in Oelwein, Iowa in 1909, the son of the founder of Chrysler Motors. At the age of 13 and then living on Long Island, he bought his first work of art, a small watercolor of a nude in a landscape by Renoir. He took the sketch with him to preparatory school where it met an unhappy end. His dorm master declared the work obscene, ripped it up and threw it in the wastebasket. Mr. Chrysler, however, continued to collect what was then modern art. So pronounced were his tastes that a few years later he overheard a conversation between his parents. His mother was lamenting his taste in art and his father suggested a potential solution "Let's buy him a Gainsborough for Christmas." The portrait had no lasting effect on his love of contemporary art.

After attending Dartmouth College, Chrysler embarked on a grand tour of Europe where he met Picasso, Braque, Gris, Matisse, Leger and other avant garde artists. Soon he was buying works by each of them and at such a rate in the 1930s that by the end of that decade he had one of the finest collections of contemporary French art in the country. At the same time, however, he was purchasing works by contemporary Americans such as Burchfield, Marin, and Benton.

In the same decade he also purchased his first piece of glass, not knowing the medium would later become one of his passions. In the early 1930s as a young man he went to have lunch with the elderly Louis Comfort Tiffany whose estate was close to his parents. In the next year he purchased a small plate by Tiffany which he discovered in a New York second-hand store. By the time of his death in 1988 Chrysler had assembled one of the largest collections of Tiffany glass in the country.

In 1934 Chrysler founded the Air-Temp division of Chrysler Motors; the forerunner of air-conditioning. In the following year he became president of the Chrysler Building, a position he held until 1953. By the 1950s Chrysler's collecting had taken a radically new direction. No longer was he collecting contemporary French art. His contemporary purchases were all American by artists of the emerging abstract expressionist school. He was also branching into then totally overlooked fields—French 19th century academic painting, Italian baroque painting and sculpture, and art nouveau furniture, decorative arts, and glass.

In 1958 his collection had become so vast that Chrysler started his own museum in an old church in Provincetown, Massachusetts. A nearby small building held his rapidly expanding collection of glass, particularly Sandwich glass. Within a decade even these quarters proved to be inadequate, and Chrysler began to think of moving his collection to another city.

Norfolk was among a number of cities being considered. Not only did Norfolk already have a small museum, but it had sentimental ties. While Chrysler was in Norfolk during the second World War, he had met and later married Jean Outland, a native of the city. Negotiations were completed in 1971; the collection moved to its new home and the old Norfolk Museum of Arts and Sciences changed its name to The Chrysler Museum at Norfolk (later shortened to The Chrysler Museum).

The Museum had been founded by the Norfolk Society of the Arts in the 1920s. The Italian style building was designed by the firm of Peebles and Ferguson of Norfolk, and the first wing opened to the public in 1933. In 1967 the Houston wing, designed by William and Geoffrey Platt of New

York and Finlay F. Ferguson of Norfolk, opened. The wing provided an auditorium and additional exhibition space, but it in no way anticipated the historic event that was to happen four years later. To help alleviate the new space requirements of the Chrysler collection, the museum added a second wing in the 1970s designed by Williams and Tazewell Associates of Norfolk.

In the 1970s several other important collections came to the museum: the Henry Clay and Elise Hofheimer collection of Worcester porcelain, a large selection of the Bernice and Edgar Garbisch collection of American primitive painting, and Pre-Columbian art from Jack Tanzer. These, added to the continually expanding Chrysler collection, necessitated a further expansion in the 1980s. As construction was in progress, the Museum added two additional collections—the Dr. Edwin Pearlman collection of Maya art and the James Ricau collection of 19th century American sculpture.

In February of 1989 the latest changes in the building will be unveiled. These include a new wing designed by Hartman-Cox of Washington, D.C., and a nearly complete renovation of all the previously existing space. The heart of the new Chrysler Museum is the new court, created by putting a skylight over an existing courtyard. All of the paintings and sculpture are on the second floor and natural light has been reintroduced to the painting galleries.

The glass collection has been completely reinstalled in its new galleries on the first floor. Elroy Quenroe of Baltimore was the designer who worked closely with Nancy Merrill, Curator of Glass, and Gary Baker, Associate Curator of Glass. The installation includes small study galleries adjacent to the central core galleries. As a result a great many more of the 8,000 pieces in the glass collection are available for study.

This handbook illustrates only a fraction of the collection. It does provide a glimpse into the range and quality of the collection and is the first in a projected series of publications on the glass collection, so carefully assembled over fifty-six years by Walter P. Chrysler, Jr.

David W. Steadman
DIRECTOR

A CONCISE HISTORY OF GLASS

ANCIENT GLASS:
500 B.C.–1000 A.D.

The discovery of glassmaking occurred sometime about 3,000 B.C. in the Near East, probably in Mesopotamia and Syria, and glass beads and rods have been found from these early times in modern excavations by archaeologists. The expansion of Egyptian power into the Near East about 1500 B.C. brought the making of glass to the fore in Egypt as well, and glass vessels in various colors were created by craftsmen in Egypt and throughout the Near East using the core-forming technique.

The oldest glass objects in The Chrysler Museum are several tiny core-formed, luxury perfume and toilet oil containers made about the 6th to 4th century B.C. in the eastern Mediterranean (Syro-Palestinian area) in shapes which are small versions of Greek pottery. These were made by trailing molten glass over a shaped, clay core which was fashioned on the end of a metal rod. The glass, mostly dark blue, was decorated with contrasting colored glass threads smoothed into the surface and often pulled with a pointed tool into zigzag designs. Upon completion, the rod was removed, the vessel annealed (gradually cooled), and the clay-mixture core scraped out.

Cast and mosaic inlays represent another use of glass in the pre-Roman world. The inlay elements were used in combination and as substitutes for semi-precious stones as decoration for furniture, boxes, for wall tiles, on shrines and coffins, and as jewelry. The solid elements, such as a face and torso of human figures, were cast and mold-pressed into open molds, then removed and annealed. Subsequently they were polished and further defined by a sharp tool. The mosaics in the Museum collection, represented by the cobra *(uraeus)* (No. 2) and other examples of early glassmaking, are complex patterns made of countless colored glass rods assembled under heat to form an image. The rods were reheated and stretched, thus reducing their overall size. After annealing, the thinner (stretched) and longer rod was sliced to form multiple, identical mosaic elements. (This is the technique the Venetians later called *millefiori*, "a thousand flowers.") Mold-pressed (cast), tooled, and lathe-cut bowls and mosaic cups (small bowls) dating from about the 1st century A.D. are objects made much like inlays.

The major portion of the ancient glass in The Chrysler Museum was created after the discovery of glassblowing, which occurred about 50 B.C., in the Syrian-Palestinian area. The use of a hollow, metal blow-pipe enabled the glassmakers to manufacture quickly and at less cost all types of containers, jugs, and tableware for daily utilitarian use. The glassblowing technique soon spread throughout the Roman Empire and revolutionized glassmaking. Glass was now no longer strictly a luxury product for the use of the well-to-do.

No doubt the technique of blowing into a mold occurred about the same time. Using a full-sized, sectioned, terracotta mold, the glassmaker could achieve in one swift operation shape, decoration, and size. An outstanding example is the Ennion jar decorated with a mold-blown inscription in Greek: "Ennion Made Me" (No. 4). Several small novelty bottles and ointment containers in the form of dates (No. 10a), several "Janus" double-headed flasks, and a beaker covered with a pattern of lotus buds (No. 10b) are among such vessels.

Trailings of glass threads, rigaree, and boss-like rosettes, often in a contrasting color, added interesting decoration to the free-blown glass. Cutting as decoration was a separate operation carried out after the vessel was cold. A large cup/bowl cut with an intricate geometric pattern (No. 12) and several jars with incised bands are examples of this technique. The most important Roman cutting can be seen in the cameo fragments (No. 5). These are from a vessel or plaque which was cameo-carved from four layers of contrasting colored glass. The carving reveals the desired design in relief; subtle shading is controlled by the depth of cutting.

The iridescence now decorating many ancient glasses was not original but represents a chemical deterioration of the glass surface which has occurred from long burial in damp soil. (This corroded, iridescent glass inspired Tiffany and others to reproduce similar effects artificially at the end of the 19th century.)

The final category of Ancient Glass is that made from the 6th to 10th century, after the collapse of the Roman Empire, in the Byzantine, Persian, and Islamic worlds. The early blown and tooled dromedary flask (No. 13) reflects the importance of this animal in the desert regions. Facet and linear cutting in stylized patterns are represented on bottles (No. 15) and on a beaker (No. 14) with a cameo design in green. Several bottles and flasks are mold-blown and tooled with various overall patterns.

With the collapse of the Roman Empire in the 5th Century, glassmaking reverted to a primitive level in Europe. In the Near East and Byzantium, however, the advanced skills and imaginative handling of glass by trained artisans continued to flourish. The heritage of Rome and its predecessors was saved by the Near East and Islam, and in time Europe would learn from the higher civilization of the Near East where learning and craftsmanship had never been lost as it had been in the former Roman Empire in the West.

Virtually all the present techniques of glassmaking in use today were known to the ancients. The tools have not changed essentially since the discovery of glassblowing, although on a technical level furnaces and chemistry have been improved. Only mechanical pressing, acid-etching, and sandblasting are 19th– and 20th– century accomplishments.

Glass in the Near East and Egypt before 100 B.C.

1. Glass Core-Formed Vessels
Eastern Mediterranean
5th–2nd Centuries B.C.

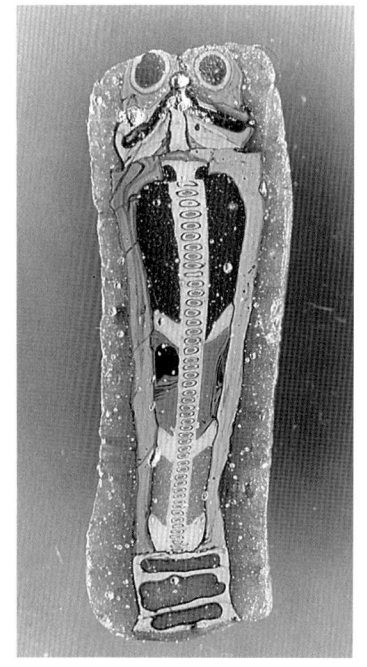

2. Glass Mosaic Inlay—Uraeus (Cobra)
Probably Alexandria (Ptolemaic Egypt)
4th–1st Century B.C.

Glass of the Roman Empire
100 B.C.–c. A.D. 500

3. Cup
Roman Empire, probably Alexandria, Egypt
Mid-first century A.D.

4. "Ennion" Bowl
Roman Empire, probably Sidon, Syria
c. A.D. 50

5. Cameo Fragments (Joining)
Roman Empire, probably Italy
1st Century A.D.

6. Flask and Cups
Roman Empire, probably Eastern
Mediterranean or Alexandria, Egypt
Late 1st Century B.C.

17

7. Krater
Roman Empire, Eastern Mediterranean
3rd Century A.D.

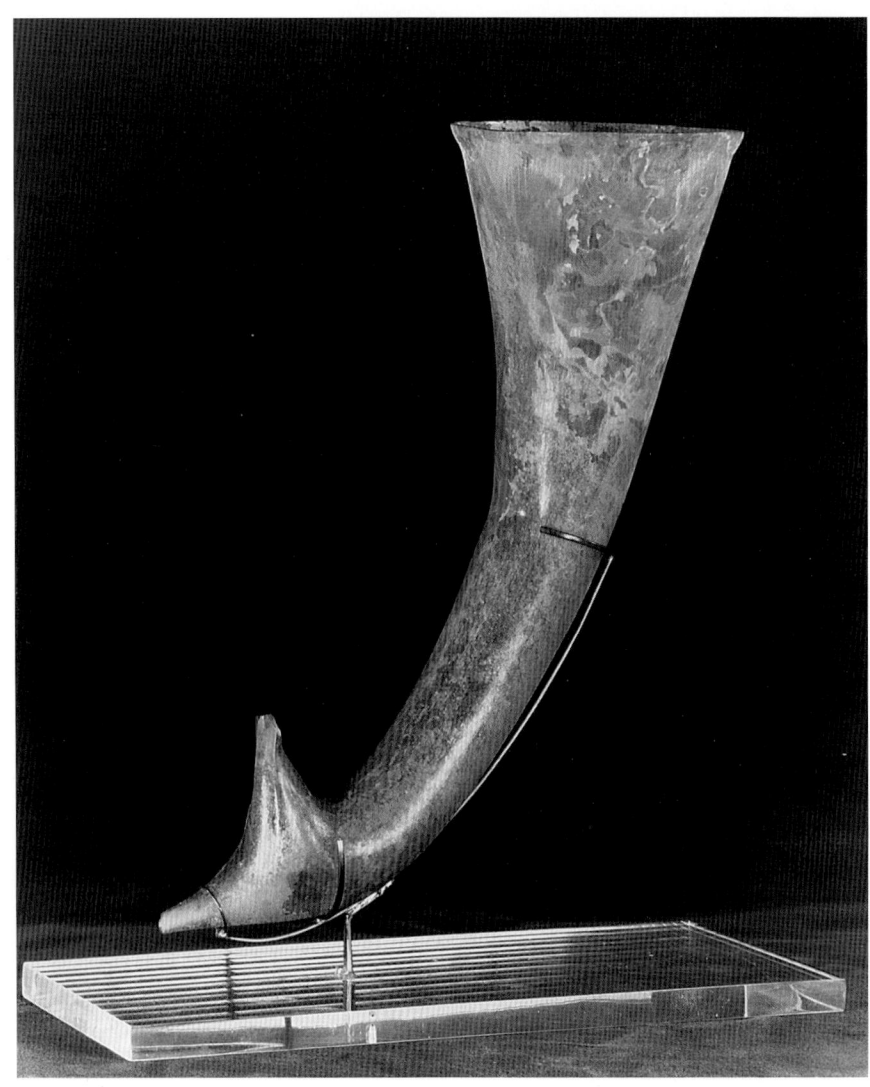

8. Rhyton
Roman Empire
3rd Century A.D.

9. Roman Deity Beaker
Roman Empire, possibly Syria
Early 2nd Century A.D.

10. Mold Blown Glass
Roman Empire, Eastern
Mediterranean
2nd–7th Century A.D.

11. Ceremonial Drinking Vessel
Roman Empire
3rd Century A.D.

12. Bowl
Roman Empire
4th–5th Century A.D.

13. Animal "Dromedary" Flask
Syria—Iran
6th Century A.D.

21

Glass of the Islamic Near East Before A.D. 1000

14. Cup
Islamic (Possibly Iran)
c. 9th–10th Century

15. Flask
Persian (Iran)
c. 9th–10th Century

VENETIAN GLASS:
1500–1800

All but the crudest forms of glassmaking were lost to Europe after the Teutonic invasions of the 5th and succeeding centuries, and the major European centers of glass fabrication disappeared. On the islands of the Venetian lagoon in northern Italy, however, the making of glass continued, at first around the Rialto area of Venice and then on the islands of Murano. After the year 1000, the Crusades brought Venice into contact with the ancient traditions of glassmaking which Islam had inherited from the Roman Empire and which had never been lost. The Crusaders brought back new skills for Venetian glassmakers, and thus the creation of exquisite glass was able to develop in Venice. Delicate objects in clear glass *(cristallo)*, glass laced with white filagree patterns, fanciful glasses with dragon stems and colorful "wings" made Venetian artistry much sought after by kings, nobles, and eventually wealthy merchants. So popular was Venetian glass that her craftsmen were often lured to other European cities to make glass *à la façon de Venise* despite the ban and threat of assassination made by the Venetian Signoria against craftsmen who might spread Venetian production secrets abroad.

16. Footed Bowl
Venice, Italy
c. 1500

17. Bowl
Venice, Italy
16th Century

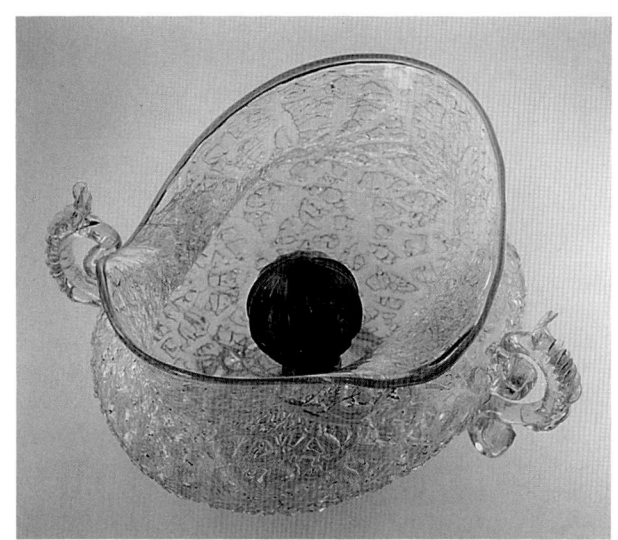

18. Bowl
Venice, Italy
Early 17th Century

19. Façon de Venice Goblet
Holland or Belgium
17th Century

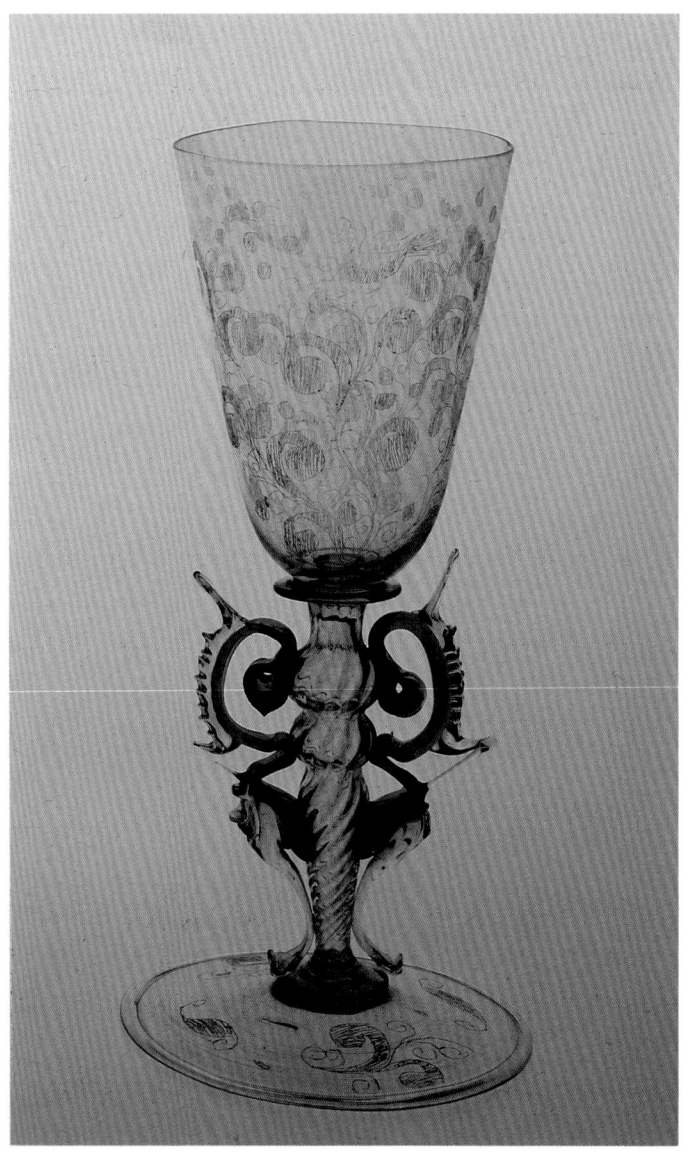

20. Beaker/Tumbler
Venice, Italy
Second half of
the 18th Century

GERMAN GLASS: BLOWN AND ENAMELED
1500–1750

One of the great glassmaking centers of northern Europe in Roman times had centered around Cologne, Germany. The destruction to learning and the crafts which ensued from the Teutonic invasions, from the 5th Century on, reduced glass centers like Cologne to a shadow of their former self. The art of making clear glass disappeared, and styles became heavy and unimaginative. With the revival of learning and contact with the heritage of the past, among the more positive aspects of the barbarian attacks on the Near East by the Crusaders, the art of making glass gradually revived in northern Europe. In addition, the example of Venetian glassmaking skills encouraged German glassmakers to create more original and fanciful, as well as useful, objects in glass once more. German glass still retained the greenish tint of its medieval *Waldglas* (glass originally made in the forest from potash), for the knowledge of how to clarify glass for a clear and untinted substance was not yet understood north of the Alps (see No. 21).

Three examples of Central European ceremonial drinking vessels in the collections of the Chrysler Museum illustrate the most popular enameled vessels made during the 200 years beginning in the mid-sixteenth century. These are the *Reichsadlerhumpen*, the *Ochsenkopfhumpen*, and the *passglas*, all making use of enameling. The two former tended to be tall, wide, cylindrical vessels which could hold a goodly amount of beer or wine; the latter was also a tall glass but generally with a more limited capacity. Decorating glass with enameling was especially inspired by the colorful Venetian imports commissioned by the aristocracy and by wealthy German merchants for their personal use as well as for their social aggrandizement. The rise of this new merchant class, with their desire for decorated glass objects, was to lead to a revival of the glass industry north of the Alps and a consequent decline in reliance on Venice for glass.

The political "Holy Roman Empire" theme, symbolizing the Empire's unity, was a popular design on the *Reichsadlerhumpen* ("Imperial Eagle Beaker") patterned on various early wood-cuts and engravings of the crowned, double-headed, Imperial eagle with outstretched wings covered with the shields of the fifty-six member states and the coat-of-arms of the ecclesiastical and secular electors.

The *Ochsenkopf* (Ox-head) enameled *humpen*, here illustrated, pictures a popular allegorical theme of the Franconia region. The illustration of a pine tree covered mountain, a church, animals, and the four rivers are praised on the reverse with an inscription saluting the mountain's riches and requesting their protection. Thus more of a "folk" theme can often be found on such drinking vessels.

The third ceremonial communal vessel is the *passglas* marked with enameled measuring bands and often images of people or animals. These glasses were particularly popular with the various guilds. A tall, cylindrical glass would have enameled bands placed equi-distant on it. As the glass was passed from hand to hand, each drinker had to drink just to the next line on the glass — or, if he missed, he had to drink on to the next line, much to the amusement of his companions. The *passglas* from the Museum collection, illustrated hereafter, is enameled with the trade insignia of a butchers' guild — with an appropriate statement toasting their sociability.

These popular themes fit the ample surfaces available on the large Germanic vessel forms. The largest illustrated, the *Reichsadlerhumpen* (No. 22), is slightly under one foot high with a capacity of about 3½ quarts. All are brightly enameled in a primitive folk style.

21. Roemer
The Netherlands
c. 1680

22. Reichsadler Humpen
Saxony, Germany
1679

23. Ochsenkopf Humpen
Franconia, Germany
1729

24. Passglas
Saxony, Germany
1713

EUROPEAN GLASS:
1700–1880

The Peace of Westphalia in 1649 ended the Thirty Years War which had wracked the Continent of Europe and set back its economy for generations. Gradually the nations returned to normal, trade revived, and industry began to flourish. In particular, the glass industry was able to rebuild its markets and to expand.

The dependency on Venice and its artisans declined as the new merchant class created glass factories which could serve an expanding economy and developing artistic tastes. In particular the discovery that the addition of lime to the formula for glassmaking could create a more sparkling and less fragile product proved a boon to the industry. A clearer and stronger glass, somewhat like the lead glass being made in Britain, could now be engraved and could be cut, and a new fashion for goblets (*Pokal* in German) developed. These potash-lime glasses became exceedingly popular from 1710 on among the well-to-do in the Courts and the merchant class.

The glassmakers of Nuremberg were among the first to produce engraved goblets, and the craftsmen in Silesia (sometimes German, sometimes Polish, depending on the vagaries of history and politics) also began to engrave and cut goblets, their best products being developed in the first quarter of the 18th century. The glasshouse in Potsdam (Berlin) was another noted producer of fine goblets in the German style. As the 1700s progressed, Bohemian glass craftsmen began to power their stone cutting wheels by water power, and newer, deeper cuts were made possible in the thick bowls of fanciful goblets.

One additional technique is of note in the 1700s, that of *Zwischengold* glass. This ancient technique, once practiced by the Romans but lost after the fall of the Roman Empire, was rediscovered about 1725, allegedly at a Bohemian monastery. Soon the most desired of glasses, its double-walled vessel encapsulated a design created in a thin foil of gold or silver, a truly luxurious glassware.

The art of engraving was carried to further heights in the Netherlands in the mid-century when diamond-stipple engraving enabled artists to create portraits or scenes on the surface of a glass with a diamond-pointed tool. Thus diversity and artistry set a new standard for glassmakers and their patrons as the 18th century developed.

25. Flask Covered Goblet
Silesia
c. 1725

26. Covered Goblet
Potsdam
c. 1730

27. Covered Goblet
Potsdam
c. 1740

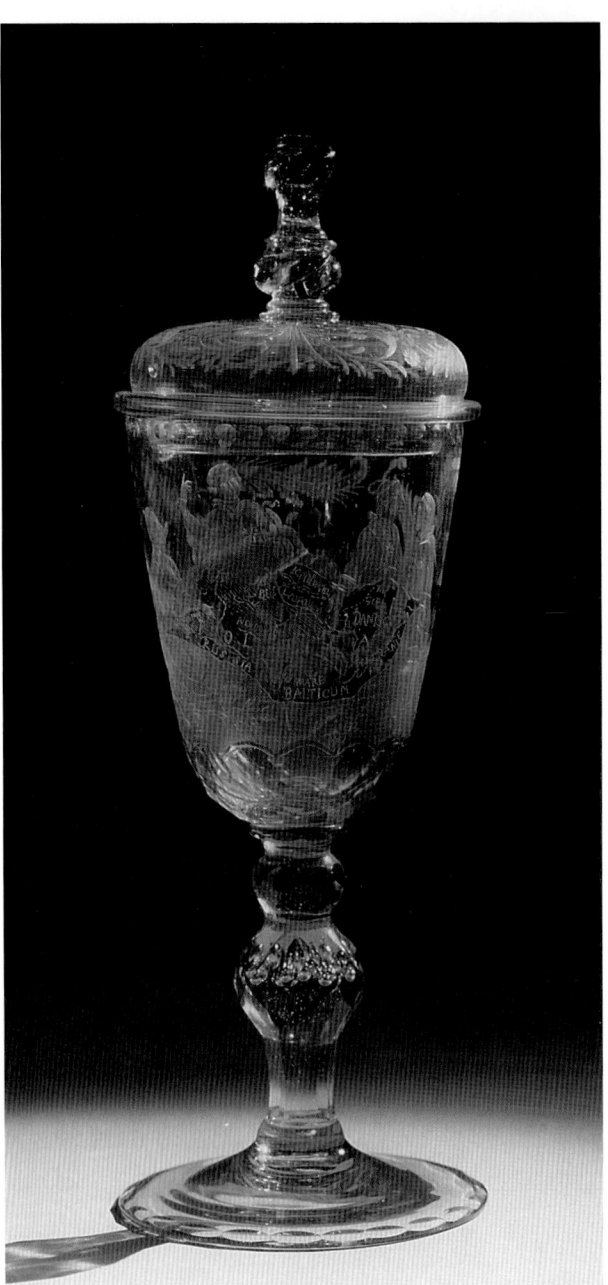

29. Covered Goblet
Silesia
c. 1773

28. Covered Goblet
Bohemia
Late 17th century

30. Covered Goblet
Saxony
c. 1740

Zwischengold Glass

The technique of creating two glasses in which one would fit inside of the other glass, with a design in gold or silver foil placed between the two vessels, was a Roman technique of glassmaking which was lost after the 500s in Europe. Rediscovered about 1725, the technique called for great skill: the two glasses had to fit tightly, and the foil had to be placed between the vessels without damage to the design. Then the tops of the two glasses had to be sealed. A luxurious glass, they were rare in their time and are even rarer now since the seal on many such glasses has broken, permitting moisture and deterioration to set in.

In Austria, Johann Josef Mildner was noted for his *Zwischengoldglas* medallions. He would cut out spaces in a glass to receive the medallions done in gold-leaf and red lacquer. Active in this technique from 1787 to 1808, he created portraits, landscapes, and still life scenes.

31. Zwischengold Tumbler
Bohemia
c. 1730–1740

33

32. Zwischengold Covered Goblet
Bohemia
c. 1730

33. Tumbler
J. J. Mildner
Gutenbrunn, Austria
1793

Diamond-Point Stippling

The use of a pointed diamond at the end of a rod enabled engravers to strike the glass with the point of the diamond, thereby leaving a slight chip which would reflect light. In the hands of a master craftsman, realistic portraits or idyllic scenes could be created on the surface of the glass in this manner. Two of the most noted artists in the Netherlands in this field were Franz Greenwood who worked from 1720 to 1755 and David Wolff whose diamond-stippled work took place primarily between 1774 and 1795. Using English lead glass, a more receptive medium for such stippling than Continental potash-lime glass, they had many followers, and, in general, unsigned diamond-stippled glass is often referred to as "Wolff-style" glass.

34. Goblet
The Netherlands
c. 1780–1785

35. Goblet
The Netherlands
Wolff-styled diamond-stipple engraving
c. 1785

36. Goblet
The Netherlands
Wolff-styled diamond-
stippled engraving
c. 1770–1775

37. Goblets
The Netherlands
Wolff-styled diamond-
stipple engraving
c. 1775–1785; 1790

38. Goblet
The Netherlands
c. 1775

39. Goblet
The Netherlands
c. 1810

37

Biedermeier-Style Glass

The end of the Napoleonic era, another of those decades of war and turmoil in Europe, led once more to a revival of glassmaking and glass engraving in Bohemia. Named for verses and drawings of a satirical nature, which lampooned the self-satisfied bourgeoisie of a newly conservative Europe, the Biedermeier style ran from 1820 to 1840. In England, its equivalent is represented by the early Victorian era in furniture and design. The most noted hallmarks of Biedermeier glass were color, a massiveness to the object, and, in general, an "over-done" quality.

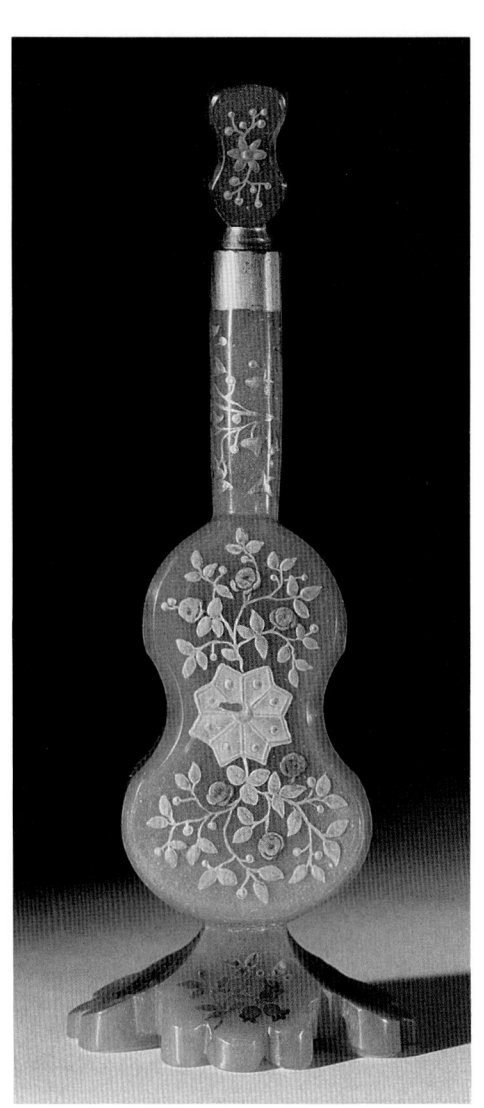

41. Cologne Bottle
Bohemia
c. 1850

40. Tumbler
Bohemia
Biedermeier-style
c. 1840

38

Franz Zach

The interest in the past, which archeological discoveries engendered in the 18th century and into the 19th century, saw a revival of Roman styles in everything from women's dress to architecture. In the field of glass, an interest in cameo glass was re-awakened, and although some of the finest of the cameo glass of the 19th century was produced in England, in the hands of Franz Zach in Bohemia such Roman techniques were employed in the glass artist's studio to fine effect.

42. Vase
"Ariadne and the Panther"
Possibly engraved by F. P. Zach
Northern Bohemia
c. 1850

43. Venetian
19th Century

The Venetian Revival
1859–1880

Glassmaking in Venice had a revival in the 19th century, and interest in Venetian techniques of the past were employed as well in glasshouses in France by Georges Bontemps, using the *latticino* technique, and at the glassworks of Count Harrach in Bohemia. In England, Apsley Pellatt also tried his hand at Venetian techniques, and some of the objects which he exhibited at the Great Exhibition of 1851 in Hyde Park used the *latticino* style.

The revivial of *latticino* glass gave an impetus to the production of paperweights, a field in which the French were to excel in the 19th century. In Venice, a number of factories fed this new interest by their production of *millefiori* canes. Moreover, Antonio Salviati opened a factory in Venice in 1859, and his reproductions of antique Venetian glass became popular at once both in Europe and America. A new day was dawning for Venetian factories.

44. Decanter–(one of a pair)
Cork Glass Co.
Cork, Ireland
c. 1783–1818

45. Bowl
Anglo-Irish,
Early 19th Century

English and Irish Glass
1780–1880

Glass had been produced in England during the years of its Roman occupation, and glassmaking probably never died out entirely—although the recorded evidence of such continued work is scanty. A native industry did develop from the 12th century on, but it was in the years of the 16th century when the influence of Venice was felt throughout northern Europe that glassmaking can be traced with some certainty in England. Some of the finest pieces of English glass were made in London by Jacopo Verzelini during Queen Elizabeth's reign. The unsettling years of the 17th century, with its political/religious antagonisms and confrontations, set back the further development of English glass. It was not until the Restoration, after 1665, the founding of the Royal Society, and a return to the main stream of European intellectual and cultural life that glassmaking was able to grow again.

The development of lead glass by George Ravenscroft in 1675 set English glassmaking in a new direction, and soon English lead glass was one of the foremost products of the glass world.

Glassmaking in Ireland in the 18th–19th centuries was the result of the English tax laws. In 1780 the tax on the exporting of glass from Ireland was lifted by the English government, and a number of English glassmakers moved their production to Ireland to avoid the heavy taxes they had to pay on their production within England. The situation changed in 1825 when an excise tax was levied on Irish-made glass as well. Much of Irish glass during this period cannot be distinguished from English-made glass.

41

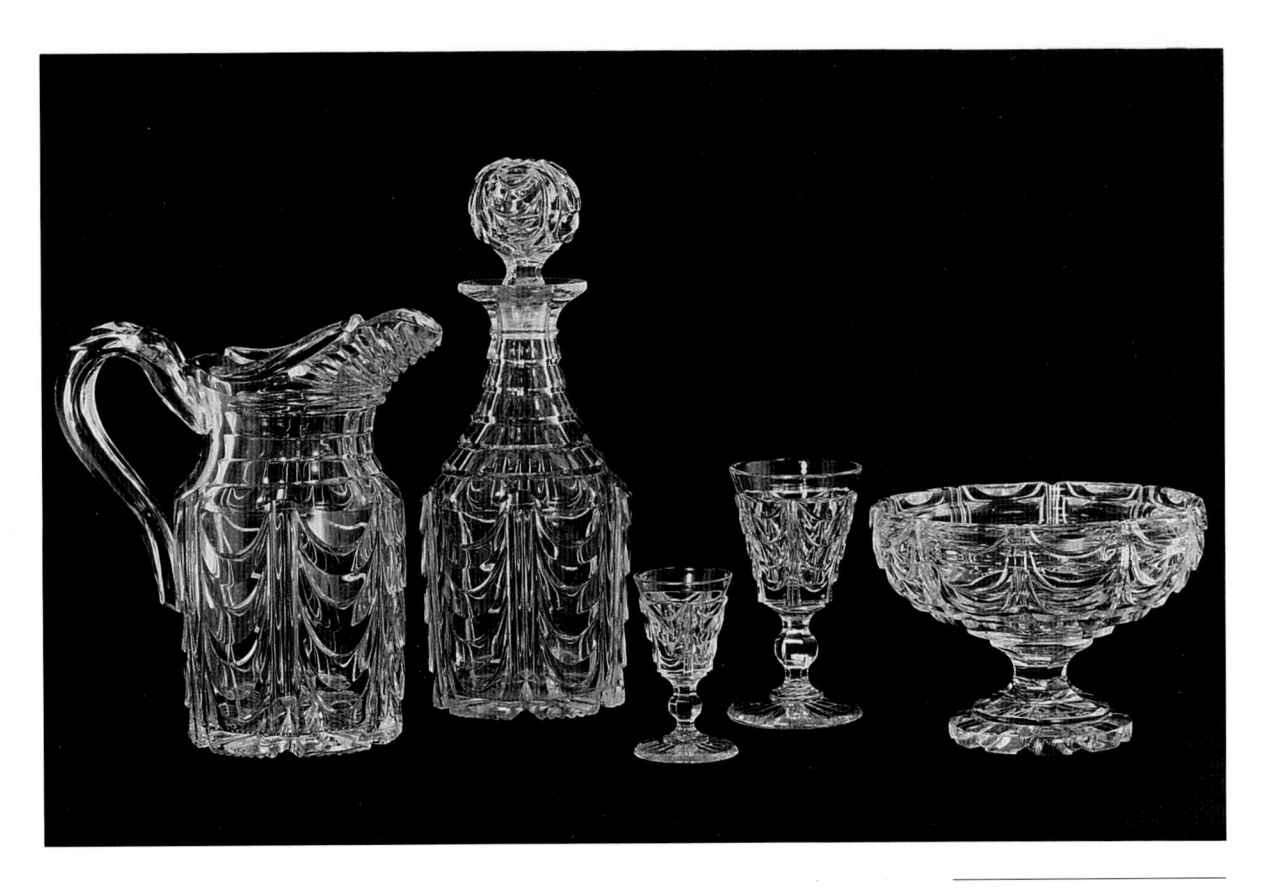

46. Cut Glass
Cork, Ireland
c. 1825 (George IV Period)

Cut Glass

The cutting wheel, a Roman-device, was again one of those techniques which had been lost to Europe until it was revived in Bohemia in the late 17th century. The use of the cutting wheel soon reached England, and English and Irish glass cutters developed an ability in decorating glass which was the envy of other countries. So successful was late 18th century Irish cut glass that its patterns were copied on the Continent. English and Irish glass cutters were often enticed to other countries, to Norway, Germany, the United States, and elsewhere, and Anglo-Irish style and lead glass became all the rage in the late 18th and early 19th centuries.

Cameo Glass

Cameo-cut glass was but one of the luxury glasses of ancient Rome, and it was one of the many specialized forms of glassmaking which disappeared with the fall of the Roman Empire. The rediscovery of Roman antiquities in the 18th century, and, in particular, the Portland Vase which came to England in 1783 awakened an interest in cameos once more.

It was in the area of Stourbridge, on the western edge of the English industrializing Midlands that cameo-cutting was to be revitalized, and the names of John Northwood and George Woodall were to become famous for their craftsmanship in cameo work as the 19th century wore on. So great was the demand for cameo glass that in the 1880s the glasshouses in Stourbridge turned to the use of acid for faster cutting of thinner layers of the white glass cased onto a blue (or other color) background. The firms of Stevens and Williams, Thomas Webb, and Hodgetts and Richardson were the noted companies which turned out cameo glass on a commercial basis.

47. English Cameo Vases
Joseph Locke
Hodgetts, Richardson and Son
Stourbridge, England
1877

47a. Close-up of incised mark on "Unhappy Child"

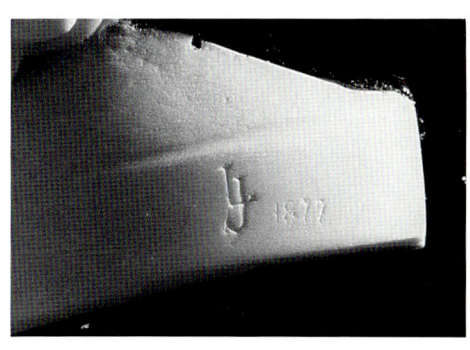

48. Antarctic Cameo Vase
Designed and carved by
George Woodall
Thomas Webb and Sons
Stourbridge, England
c. 1909–1910

Art Glass

The competition among glass firms, particularly in light of the heightened interest in glass which came from the numerous "World Expositions" of the late 19th century, demanded new types of glass and novelty on a continuing basis. The use of color became a primary concern of glassmakers in order to attract customers, and one of the approaches they found useful was to employ heat-sensitive glass. Heat-sensitive glass could be shaded from one color to another as heat was applied to the glass during its production. Joseph Locke was one of the originators of this new approach, and his Amberina glass, a clear amber glass which became a deep ruby color when reheated at the furnace (due to gold in solution in the glass batch) became most popular. His departure for the United States was a loss to the English glass world, for his inventiveness was now a part of the American story.

49. Vase
English
Stourbridge Area
c. 1880

50. Vase
Stevens & Williams
Brierley Hill Glass Works
Stourbridge, England
c. 1888–1890

45

Reflections of Art Nouveau

Although the Art Nouveau movement was primarily a French development, the same currents of artistic thought which inspired French glassmakers were available to English glass producers as well. The Art Nouveau style began in France in the late 1880s and early 1890s, and it is interesting to see how some of the new concepts began to be reflected in glass from the Stourbridge area. One of the more inventive glass designers in Stourbridge was Frederick Carder, who, like Joseph Locke, was to transfer his genius to the United States.

51. Vase
Stevens & Williams
Brierley Hill Glass Works
Stourbridge, England
c. 1890–1895

52. Vase
Stourbridge Area, England
Designed and enameled by Jules Barbe
c. 1900

EUROPEAN ART NOUVEAU GLASS: 1878–1920

The end of the nineteenth century saw a new development in the field of art, and particularly in artistic glass production. Known as the Art Nouveau movement, it took its name from a gallery which showed the work of contemporary, and, at first, often unrecognized artists of the day, a shop entitled *La Maison de l'Art Nouveau* which opened in 1895 in Paris.

The movement had its roots early in this last decade of the century when artists turned toward the past and to nature for inspiration. Motifs from the medieval past and stylistic approaches of other lands, particularly of the Near and Far East found their way into the artists' ateliers. Intrigued as well by the virility and force within nature, the elaborate, twirling, and twisting tendrils of plants which appear in the designs of many of the artists of the day show another aspect of the Art Nouveau style.

Various techniques of glassmaking were employed, and forms which were often in a less than "classical" mode than had hitherto been associated with glass were to come into use. In the hands of masters like Gallé, twisted and even shapeless forms became artistic when associated with nature. The decorative style was emphasized, many of the floral motifs appearing in relief and in enameling. Experimentation with cameo glass in double and triple layers was frequently used, and eventually a new type of glass made of pulverized glass (*pâte de verre*) was mastered by a handful of more adventurous glassmakers. The *pâte de verre* glass, because of its individualistic nature, is listed separately at the end of the section on Art Nouveau/*Jugendstil* glass.

Art Nouveau in France:

Emile Gallé
Nancy, France
(1846–1904)

Emile Gallé, the pre-eminent French Art Nouveau glass artist and designer, the amateur painter, botanist, philosopher, and mineralogist became artistic director of his father's ceramic and glass firm in 1874. He developed a fresh, new, and original style based on nature and using unconventional exotic shapes and decorations.

The Gallé Glass Collection in The Chrysler Museum numbers about 180 objects beginning with an early (c. 1873) colorless, cut casket enameled in an historical style. Other enameled vessels are of the type exhibited in the 1878 *Exposition Universelle*, in Paris, when Gallé first received public recognition. An interesting group (c. 1884) contains pieces which are acid-cut, carved, and enameled in medieval designs inspired by *La ballade des dames du temps jadis* by François Villon. Several 1880s items are enameled in Persian designs whose inspiration can be traced to the glass by Brocard.

The Museum collection includes a unique bowl, a *verrerie parlante* ("talking glass") engraved with a mournful poem by Maurice Rollinat. The mark on the bottom of the foot is *Emile Gallé/Nancy/ 1892* around the outline of a snail. Another object, marked on the bottom *1892* with a blossom carved in high relief, is the soft blue-green Columbine Vase which is probably the one in the much illustrated painting of Gallé by Prouvé. The Columbine Vase is part of a limited edition, and the Museum selection is marked *1892 Emile Gallé fecit* and is a major example of Gallé's work. Other objects made in limited editions are the Seahorse Ewer and the Dragonfly Bowl. Even the "standard" Gallé glass which is acid-cut and carved on two or three layer blanks reveals the creativity of Gallé production.

53. Bowl
Emile Gallé
Cristallerie d'Emile Gallé
Nancy, France
c. 1878–1884

Emile Gallé died in 1904 and, from then until the closing of the factory in 1931, the work of the company was carried on under the direction of various family members. Eventually the designs lost their appeal for the public as tastes for the Art Nouveau became jaded. Nonetheless, large post-World War I vases called "blowouts" do reveal a new fashion for Gallé glass, using what is almost an Art Deco approach. This is especially true of the Elephant Vase.

The signature/marks on the objects are interesting, and few are alike. The first vessels are engraved and usually gilded with *E. Gallé Nancy*. Later some read *Cristallerie d'Emile Gallé/Nancy/modèle et décor déposés* and are also marked around a blossom or leaf, repeating the decoration of the vessel. There is one marked *Noël Series* ("Christmas Series") and one *Etude* ("Study"); several include the *E ǂ G* (Emile Gallé) and the cross of Lorraine. The cameo objects, acid-cut and carved, are marked in relief on the side, usually a planned part of the design and often with an additional mark on the bottom. An unusual mark appears on the cut and engraved bowl *Escalier de Cristal Paris* on both the gilded bronze stand and the glass. The glass is also engraved *Emile Gallé/Nancy 315* together with a deeply engraved pitcher marked *E.G.*

The Museum collection is fortunate in being able to offer a broad review of Gallé glass production.

54. Vase
Emile Gallé
Cristallerie d'Emile Gallé
Nancy, France
c. 1878–1884

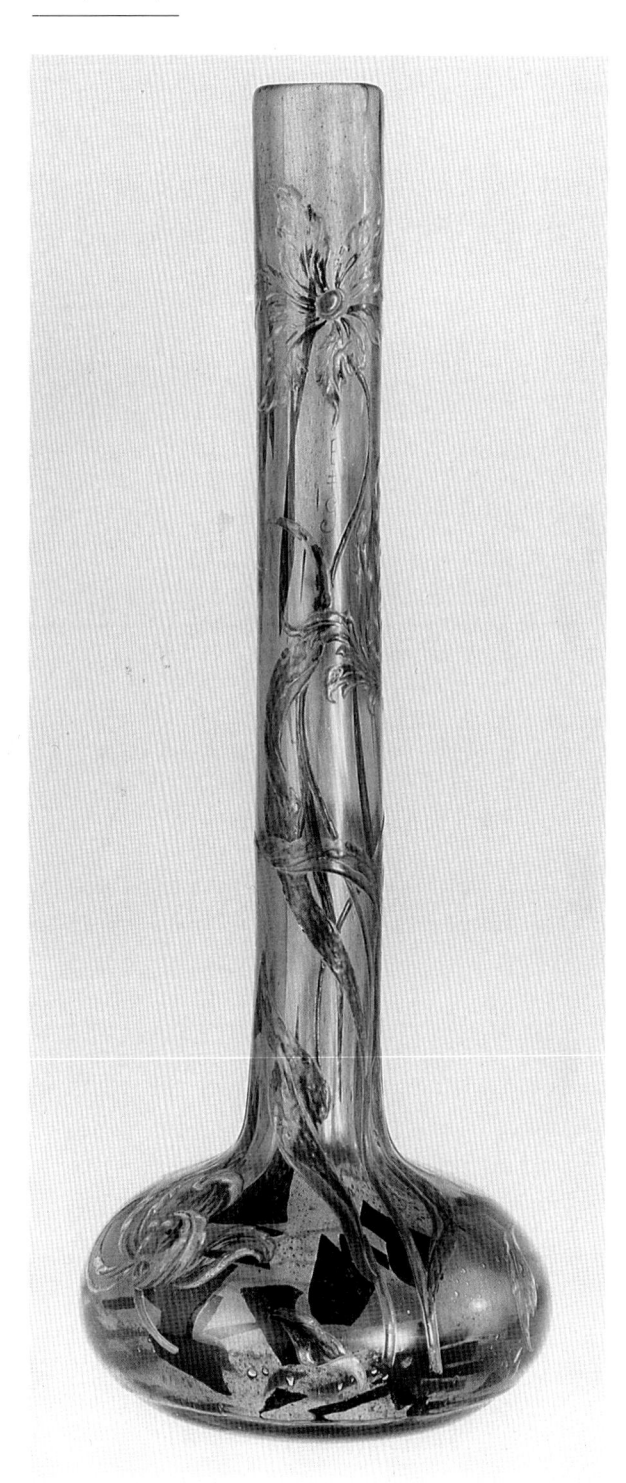

55. "Marine" Bowl in Gilded Bronze Stand
Emile Gallé
Cristallerie d'Emile Gallé
Nancy, France
c. 1884

55a. Close-up of Mark

56. Enameled and Etched Vase
Emile Gallé
*Cristallerie
d'Emile Gallé*
Nancy, France
c. 1885–1900

57. Medieval Designs
Emile Gallé
*Cristallerie
d'Emile Gallé*
Nancy, France
c. 1884–1890

51

58. Vase
Emile Gallé
*Cristallerie
d'Emile Gallé*
Nancy, France
c. 1889

59. Dragonfly Bowl
Emile Gallé
*Cristallerie
d'Emile Gallé*
Nancy, France
c. 1889

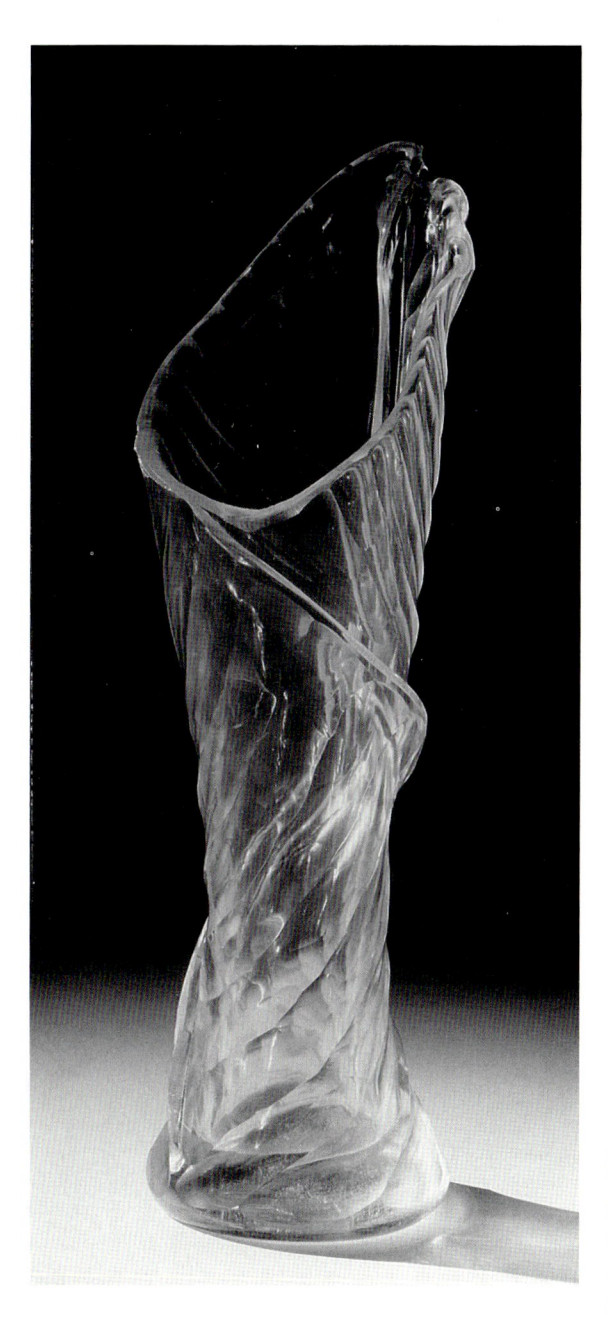

60. Arum Lily Flower Form Vase
Emile Gallé
Cristallerie d'Emile Gallé
Nancy, France
c. 1889–1897

61. "Marine" Bowl
Emile Gallé
Cristallerie d'Emile Gallé
Nancy, France
c. 1889–1895

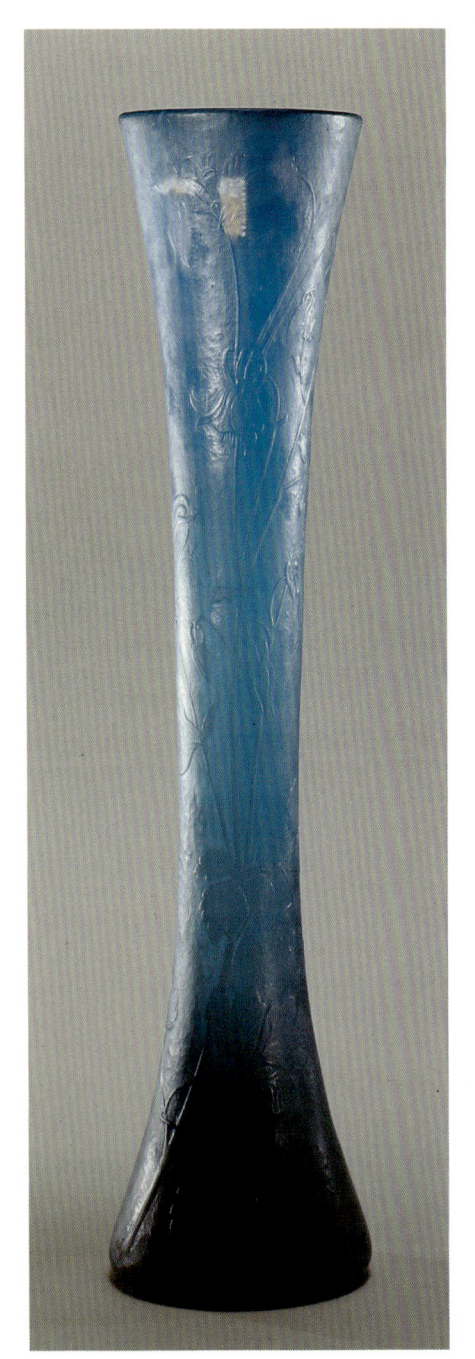

62. Vase
Emile Gallé
*Cristallerie
d'Emile Gallé*
Nancy, France
1892

63. Bowl
Emile Gallé
*Cristallerie
d'Emile Gallé*
Nancy, France
1892

64. Vase
Emile Gallé
*Cristallerie
d'Emile Gallé*
Nancy, France
1895

65. Pitcher
Emile Gallé
*Cristallerie
d'Emile Gallé*
Nancy, France
c. 1898

66. Vase
Emile Gallé
*Cristallerie
d'Emile Gallé*
Nancy, France
c. 1895

68. Vase
Emile Gallé
*Cristallerie
d'Emile Gallé*
Nancy, France
c. 1898

67. Nautilus Bowl
Emile Gallé
*Cristallerie
d'Emile Gallé*
Nancy, France
c. 1895

69. Vases
Emile Gallé
*Cristallerie
d'Emile Gallé*
Nancy, France
c. 1900–1904

70. Vase
Emile Gallé
*Cristallerie
d'Emile Gallé*
Nancy, France
c. 1900

71. Seahorse Ewer
Emile Gallé
*Cristallerie
d'Emile Gallé*
Nancy, France
c. 1901

72. Dragonfly Bowl
Emile Gallé
*Cristallerie
d'Emile Gallé*
Nancy, France
c. 1902

73. "Elephant" Vase
Emile Gallé
*Cristallerie
d'Emile Gallé*
Nancy, France
c. 1925

Verrerie d'Art de Lorraine
Burgun, Schverer & Cie.
Meisenthal
Alsace-Lorraine (Germany)
(1711–1969)

Burgun Schverer was a leading Alsace-Lorraine glass house from 1711 to 1969. It was here that Emile Gallé received his glass training and, although in German-occupied France after the Franco-Prussian War, this company and the Gallé firm remained on good terms. When the glass production of the Gallé company could not meet its own demands, it commissioned Burgun to supply glass to specific design some of which was later decorated at the Gallé Studios. By 1895 Gallé's expansion eliminated the need for this arrangement.

The two vases illustrated here are a popular "new" style of enameling between layers of glass which Burgun Schverer displayed at the 1895 Strasbourg exhibition.

74. Vases
Verrerie d'Art de Lorraine,
Burgun, Schverer & Cie.
Meisenthal, Alsace-Lorraine,
Germany
c. 1895–1900

Verrerie de Nancy
1878–
Daum Frères, 1892–

The brothers Auguste and Antonin, sons of Jean Daum, the founder of *Verrerie de Nancy*, established an art glass division in the company in 1890 and began producing colored glass. A year later, they created a decorating shop, and cased glass was enameled, acid-cut, and carved in the Gallé Art Nouveau style.

The Chrysler Museum collection of just over 100 objects illustrates the production of Daum glass from about 1892 to the present. Several original techniques were perfected. The first, called *martelé*, is like the hammered metal for which it was named. The background of the glass was wheel engraved with numerous facet cuts to give it this special effect.

Another technique, vitrification, decorated the surface by rolling a hot bubble of molten glass over a prepared design of pulverized colored glass. Afterwards, the object could be given better perspective by carving or acid-cutting.

Interior background colors, called *verre de jade*, also came from the use of pulverized, colored glass which was trapped and fused between other layers of glass during its fabrication. Another more complicated technique was called *intercalaire* which was patented in 1899. This was like the later Frederick Carder, Steuben "Intarsia" glass. It used a technique which involved the creation of decoration between layers of glass by employing pulverized glass which was etched or carved prior to reheating, casing, and reshaping.

After World War I, interesting vessels were blown into wrought iron and brass decorated frames. Usually the glass was cased, often with metallic foil inclusions. The metal for these selections was supplied by Louis Majorelle of Nancy, noted for his furniture. These pieces were marked by engraving on the glass bottom *Daum ‡ Nancy* and *L. Majorelle*.

As with Gallé glass, Daum objects were also marked. *Daum ‡ Nancy* was engraved on the bottom, the foot top, or in cameo relief on the side. The marks always included the cross of Lorraine ‡.

Daum's *pâte de verre* atelier (1906–1914) and the production under Amalric Walter is covered in the section on *pâte de verre*.

75. Vase
Daum Frères.
Verrerie de Nancy
Nancy, France
c. 1894–1900

76. Vase
Daum Frères.
Verrerie de Nancy
Nancy, France
c. 1895

77. Compote
Daum Frères.
Verrerie de Nancy
Nancy, France
c. 1900

79. Vase
Daum Frères.
Verrerie de Nancy
Nancy, France
c. 1903–1905

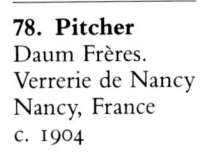

78. Pitcher
Daum Frères.
Verrerie de Nancy
Nancy, France
c. 1904

80. Chandelier
Daum Frères.
Verrerie de Nancy
and Louis Majorelle
Nancy, France
c. 1905

81. Mushroom Vase
Daum Frères.
Verrerie de Nancy
Nancy, France
c. 1907

83. Vase
Daum Frères.
Verrerie de Nancy
Nancy, France
c. 1912–1913

82. Vase
Daum Frères.
Verrerie de Nancy
Nancy, France
c. 1908

64

85. Vase
Daum Frères.
Verrerie de Nancy
and Louis Majorelle
Nancy, France
c. 1921–1922

84. Vase
Daum Frères.
Verrerie de Nancy
Nancy, France
c. 1910

86. Footed Bowl
Daum Frères.
Verrerie de Nancy
Nancy, France
c. 1925–1930

87. Vase
Daum Frères.
Verrerie de Nancy
Nancy, France
c. 1925–1930

**Muller Frères
Grandes Verreries de
Croismare et Lunéville**
Lunéville, France
1895–1936

The nine Muller brothers and one sister were at one time or another involved in the Muller glass decorating shop established by Henri in 1895 at Lunéville, near Nancy. Specially designed glass blanks were secured at the Hinzelin factory in Croismare.

At least five of the Muller Brothers had been employed by Gallé, and the Muller products reflect the style of Gallé.

After the interruption of World War I, the Mullers acquired the Hinzelin plant in Croismare, although they continued to decorate the glass at the Lunéville studio. Economic reverses forced the business to close in 1936.

88. Vase
Muller Frères
Lunéville, France
c. 1900–1905

89. Vase
Muller Frères
Lunéville, France
c. 1900–1905

91. Vase
Muller Frères
Lunéville, France
c. 1920s

90. Vase
Muller Frères
Lunéville, France
c. 1910

Other French Art Nouveau Artists and Glasshouses:

Philippe-Joseph Brocard & Fils
d. 1896

Philippe-Joseph Brocard was fascinated by the Islamic Mamluk style of glass of the 13th and 14th centuries as seen in mosque lamps of these times. Brocard revived this Islamic style, and his work first attracted attention at the 1867 Paris *Exposition* and again in 1874 and 1884. He thus represents that aspect of the Art Nouveau movement which turned to other times and cultures in the movement's attraction to the exotic and different in art.

92. Ornament
Philippe-Joseph Brocard & Fils
Paris, France
1884

Eugène Michel
1848–1905

In 1900, after working as an engraver and decorator for glass artists E. Rousseau and Léveillé, Michel became an independent glassmaker in Paris. He produced thick, brightly colored and deeply carved glass in a style influenced by Chinese cameo glass. His production must have been small as his glass is scarce.

Amédée de Caranza and Jeanne Duc (Descôtes)
Paris, France 1902–1904
H. A. Copillet & Cie
1903–1906
Noyon-sur-Seine, France

Amédée de Caranza was the expert who produced the unusual lustered designs on glass similar to that made at the ceramic firm of Clément Massier, Vallauris, France, where Caranza worked at the end of the 19th century. From 1902–1904 he worked with Jeanne

93. Vase
Eugène Michel
Lunéville, France
c. 1895–1900

94. Vase
Duc-Amédée de Caranza
Paris, France
c. 1902–1904

Duc and it was during this time that they applied for both French and German patents describing a heat reduction technique after painting the glass with various metallic oxides. In 1903 Caranza became a designer for Copillet where lustered decorated glass continued to be made.

95. Vase
H. A. Copillet & Cie.
Noyon-sur-Seine, France
c. 1903–1906

Cristallerie de Pantin
Verreries et Cristalleries
de St. Denis et Pantin Réuniés
Pantin (Seine), France
1851–

The Pantin glasswork was established in 1851. After a move to Pantin, a suburb of Paris, and several reorganizations, interesting Art Nouveau-style glass was produced about 1900. Other Art Nouveau acid-cut cameo vases in the style of "standard" Gallé designs were made. The identifying mark on these was *De Vez*, the pseudonym for the art director Camille Tutré de Varreux. *Mont Joye* was another Pantin mark. (Pantin underwent a number of name changes in the 19th century, and *Stumpf, Touvier, Viollet et Cie.* was one of the company names which was also used.)

Pantin merged with *Legras & Cie.* (see below) and the firm eventually became *Verreries et Cristalleries de St. Denis et Pantin Réuniés*.

Legras et Cie.
St. Denis, Paris

Legras et Cie., a large and prosperous table and decorative glass manufacturer, produced colorful, popular art glass. After World War I it merged with the Pantin Glassworks—see the above entry under *Pantin*.

97. Vase
Legras & Cie.
Saint Denis (Seine), France
c. 1912

96. Vase
Cristallerie de Pantin:
Stumpf, Touvier, Viollet & Cie.
Pantin (Seine), France
c. 1901

71

98. Bowl
Legras & Cie.
Saint Denis (Seine), France
c. 1925

Jugendstil—Art Nouveau in Germany, Austria, and Bohemia:

The Art Nouveau movement in Central Europe appeared under the name of *Jugendstil*, the youthful style, named from the German magazine *Die Jugend (Youth)*. Inspired by the decorative movement popular in France, it looked to Tiffany in America for inspiration as well. In its use of iridized glass, the Loetz firm, for example, was clearly looking toward the American Tiffany in its glass production. In Austria, another trend developed as the Secessionist movement moved away from the curvilinear lines of Art Nouveau and employed geometric styles. A group of Austrian artists, deciding to work together, banded into the *Wiener Werkstätte*, and they became noted for one of the more creative movements which deviated from the Art Nouveau style.

Ludwig Moser & Söhne
Karlsbad, Bohemia
1857–

Ludwig Moser (1833–1916) founded a glass engraving and polishing firm in 1857 in Karlsbad, a factory which grew into a full luxury glass operation. The influence of the French Art Nouveau movement soon reached Bohemia, and the company concentrated on deep cutting of curvilinear floral designs, often accompanied by gilding. (The company continues today in the same city in which it began, now named Karlový Vary, Czechoslovakia, as a part of the nationalized industrial system of the C.S.S.R.)

The following two pieces from The Chrysler Museum collection of 30 objects illustrate the range of luxury glass produced.

99. Ewer
Ludwig Moser & Söhne
Karlsbad, Bohemia
c. 1890

100. Covered Jar
Ludwig Moser & Söhne
Karlsbad, Bohemia
c. 1925

101. Pair of Cordials
Karl Koepping
(Dresden, 1848–Berlin, 1914)
c. 1895–1900

102. Vase and Bowl
Johann Loetz Witwe
Klostermühle, Bohemia
c. 1900

Karl Koepping
1848–1914

Karl Koepping, a painter and etcher, began experimenting with glass designs about 1895 using the lampwork technique of manipulating tube glass at the torch. His stained glasses, some with iridescence and often in the shape of a flower, are usually thin and fragile. His goblets were carried in Siegfried Bing's famous Paris shop, *La Maison de l'Art Nouveau*, from its inception in 1895.

Johann Loetz Witwe
Klostermühle, Bohemia
1836–1930

The Loetz collection of about 30 pieces in The Chrysler Museum displays quality iridescent and Tiffany-type Art Nouveau glass made about 1900 under the direction of Max Ritter von Spaun, the step-grandson of the founder, Johann Loetz. Under von Spaun, new equipment was acquired, marketing procedures were reorganized, and talented artisans were employed. This revitalization of the firm helped to win international fame for the company. Loetz received awards at several world fairs, even exhibiting in the St. Louis, U.S.A. 1904 Louisiana Purchase Exposition.

The French-style acid-cut cameo was introduced into the Loetze line, and designs by the *Wiener Werkstätte* group were employed. Many pieces are marked on the bottom with the engraved *Loetz—Austria*—probably intended for the American or English markets.

The glasswork's fortunes began to decline after Max Spaun's death in 1909 and the interruptions of World War I. Following a factory fire, the glassworks closed in 1930.

103. Vase
Johann Loetz Witwe
Klostermühle, Bohemia
c. 1905

Meyr's Neffe Glassworks
Adolf, Bohemia

The Meyr's Neffe Glassworks in the Wimperk (Winterberg) region of southern Bohemia made glass in its own right, but it was also one of the chief suppliers of glass to Lobmeyr of Vienna. (A daughter of the Lobmeyr founder married the owner of Meyr's Neffe Glassworks.) One of the designers used by the firm was Otto Prutscher of the *Wiener Werkstätte*, an organization which provided studio space for young artists, many of whom were in reaction to the "flowery tendril" style of Art Nouveau. Their work tended toward the geometric. Prutscher's drinking glasses were noted for the elegance of their style.

104. Wine Goblets
Meyr's Neffe Glassworks
Adolf, Bohemia
c. 1906–1914

EUROPEAN *Pâte de Verre* GLASS:
1890–1970

Pâte de verre (glass paste), which had been made in antiquity, was revived in France at the end of the 19th century. The technique is similar to that of pottery. Powdered colored glass is mixed to a paste with a binder, usually water, packed into a mold, and fired in a kiln at a lower than normal temperature for melting glass. The annealing (gradual cooling) time is lengthened. It was a novel approach for glassmakers at the end of the 19th and beginning of the 20th centuries, and a number of French artists became masters in the art.

The following entries are a few examples of the extensive collection of *pâte de verre* in The Chrysler Museum. These selections range from the turn-of-the-century (c. 1900) heavy, sugary-like pieces by George Despret (1862–1952) to the later, thinner, more translucent objects by Gabriel Argy-Rousseau (1885–1953) and François-Emile Décorchement (1880–1971).

The Daum items made prior to World War I (1906–1914) were by Amalric Walter (1859–1942) at Daum's *pâte de verre* atelier. After that war, Walter established his own studio and continued producing *pâte de verre* objects. These were marked with his name or initials and usually those of his associate sculptor-designer. After a hiatus toward the middle of this century, there has been a recent revival in interest in the technique of *pâte de verre*. In 1968 Daum commissioned contemporary sculptors to supply appropriate models which used this technique. The 1970 Salvador Dali design is one example. Now several studio artists are working in this field in the United States and in Europe. Thus *pâte de verre*, which began as a part of the Art Nouveau movement, continues to flourish a century after it was revived and, in a sense, it serves as a bridge between the pre-World War I artists in glass and those who came after the war.

105. Vase
George Despret
Jeumont, France
c. 1906

106. Statuette/(Tanagra Style)
George Despret
Jeumont, France
c. 1906

George Despret
1862–1952

George Despret began his work in his studio in Jeumont, France, where he showed an interest in overlay glass and glass with entrapped air bubbles. From 1890 on, however, he specialized in the *pâte de verre* technique, especially in Tanagra style figures and fish and animals in the round. His factory was destroyed during the First World War but re-opened in 1920. It finally closed in 1937.

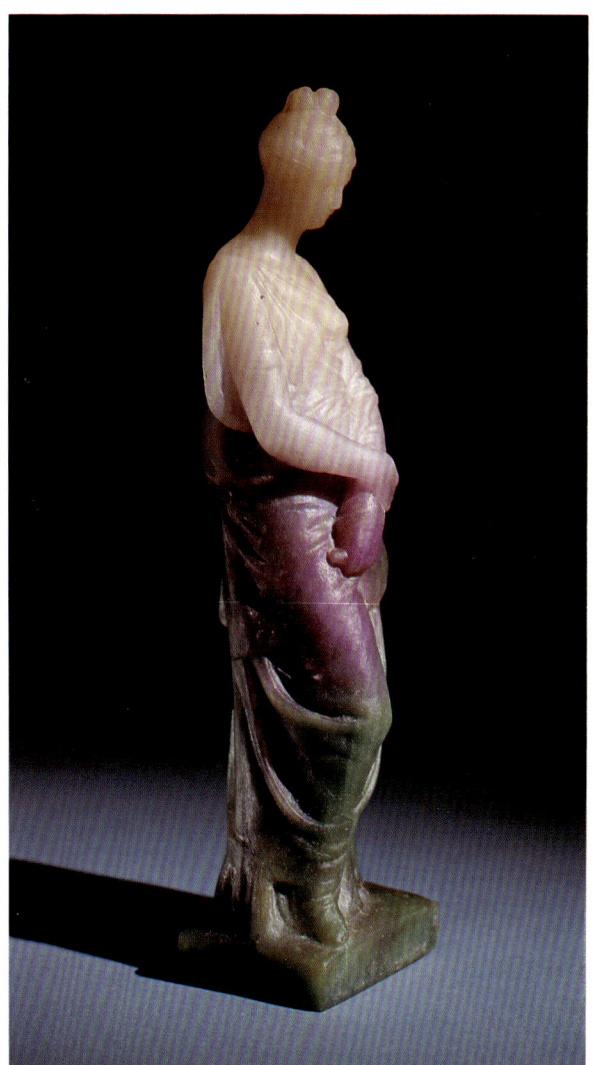

107. Cup
Jules-Paul Brateau
France
c. 1910–1912

108. Statuette/ Tanagra Figure
Amalric Walter
Daum & Cie.
Nancy, France
c. 1905–1906

108a. A Bronze Duplicate of This Figure
H: 12¾ in. (32.5 cm.) 88.75
Mark: On the side a circular impression:
GART AU TITRE A.L.

Jules-Paul Brateau
1844–1923

Jules-Paul Brateau, a trained sculptor noted for his jewelry and objects made of pewter, exhibited in the 1889 and 1900 Paris *Exposition Universelle*. Subsequently he produced small, delicate *pâte de verre* pieces. These were probably inspired by those of the early *pâte de verre* master Albert-Louis Dammouse (1848–1926) whose work was highly acclaimed when it was seen at the 1900 Paris *Exposition*.

Amalric Walter
1849–1942

The Daum *pâte de verre* from 1906–1914 was made by Amalric Walter. After World War I, he opened an independent atelier where he made a wide range of decorative objects with animal and insect motifs. His glass was usually composed of opaque, dense colors. The spelling of Walter's name differs in several publications as follows:

Amalric is used in the books and catalog by Daum and will be the one used here.
Almaric is used by the Musée des Arts Décoratifs, Paris, by Yvonne Brunhammer.
Alméric is used by Newman, *An Illustrated Dictionary of Glass* and in *Glass: Art Nouveau to Art Deco* by Victor Arwas.

Amalric is the German version of the name, Almaric is the Gallic, and Alméric is the French. A paperweight/bookend is incised on one side: *MALRIC*, and this may be the "pen" or nickname Amalric Walter used.

109. "Loïe Fuller" Statuette
Amalric Walter
Nancy, France
c. 1920

110. Vide Poche or Cendrier
Amalric Walter
Nancy, France
c. 1920

111. Vide Poche
Amalric Walter
Nancy, France
c. 1920

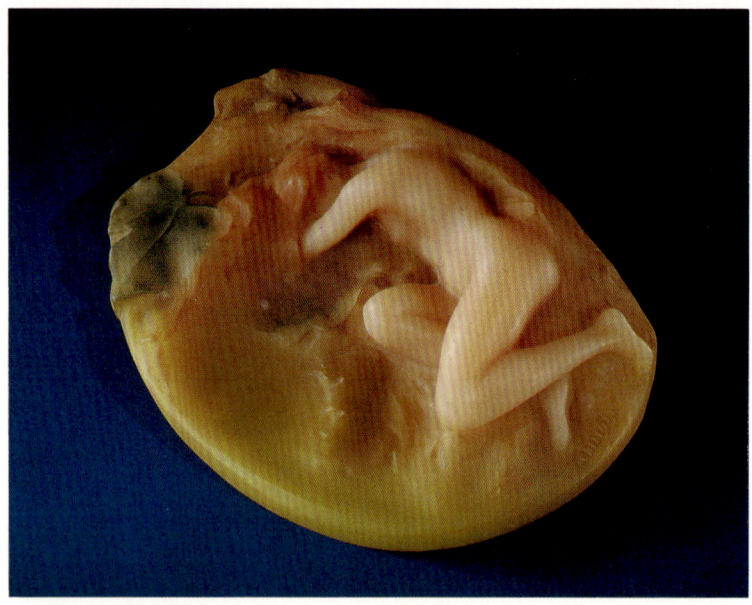

112. Vide Poche
Amalric Walter
Sculptor: Alfred Finot,
Nancy, 1876–1947
Nancy, France
c. 1920

113. Vase
Amalric Walter
Sculptor: L. E. Jan
Nancy, France
c. 1925

114. Plaque à La Rose
Amalric Walter
Nancy, France
c. 1925

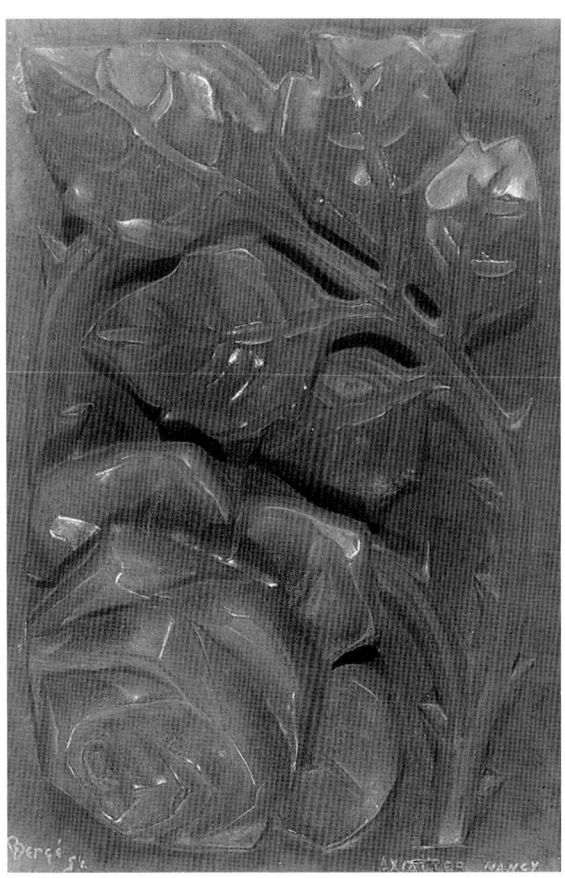

Gabriel Argy-Rousseau
1885–1953

Gabriel Argy-Rousseau graduated from the ceramic school at Sèvres in 1906 in the same class with Jean Cros, son of Henry Cros, the one who rediscovered the *pâte de verre* technique. After working in the ceramic field a few years, Argy-Rousseau turned to *pâte de verre* and his first designs were exhibited in 1914. Following the World War I interruption, he became managing director of the company, *Les Pâtes-de-Verre D'Argy-Rousseau*, in partnership with a financial backer. From then until its close in 1931 he developed new, innovative Art Deco designs in a semi-industrial operation with a few dozen workers and decorators. They produced a wide range of thin-walled vases and bowls in a mold technique which could be repeated numerous times, often using *pâte de cristal* to make a translucent finished product.

Reference: Arwas, Victor. *Glass: Art Nouveau to Art Deco*, Harry N. Abrams, Inc. New York, 1987, pp. 27–35.

115. Vase
Gabriel Argy-Rousseau
Paris, France
c. 1925

116. Vase "Nu Couché"
Gabriel Argy-Rousseau
Paris, France
c. 1927

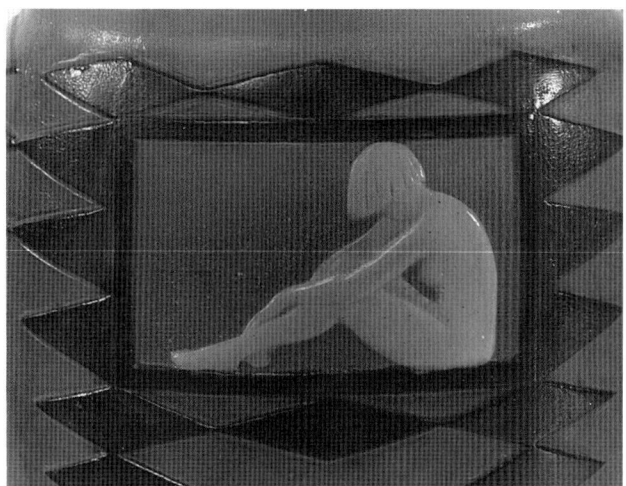

116a. Reverse Medallion—Close Up.

83

François Emile Décorchemont
1880–1971

In 1902, Décorchemont started his factory in Conches (Eure), France, where he made vases in the *pâte de verre* technique in subdued colors and with a cloudy transparency. From 1905 to 1910 he worked in a new style in which rough surfaces were decorated in relief with floral motifs and insects. After 1912 he worked in the *pâte de cristal* technique, making objects of a massive nature with marbled colors. He also experimented with the *cire perdue* (lost wax) technique. After the Second World War he began to create stained glass windows.

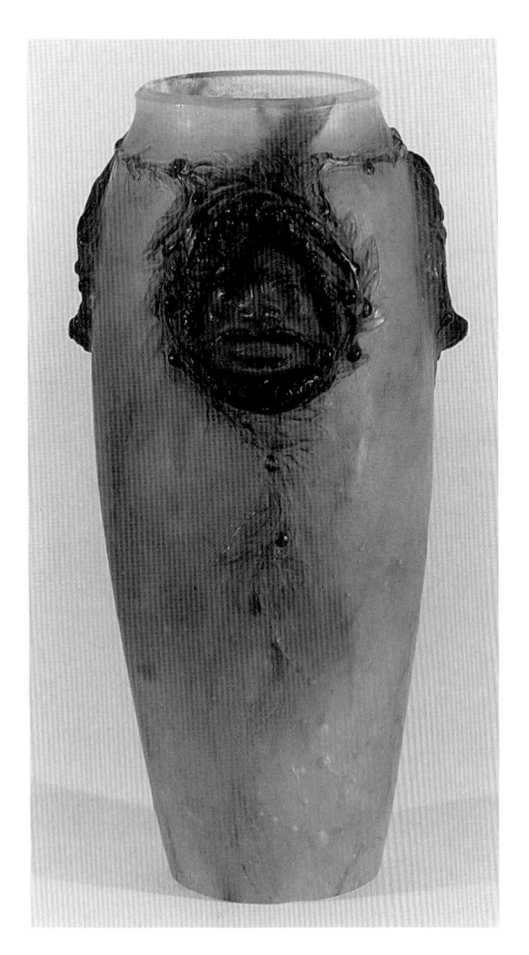

117. "Loïe Fuller"
François-Emile Décorchemont
Conches, France
c. 1912

118. Vase
François-Emile Décorchemont
Conches, France
c. 1919–1920

119. Vase
François-Emile
Décorchemont
Conches, France
c. 1924

Post-World War II Glass:

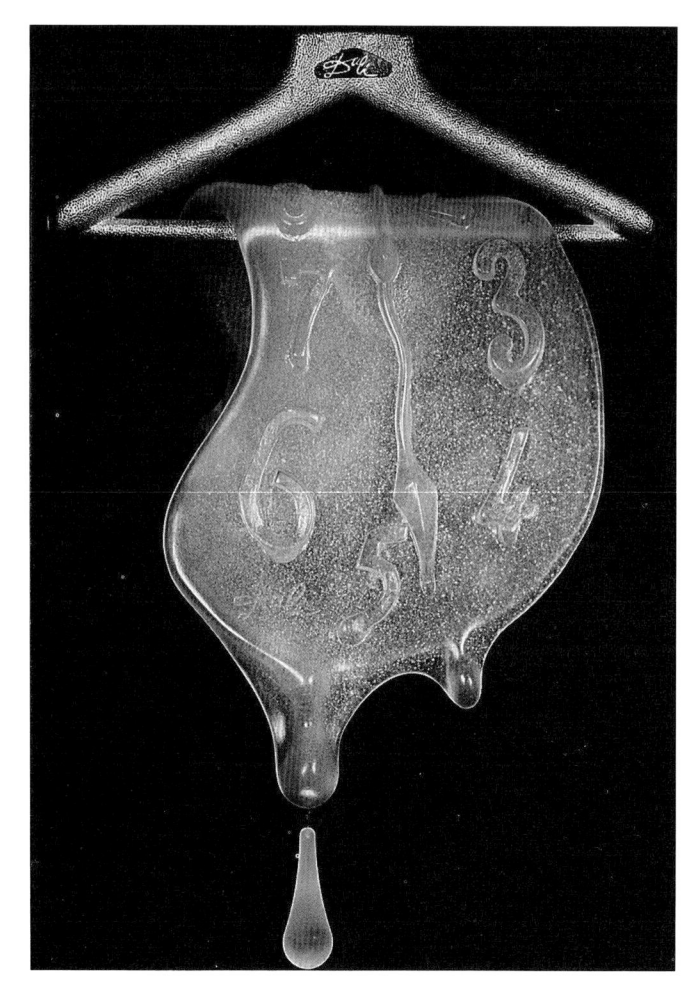

120. Porte-Manteau Montre
Salvador Dali
Daum & Cie.
Nancy, France
1970

85

EUROPEAN GLASS:
1920 TO THE PRESENT DAY

The interest in Art Nouveau virtually came to an end in Europe with the beginning of the First World War. Certain aspects of the pre-war era did persist beyond 1918, the interest in *pâte de verre*, for example, continued to attract some noted French glass artists, and this glassmaking technique continues to fascinate glassmakers world-wide to the present time. If one new style captured public and artistic interest, however, it was that of Art Deco.

Whereas Art Nouveau had favored the sinuous line in dealing with nature and often turned to other times and other lands for inspiration, the Art Deco style called for a new simplicity. The seeds of the movement can be seen in the Wiener Werkstätte movement before 1914, when an interest in the geometric design became attractive to artists in that movement. Thus the simple line and a "streamlining" of design came to the fore in 1925. The name "Art Deco" comes from the 1925 *Exposition Internationale des Arts Décoratifs et Industriel Moderne*, and Maurice Marinot, René Lalique, and André Thuret are among the most important artists in Art Nouveau design and implementation in the field of glass.

But there were other directions being taken in glass as well. In Sweden the decision by Orrefors to hire designers led to a new development in glass artistry, and the work of Gate and Hald set a new standard for artistic endeavors in glass. In Norway, Hadelands Glass opted for the modern vein in design, as did Holmegaard in Denmark. In Finland, toward the end of this period, the work of Alvar Aalto brought new visions to glass design. The influence of the Bauhaus in Germany in the 1920s gave impetus to the Modernist movement, which, like French Art Deco, looked for a new simplicity in glass and became an international movement which was to remain an influence after the debacle of the years of the Second World War.

Individuals continued to go their own way, and the most noted of these, perhaps, was Maurice Marinot, who not only designed his own glass but created it himself at the furnace. In a sense, he was the fore-runner of the Studio Glass artists of the post-1945 era. Thus a number of directions can be found in the period between the wars, ranging from designer glass in Scandinavia (and elsewhere), to the simpler and geometric glass of the Art Deco style, to the Modernist sensibilities of the Bauhaus group and their successors.

The post-Second World War period saw a flourishing of glass art in Scandinavia, particularly in Finland and in Sweden. The work done by Venini in Italy, which began in the 1920s, continued after 1945, and the company not only generated its own designs but invited leading artists in glass from other countries to work in this Venetian glass house.

The Studio Glass movement began in the United States in the 1960s, albeit it had its origins in Europe with Marinot and others, and it came to influence European artists as well. A new generation of European glass artists began to experiment with hot glass, both designing and producing their own objects. Much of their work can be seen in the *New Glass Review* which began publication in 1979 and offers illustrations of the newest in glass artistry by glassmakers world-wide.

121. Flasks
Maurice Marinot
Paris, France
1912–1915

122. Decanter
Maurice Marinot
Paris, France
c. 1925

Maurice Marinot
Troyes, France
1882–1960

Maurice Marinot was a trained artist who discovered glass in 1911 when he visited a friend's glass factory at Bar-sur-Seine, near his hometown of Troyes. He soon was designing and directing the production of simple shapes which he later enameled. The three flasks illustrated above, dated 1912, 1915, and 1914, are examples of his early work in glass.

Marinot had begun his painting career in 1901 at the Ecole des Beaux-Arts in Paris, working in the studio of Fernand Cormon. His radical views on painting led to his expulsion from the school although he continued to take advantage of Cormon's studio whenever the master was absent. He was associated with the *Fauves*, and he included among his friends Derain, Villon, and André Mare of the Paris art scene. His paintings were exhibited at the *Salon d'Automne* and *Salon des Indépendants* in Paris as well as in the famous 1913 New York Armory Show.

Marinot considered glass a proper medium for aesthetic expression and worked with it from 1911 to 1937. Until 1922 he enameled glass in the fashion of his paintings, using strong colors, as in the two examples above, which show figures dressed in the style of a leading Parisian couturier, Paul Poiret. After World War I, unusual surface texture effects were accomplished by acid-etching thick vessels, often combined with enameling in more geometric styles. Late in the 1920s, after learning glass blowing, he produced heavy, simple container forms inlaid with minute bubbles and shaded smokey colors. The decanter, shown right, is such an example. When the glass factory at Bar-sur-Seine closed in 1937, Marinot abandoned glassmaking but continued painting.

Marinot was one of the first artists to learn the entire glassmaking craft. His successful work under ideal conditions with no commercial restraints influenced not only his generation but continues today to be a major inspiration to modern studio glass artists.

123. Cluny Vase
René Lalique
Wingen-sur-Moder, France
c. 1925

René Lalique & Cie.
Wingen-sur-Moder, France

In 1908, after René Lalique had achieved fame as an Art Nouveau jeweler, he established a glass manufactury which still bears his name. The Chrysler Museum collection of Lalique glass consists primarily of the well-designed, molded glass which successfully captured the mood of the 1920s and 1930s. The repetitive stylized designs of birds, fish, flowers, or the female nude, often in high relief, in colorless opalescent or in a clear color glass selectively etched (frosted) had wide appeal, and they gained an international reputation for Lalique glass. Imitative molded, matte surface Lalique-style glass was made on both sides of the Atlantic, and the name "Lalique" has become the generic name for this popular style.

124. Tourbillons Vase
René Lalique
Wingen-sur-Moder, France
c. 1925

125. Poissons Vase
René Lalique
Wingen-sur-Moder, France
c. 1930

126. Aigrettes Vase
René Lalique
Wingen-sur-Moder, France
c. 1930

127. Alicante Vase
René Lalique
Wingen-sur-Moder, France
c. 1930

128. Druides Vase
René Lalique
Wingen-sur-Moder, France
c. 1930–1932

Cristallerie de Schneider
Epinay-sur-Seine, France
1909–

Two Schneider brothers, Charles, the artistic director, and Ernest, the business manager, established a glass factory in 1909 for the production of a variety of lighting devices, art glass, and tableware. It is still in business in Lorris, where it moved in 1962, now under the direction of Charles's sons.

The glass is marked with an engraved *Schneider*, the trademark *Le Verre Français* or *Charder* (for *Char*les Schnei*der*—Charles Schneider).

The glass in the Chrysler Museum collection is that of the 1920s colorful Art Deco style.

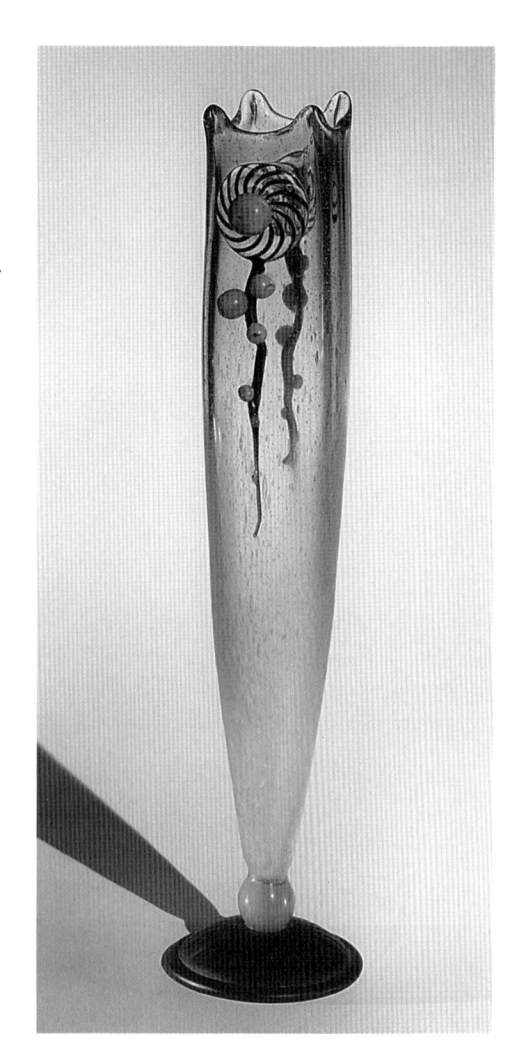

129. Vase
Cristallerie de Schneider
Epinay-sur-Seine, France
c. 1925

André DeLatte
Nancy, France

André DeLatte founded a glass factory in 1921. Information is scant, but it is believed that the business lasted about ten years, producing interesting Art Deco-style acid-cut and enameled pieces.

130. Vase
André DeLatte
Nancy, France
c. 1922

131. Vase
André DeLatte
Nancy, France
c. 1925

Orrefors Glasbruk

The management of a small glass factory in the province of Smålands in Sweden made a decision in 1915 which was to bring Swedish glass to the fore in the twentieth century. It was a decision which led to an artistic influence that was to affect other glass houses throughout Europe. That decision was to hire a designer who could set a style for the glassblowers in the factory. Swedish glass had been under the influence of Gallé, but under Simon Gate after 1915, and then his colleague, Edward Hald, who joined him in 1917, Orrefors began to move in new directions. A concern for simple tablewares in the modern spirit led to a new "modern" style in glass design. The use of wheel engraving was employed, and a variety of designs ranging from the classical to the whimsical poured forth. Other designers joined Gate and Hald in time, and Kosta, Boda, and other Swedish glassworks rose to the challenge of the new movement in Sweden in the 1920s and the decades thereafter. Swedish and Scandinavian design helped to establish new norms for glass design throughout the world.

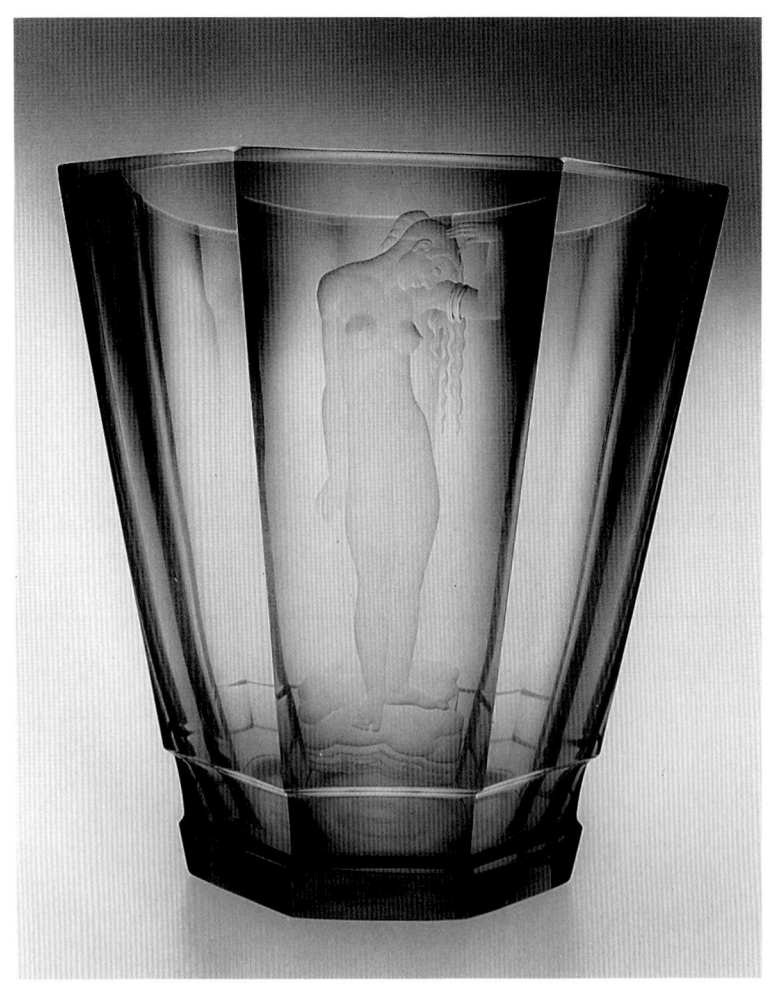

132. Vase
Simon Gate (1883–1945)
A. B. Orrefors Glasbruk
Orrefors, Sweden
c. 1928

Monart Glass
John Moncrieff, Ltd.
Perth, Scotland
1924–1939
World War II Interruption
1950–1962

John Moncrieff, Ltd. a glass factory producing industrial bottles and chemical glassware, opened a decorative arts glass division in 1924 under the direction of Salvador Ysart, a glassman from Barcelona with additional experience with various French firms. The blown ware, mostly vases and bowls, reflect the Venetian tradition with swirls of colors, some with metallic flecks using various color backgrounds.

Only paper labels were used. Many objects were finished with slightly protruding partly polished pontil marks, and, if a label survived, it would be found here.

The name for this glass came from the factory: *MON*crieff and Ys*ART*.

133. Vase "Monart"
John Moncrieff, Ltd.
Perth, Scotland
c. 1935

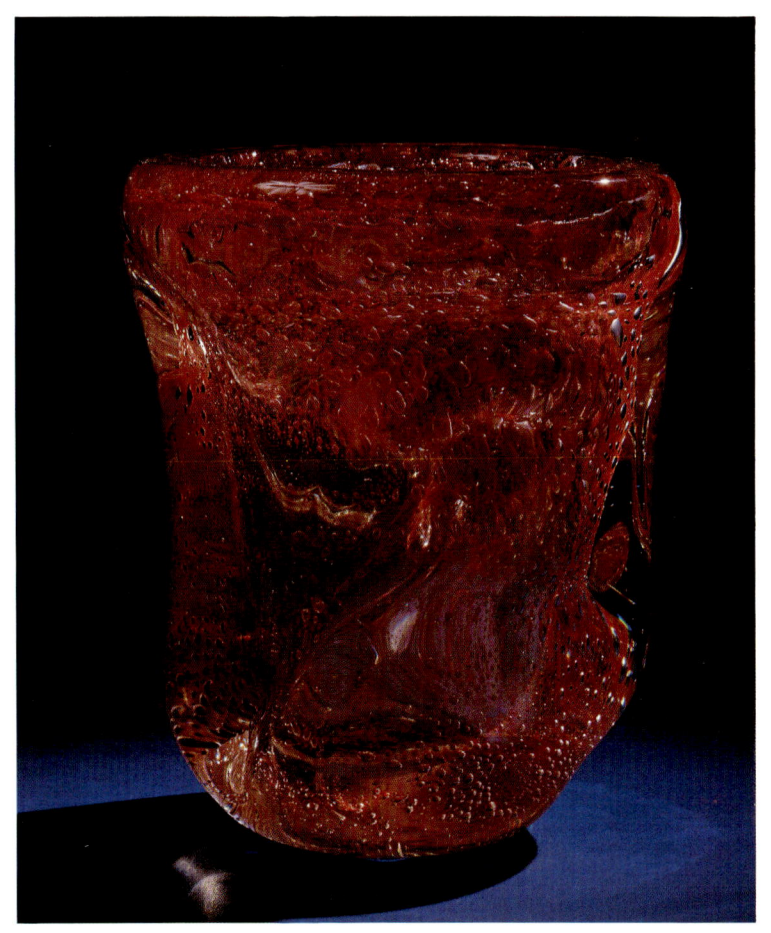

André Thuret
1898–1965
Paris, France

André Thuret combined a career as a glass engineer, researcher, and advisor to L'Institut du Verre (glass) with one as a glass artist. Beginning in 1924, he created colorful blown vessels using various colors and metallic flakes to produce foamy inlays. Thuret did pioneering work as a studio glass artist in France.

134. Vase
André Thuret
Paris, France
c. 1935–1940

Société Anonyme Holophane
Les Andelys, France

Holophane was an industrial glass factory which produced decorative glass, both blown and pressed, in the Lalique style from about 1925 to 1955. Some of the molds for the latter were acquired by the United States subsidiary, Verlys of America, Inc. See the American example in the section on American glass.

135. Vase
Les Andelys, France
c. 1935

Post-World War II Glass:

The end of the Second World War gradually saw a revival of glassmaking after the hiatus of the seven years of conflict (1939–1945). Scandinavia in particular, offered a new leadership in design, and the work of Kaj Frank, Gunnel Nyman, Saara Hopea, and Tapio Wirkkala in Finland gave a new impetus to modern glass design. The work in Italy which had begun in the 1920s continued under Venini, and the Barbini factory was able to produce a variety of wares, many of which had the distinguishing mark of the able talent of its founder.

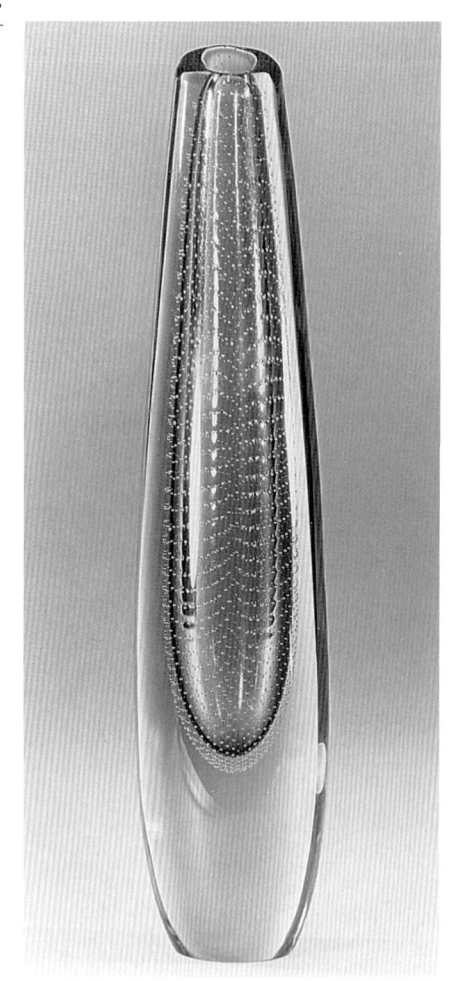

136. Vase
Gunnel Nyman (1909–1948)
Notsjö Glassworks
Nuutajarvi, Finland
c. 1945–1947

Gunnel Nyman
1909–1948

Gunnel Nyman was a graduate of the Design School in Helsinki. She was an important designer of modern glass, and she was responsible for creating many original designs which served as an inspiration to other designers.

137. Vase
Alfredo Barbini
Murano (Venice), Italy
1948

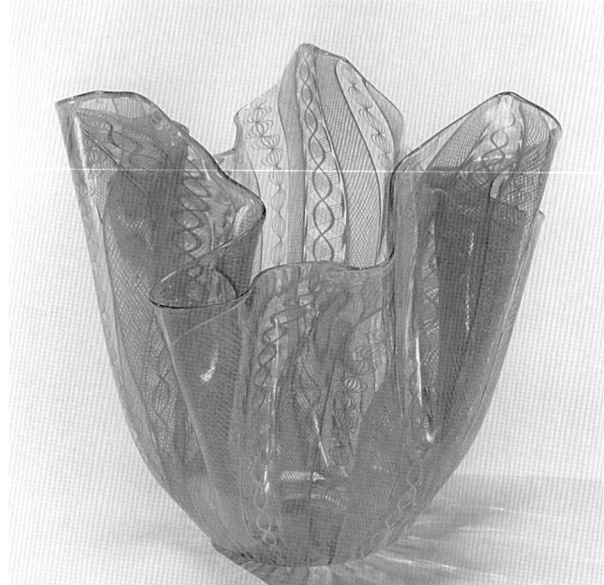

Alfredo Barbini
Murano, Italy
1912–

Descended from a family of glassmakers in Murano (Venice), Italy, since the 1600s, Barbini worked for a number of leading Venetian glass factories. In 1950 he set up his own glass house in a former chapel on the island of Murano where he produces general glasswares as well as particularly finely designed items. A technique which he developed, *a masello*, involves the sculpting of a solid block of molten glass.

Paolo Venini
1895–1959

In 1926, Paolo Venini formed his own glass firm, Venini & Cie. Reviving the traditional *millefiori* ("a thousand flowers") and *filigrana* (filigree) techniques of Venetian glass production, he began to do his own designing, as well as inviting outside designers (ranging from Tapio Wirkkala to Salvador Dali) to design for the firm. Venini himself is responsible for numerous new designs, but perhaps the most famous is his *vaso fazzoletto*, the "handkerchief bowl," first introduced at the 1948 Venice Biennale. The cupped and folded shape was made in several colors and sizes for about two decades. The vase, described below, imitates a linen effect with white, crisscross, spiral filagree imbedded in the grayish glass. It is a large, early example of this design which has had many imitators.

138. Fazzoletti (Handkerchief) Vase:
Paolo Venini
Venini & Cie.
Murano (Venice), Italy
c. 1950

AMERICAN BLOWN AND MOLD-BLOWN GLASS:
1790–1840

Glassmaking in the United States almost pre-dates the founding of European civilization on the shores of the New World. In 1608, a number of glassmakers of varying nationalities were set ashore in Virginia, sent by a group of London entrepreneurs, to begin the making of glass. This first industrial enterprise on American shores was the result of the rapid disappearance of wood for fuel in England, with its concomitant effect on the firing of glass furnaces. The New World had timber a-plenty, and it seemed as though the glass industry would flourish on these alien shores.

Unfortunately, the making of glass could not succeed under the conditions prevalent at the time. Additional attempts were made to start a glass industry during the Colonial period but none were successful until 1737 when a glassworks for making of window glass, bottles, and hollow ware was established by Caspar Wistar in Salem County, New Jersey, near Philadelphia. The business continued under Wistar's son Richard until the Revolutionary War.

Two other eighteenth century glass factories were successful for a short time. Henry William Stiegel produced glass at Manheim, Pennsylvania, 1763–1774, and John Frederick Amelung's New Bremen Glass Manufactory at Frederick, Maryland, 1784–1795. Both made window glass, blown and mold-blown bottles, flasks, and tablewares. Stiegel glass is mostly unidentified. Several splendid engraved Amelung vessels are known, identified by matching shapes and engraving with a few surviving presentation glasses which include the engraved New Bremen Glass Manufactory name.

It was Deming Jarves who was to see to the development of the first truly successful American glassworks in the new United States. In part, the War of 1812 gave the needed economic lift to the infant glass industry when an embargo was placed on English glass, and the American industry was thus given a protection formerly lacking in its competition with imported glass. In 1818, Jarves and associates incorporated the New England Glass Company in East Cambridge, Massachusetts, and in 1825 he moved on to found The Boston & Sandwich Glass Company, two of the most successful glass factories in the life of the new nation.

The spread of the United States into the lands of the west of the original thirteen colonies led to the development of a glass industry in the Pittsburgh area, a growth which was to see the further development of the glass industry into West Virginia and Ohio. The Bakewell Company founded in 1808 at Pittsburgh was one of the most successful of these operations, and it was soon sending glass to all areas of the nation as well as in exporting its wares beyond the borders of the United States.

Most glass in this early period of American glassmaking was made by the traditional blowing and mold-blowing techniques with the use of a dip or part-size mold for a design which was then expanded by additional blowing. Recessed panels and checkered diamond patterns are examples. It was not until the invention of glass pressing equipment that the industry would really flourish after the mid-1820s.

139. Salt
John Frederick Amelung
New Bremen Glass Manufactory
Frederick County, Maryland
c. 1790

140. Covered Sugar Bowl
New England Glass Company
Cambridge, Massachusetts
c. 1820

141. "Petticoat" Whale Oil Lamp
New England Glass Company
Cambridge, Massachusetts
c. 1820

142. Vase
Pittsburgh Area
c. 1830

144. Decanter, Pint Size
Pittsburgh Area
c. 1825–1840

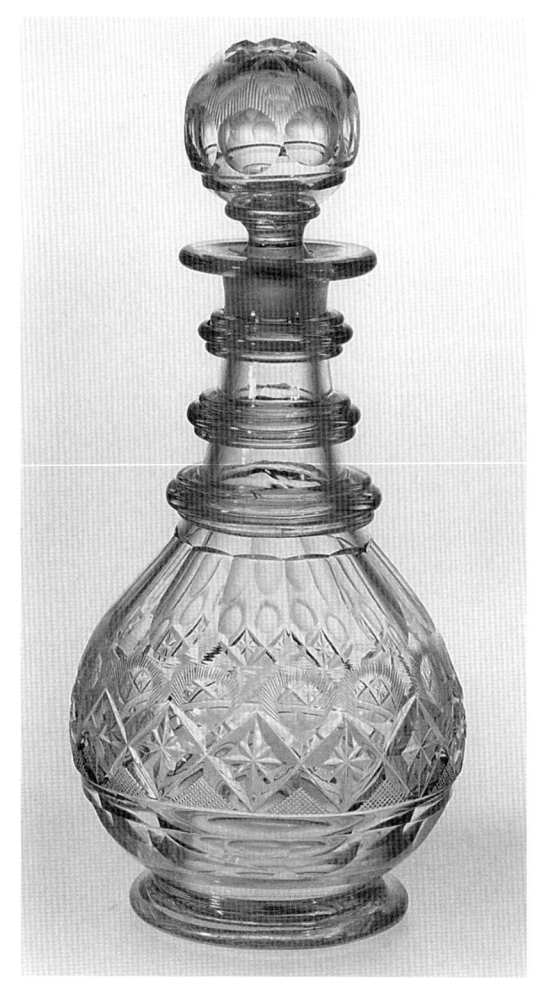

143. Bank (Whimsey)
New England Area
Probably The Boston &
Sandwich Glass Company
Sandwich, Massachusetts
c. 1830–1840

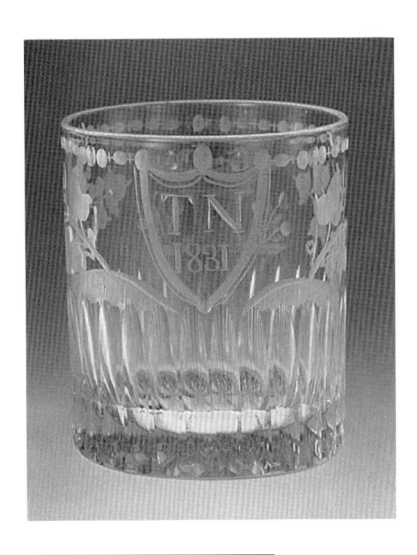

145. Tumbler
Pittsburgh Area
Perhaps Bakewell
and Company
Pittsburgh, Pennsylvania
c. 1831

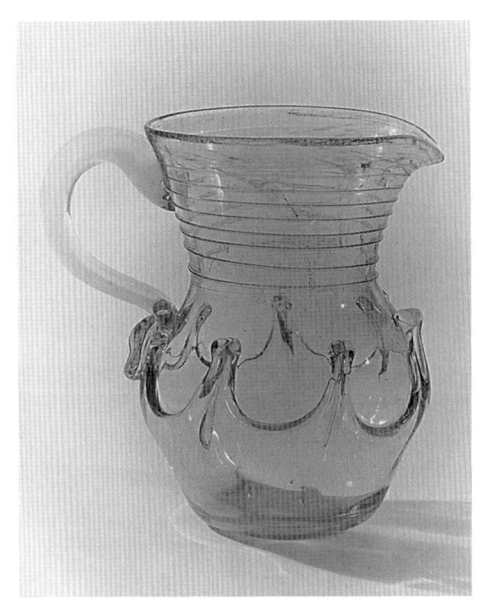

146. "Lily Pad" Pitcher
South Jersey or New York Area
c. 1830–1850

147. Compote
Pittsburgh Area
c. 1835–1870

148. Tea-Caddy
New England Area
Probably New England
Glass Company
Cambridge, Massachusetts
c. 1840

149. Sugar and Creamer
New England Area
Probably The Boston &
Sandwich Glass Company
Sandwich, Massachusetts
c. 1840

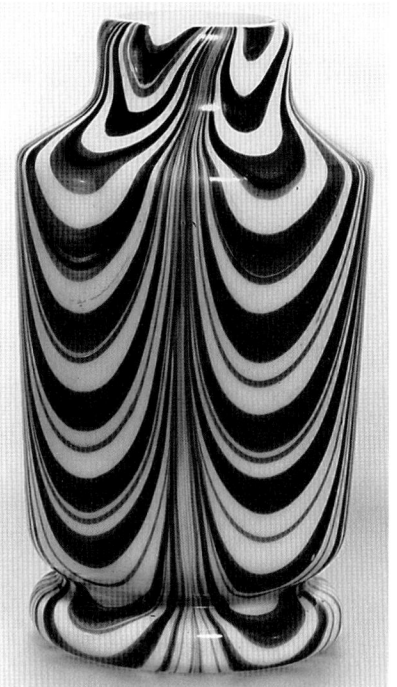

150. Cream Pitcher
Pittsburgh Area
c. 1840

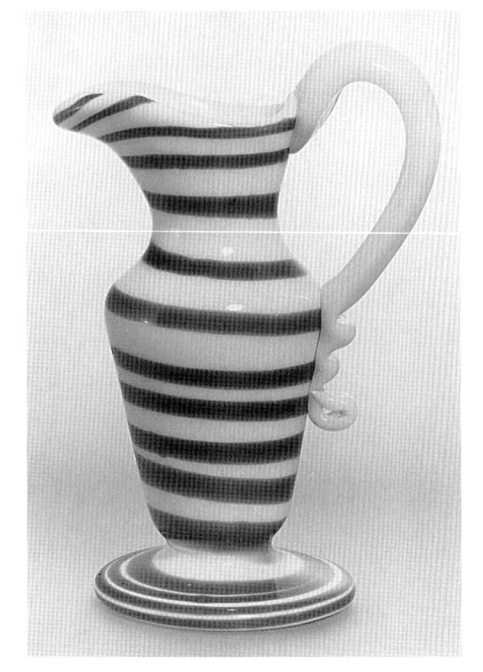

101

Mold-Blown Glass

The discovery that glass could be blown at the end of a hollow metal pipe, about 50 B.C., revolutionized the art of glassmaking and made a form of "mass production" possible for Roman glassmakers. The fact that glass could also be blown into a mold made for even greater efficiency and speed of glassmaking, for the same form could be created time after time. In later times, with the advances in technology, molds could be made of metal, and such molds could be used over and over, being less fragile than molds made of ceramics (or, even earlier, of wood). The Roman Empire "Ennion" bowl (see Ancient Glass No. 4) was made in so-called blown-three-mold technique, although the Roman example is a sharper, finer image.

The production of mold-blown wares was further developed about the 1820s when the technique known as "blown-three-mold" became popular, especially at Sandwich and other factories in the eastern United States. Full-size hinged metal molds, usually made with three sections, although two and four were also used, produced size and decoration in one quick operation. Manipulation followed, such as making a pouring spout and handle for a pitcher, extending the top to produce a neck for a decanter, or tooling to form a bowl or plate. The

152. Vase
The Boston & Sandwich Glass Company
Sandwich, Massachusetts
c. 1830–1840

151. Pitcher
New England Area
Probably New England Glass Company
Cambridge, Massachusetts
c. 1820–1840

designs originally were an adaptation of the popular Anglo-Irish cut glass. Soon patterns now known as "arch" and "baroque" used original patterns, more appropriate for the "new" blown-three-mold technique. Glassware mass produced in this way was available at a low price, and the resulting popularity helped expand American glass production.

153. Vase (Celery)
Pittsburgh Area
Probably Bakewell & Company
Pittsburgh, Pennsylvania
c. 1820–1840

154. Vase (Celery)
Pittsburgh Area
Probably Bakewell & Company
Pittsburgh, Pennsylvania
c. 1820–1840

155. Bar Decanter
Midwest or Pittsburgh Area
c. 1850

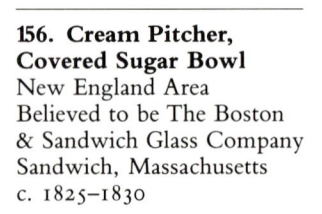

**156. Cream Pitcher,
Covered Sugar Bowl**
New England Area
Believed to be The Boston
& Sandwich Glass Company
Sandwich, Massachusetts
c. 1825–1830

104

157. Lamp, Decanters
Probably The Boston
& Sandwich Glass Company
Sandwich, Massachusetts
c. 1825–1830

158. A Pair of Whale Oil Lamps
The Boston & Sandwich
Glass Company
Sandwich, Massachusetts
c. 1830

AMERICAN EARLY PRESSED AND LACY GLASS:
1827–1860

While the blown-three-mold technique improved the efficiency of glassmaking, it was the invention of the glass pressing machine in the United States in the 1820s that brought another revolutionary change to glassmaking. The technique consisted of cutting a gather of hot glass into a metal mold and then using a plunger operated by a lever to press the molten glass into all parts of the mold. The pressing machine had grown from a late eighteenth and early nineteenth century hand-press squeezer device, used to make feet for goblets, salts, lamps, and stoppers, among other objects, by a few United States and European glassworks. The earliest recorded patent for pressing glass was one issued to John P. Bakewell, September 9, 1825, for an improvement in making glass furniture knobs. Numerous other patents for most flint glass manufacturers followed rapidly.

The cloudy surface of the early pressed products caused by the uneven temperature of the mold and molten glass posed a problem. It proved difficult to keep the mold and the glass at the same temperature, but soon the glassmakers discovered that this and other imperfections of the early technique, such as seeds or stress lines or shear marks, could be disguised by patterning the background with small stipples. Lacy pressed glass was born. By the 1840s, techniques were improved, and thereafter simpler designs could be employed without detriment to the overall surface of the glass objects.

This important American contribution to world glassmaking soon found a home in Europe, and the production of glass increased as the cost of the finished product fell. The price of glass was so reduced that families could now consider the purchase of glassware in quantity.

Pre-Lacy Period Pressed Glass

159. Cream Pitcher
New England Glass Company
Cambridge, Massachusetts
c. 1827

160. Plate
The Boston & Sandwich
Glass Company
Sandwich, Massachusetts
c. 1827–1830

Lacy Period Pressed Glass

161. Lacy Period Cup Plates
The Boston & Sandwich
Glass Company
Sandwich, Massachusetts
c. 1827–1955

162. Bowl/Plate
New England
Probably The Boston &
Sandwich Glass Company
Sandwich, Massachusetts
c. 1830

163. Lacy Candlesticks
Probably The Boston &
Sandwich Glass Company
Sandwich, Massachusetts
c. 1830

164. Lamp
Pittsburgh Area
Probably Bakewell & Company
Pittsburgh, Pennsylvania
c. 1835–1840

109

165. Oval Bowl
The Boston & Sandwich
Glass Company
Sandwich, Massachusetts
c. 1830

166. U.S.F. Constitution Tray
The Boston & Sandwich
Glass Company
Sandwich, Massachusetts
c. 1830–1835

167. Union Plate
Midwestern
c. 1830–1845

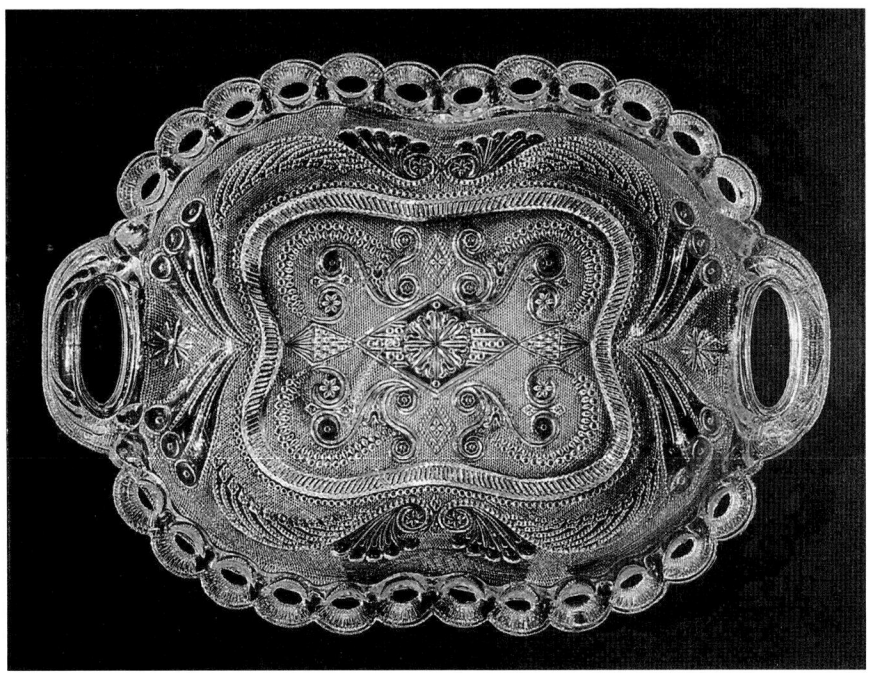

168. Lacy Dish
The Boston & Sandwich
Glass Company
Sandwich, Massachusetts
c. 1830–1835

111

169a. Lacy Covered Bowl
New England Area
Probably The Boston &
Sandwich Glass Company
Sandwich, Massachusetts
c. 1830–1840

169b. Lacy Bowl
Same item as above but
with a cover design of
three medallions.

170. Whale Oil Peg Lamp
The Boston & Sandwich
Glass Company
Sandwich, Massachusetts
c. 1825–1830

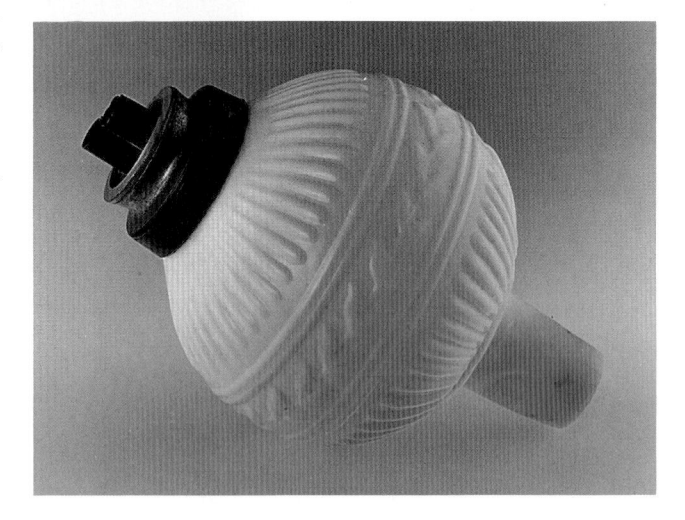

171. Lamp
New England Area
Probably The Boston &
Sandwich Glass Company
Sandwich, Massachusetts
c. 1830

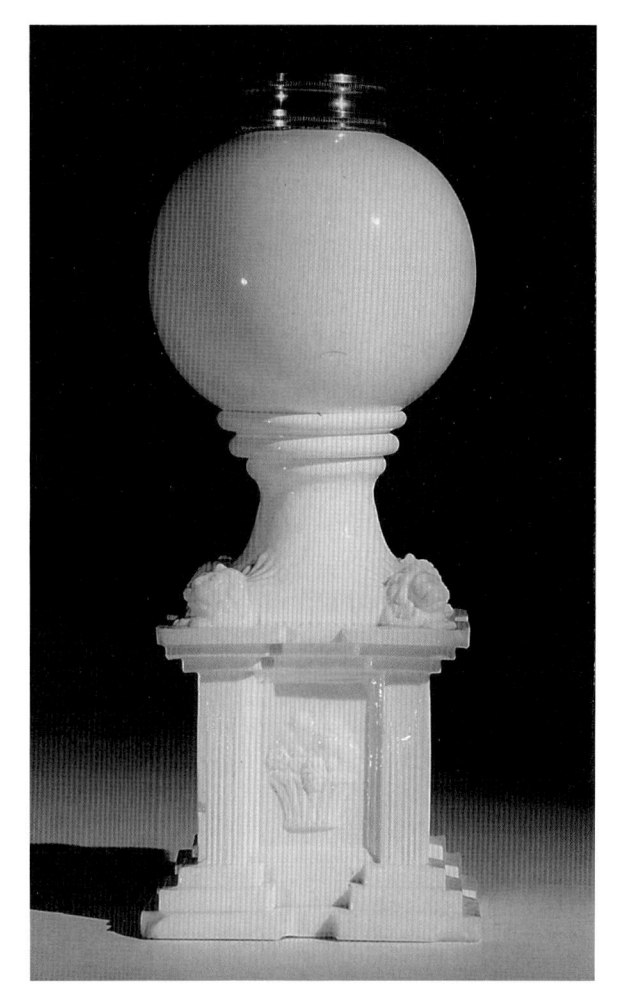

172. Lacy Period Salts
The Boston & Sandwich
Glass Company
Sandwich, Massachusetts
c. 1830–1845

173. Window Pane
J. & C. Ritchie
Wheeling, West Virginia
c. 1833–1835

174. Lacy Window Pane
Midwestern, probably
Pittsburgh, Pennsylvania
c. 1835–1840

175. Lacy Window Pane
Pittsburgh Area
c. 1835–1845

176. Gothic Style Lacy Window Pane
Bakewell & Company
Pittsburgh, Pennsylvania
c. 1836–1839

177. "Industry" Bowl
New England Glass Company
Cambridge, Massachusetts
c. 1840

178. Lacy Compote
The Boston & Sandwich
Glass Company
Sandwich, Massachusetts
c. 1840

116

179. Dish
The Boston & Sandwich
Glass Company
Sandwich, Massachusetts
c. 1835–1840

180. Fruit Bowl
The Boston & Sandwich
Glass Company
Sandwich, Massachusetts
c. 1845

117

181. Compote
The Boston & Sandwich
Glass Company
Sandwich, Massachusetts
c. 1845–1855

182. Dish
The Boston & Sandwich
Glass Company
Sandwich, Massachusetts
c. 1840

183. Pressed Glass Selections
The Boston & Sandwich
Glass Company
Sandwich, Massachusetts
c. 1850–1860

AMERICAN PATTERN (PRESSED) GLASS:
1850–1875

As glass pressing skills improved, it was unnecessary to use lacy designs to disguise imperfections. Not only had the cost of extremely detailed molds become prohibitively expensive, but elaborate styles were no longer considered tasteful. The depression of 1837 must have had an influence as well. Broad panels such as the tulip vases or the Huber pattern and the simple block design of the Ashburton pattern appeared.

Most major factories had their own mold making shops where the molds for pressed glass could be created. The more creative the mold maker, the more designs in glass a company could offer. By the mid-nineteenth century full tableware sets were being made, now known as pattern glass. Patterns reflected a variety of themes: elements from nature (shells, flowers), patriotic motifs, natural events (e.g. the popular "Comet" pattern; a "Star" pattern, etc.). Patterns were particularly appealing in full sets of glassware for the table, for they brought an elegance to the American middle-class table which had not previously been available.

Eventually, a vast number of patterns were created. Popular ones were copied throughout the glass-making world and the identification of the manufacturers today is almost impossible.

184. Lamp
The Boston & Sandwich
Glass Company
Sandwich, Massachusetts
c. 1850–1860

**185. Sugar Bowl and Creamer—
Ashburton Pattern**
New England Glass Company
Cambridge, Massachusetts
c. 1850–1860

186. Vases, Compote, Bowl — Leaf Design
The Boston & Sandwich Glass Company
Sandwich, Massachusetts
c. 1840–1850

187. Covered Butter Dish — Comet Pattern
The Boston & Sandwich Glass Company
Sandwich, Massachusetts
c. 1850–1870

188. Compote, Covered Sugar Bowl, Decanter — Sharp Diamond Pattern
New England Glass Company
Cambridge, Massachusetts
c. 1850–1870

189. Compote — Sandwich Star Pattern
The Boston & Sandwich Glass Company
Sandwich, Massachusetts
c. 1860

190. Dolphin Candlesticks
The Boston & Sandwich
Glass Company
Sandwich, Massachusetts
c. 1855–1870

**191. Bar Decanter —
Washington Pattern**
New England Glass Company
Cambridge, Massachusetts
c. 1865

192. Pitcher, Sugar Bowl, Covered Butter — Paneled Wheat Pattern
Hobbs, Brockunier & Company
Wheeling, West Virginia
c. 1870–1880

193. Tumbler, Candlestick
Pittsburgh Area
c. 1860

194. Perfume Bottle
New England Glass Company
Cambridge, Massachusetts
c. 1865–1875

194a. Perfume Bottles
1865–1875

195. Inkwell
New England Glass Company
Cambridge, Massachusetts
c. 1870

196. Vase
Pittsburgh Area
c. 1860

127

AMERICAN CUT, ENGRAVED, AND ENAMELED GLASS:
1850–1880

While early pressed and later mass-produced pressed pattern glass was being made, cut, engraved, and enameled table and decorative glassware was still being created for the "Carriage Trade." Bakewell & Company, Pittsburgh, Pennsylvania, the longest operating nineteenth century American flint glass manufactory (1808–1882) was noted for the splendid cutting of their brilliant glass. Number 144 is a good example of their early cut style.

The New England Glass Company, Cambridge, Massachusetts (1818–1888) advertised cut glass from the company's beginning, recording 24 steam cutting mills in operation. Considerable glass must have been cut during the early years, but the quality seems indistinguishable from the imported Anglo-Irish wares. The Boston & Sandwich Glass Company's cut glass probably parallels that made by the New England Glass Company but in smaller quantity. In 1842 Sandwich received special mention of cut glass at the Franklin Institute Exhibition in Philadelphia.

Engraved glass seems easier to identify. The cut and engraved 1831 Thomas Norton tumbler made in Pittsburgh, or possibly Wheeling, West Virginia, illustrates early techniques. Other typical Pittsburgh engraved glass is that with the daisy and leaf band, numbers 153, 154, and 164.

Colorful Bohemian cased and cut glass (now called overlay) exhibited in the London Crystal Palace Exhibition in 1851 was soon produced by the New England Glass Company and exhibited in The New York Crystal Palace of 1853–1854. The ruby cased and cut compote, number 206, and the green tumble-up, number 211, both from the Smith Collection, could well be such pieces.

Although The Boston & Sandwich Glass Company, Sandwich, Massachusetts, is incorrectly thought to have produced only lacy and later pressed pattern glass, Sandwich made all types of table and decorative glassware. Sandwich's display at the 1876 Philadelphia Centennial Exposition included blown, cut, engraved, and enameled glassware. The one surviving Sandwich catalog, c. 1874, illustrates hundreds of similar quality glass. Number 202 and 204 show typical engraved and cut designs and number 197 illustrates various enameled ware.

In the last quarter of the nineteenth century, at the height of the Victorian era, the taste for the exotic and for elaborate decoration led to new glass effects, colors, and decorations. Bright cut, Amberina, Peach Blow, Burmese, Royal Flemish, and so forth, were created and are described in the following section.

197. Enameled Opal Glass
The Boston & Sandwich
Glass Company
Sandwich, Massachusetts
c. 1874

198. Engraved Glass
New England Glass Company
Cambridge, Massachusetts
c. 1850–1860

199. Decanter and Spoon Holder
New England Glass Company
Cambridge, Massachusetts
c. 1850–1870

200. Oil Lamp
The Boston & Sandwich Glass Company
Sandwich, Massachusetts
c. 1860

201. Celery Vase, Compote, Covered Sugar Bowl
New England Area
Probably The Boston & Sandwich Glass Company
Sandwich, Massachusetts
c. 1855

202. Decanter and Two Goblets
The Boston & Sandwich Glass Company
Sandwich, Massachusetts
c. 1870–1880

203. Pitcher, Tumbler, Jar
The Boston & Sandwich
Glass Company
Sandwich, Massachusetts
c. 1870–1886

204. Finger Bowl and Wine
The Boston & Sandwich
Glass Company
Sandwich, Massachusetts
c. 1874

132

205. Newel Post Finial
New England Glass Company
Cambridge, Massachusetts
c. 1850–1860

206. Compote
New England Glass Company
Cambridge, Massachusetts
c. 1855

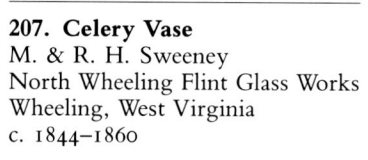

207. Celery Vase
M. & R. H. Sweeney
North Wheeling Flint Glass Works
Wheeling, West Virginia
c. 1844–1860

208. Castor Set
New England Glass Company
Cambridge, Massachusetts
c. 1857–1862

209. Spoonholder
New England Glass Company
Cambridge, Massachusetts
c. 1860

210. Paperweights
New England Glass Company
Cambridge, Massachusetts
c. 1852–1880

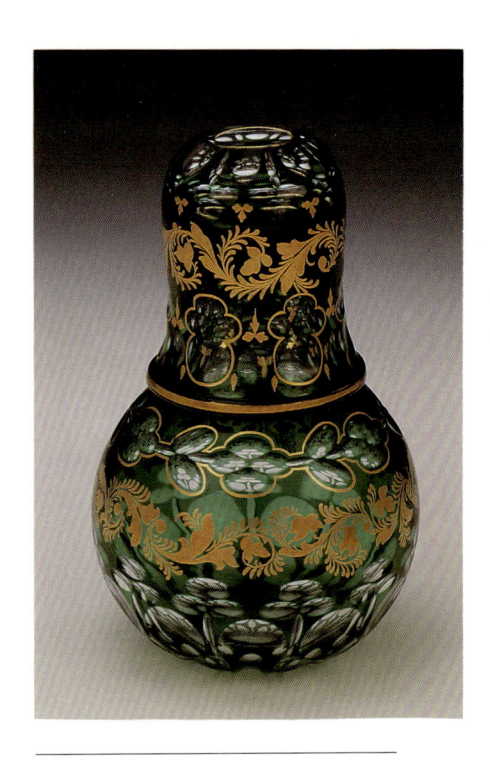

211. Bohemian Style Tumble-Up
New England Glass Company
Cambridge, Massachusetts
c. 1850–1860

212. Kerosene Lamp
The Boston & Sandwich
Glass Company
Sandwich, Massachusetts
c. 1865–1875

AMERICAN ART GLASS: 1878–1900

The prosperity brought to the new American middle-class by growing industrialization after the Civil War also brought an increase in their desire to enhance their surroundings with items of artistic appeal. Where the glass factories of the East Coast of the United States were concerned, this was a challenge which not only needed to be met but which might assist them in competing with the glass factories in the American Midwest where nearby fuel and the perfection of the cheaper soda-lime glass formula enabled them to turn out vast quantities of less expensive pressed glass. Thus it was that the "Art Glass" period of the last quarter of the 19th century developed.

The development of pressed glass had made utilitarian glass products readily available to most Americans, and, if the East Coast factories were to compete with the glasshouses of western Pennsylvania, West Virginia, and Ohio, which were turning out such products en masse, it seemed natural to try to appeal to a more affluent audience which might be interested in glass as an "art" rather than a purely "utilitarian" form.

The creation of new techniques in glassmaking would lead to a more colorful type of glass, often heavily decorated in a manner which appealed to late Victorian sensibilities. The realization that certain types of glass could develop "shading" in its colors if it were heated, cooled, and then re-heated made it possible to create the new "Art Glass." (See the description of the technique in the discussion of individual glasshouses hereafter.)

Imaginative names added to the attractiveness of the new glass: Amberina, Peach Blow, Wild Rose, Pomona, Burmese, Crown Milano, Napoli are but a few of the names which were conjured to lure the public to the market. The period of each of these products was brief, and in time they were replaced by a new interest in cut glass and then in the glass of Tiffany, Steuben, and their imitators. The "Art Glass" period, however, does reflect a time in American taste, one, which for the most part is more honored historically than artistically.

213. Lava Glass Vases
Mt. Washington Glass Company
New Bedford, Massachusetts
c. 1878

The Mt. Washington Glass Company
1837–1900

The Mt. Washington Glass Company was established in 1837 in South Boston by Deming Jarves of Sandwich Glass fame. In 1870 William L. Libbey, the then owner (and later principal of the New England Glass Company), moved the business to New Bedford. It was incorporated as The Mt. Washington Glass Company in 1871, and in 1894 it merged with its neighbor, the silver-plating firm, the Pairpoint Manufacturing Company. From 1900 to 1938 it was the Pairpoint Corporation. In the following years there were other reorganizations. It was Gundersen Glass Works from 1939 to 1952 and the Gundersen-Pairpoint Glass Works to 1957. Its current successor, the Pairpoint Glass Company, still operates in Sagamore, Massachusetts.

No documented South Boston period glass can be identified, but the products must have been similar to those made by The Boston & Sandwich Glass Company, the New England Glass Company, and other eastern factories. However, the celebrated "Art Glass" produced in New Bedford during the last two decades of the 19th century are the predominately blown ornamental pieces. The exotic styles and colors, often with enameling, were usually patented and assigned romantic names such as Lava, Burmese, Albertine, Royal Flemish, Crown Milano, Napoli, Verona, Rose Amber (Amberina), and Peach Blow.

Mt. Washington's Lava Glass, patented on May 28, 1878, by Frederick Shirley, was known at first as Sicilian Glass. It was one of the early Art Glass styles to attract the attention of the glass buying public, and it was soon followed by Mt. Washington's Rose Amber—see the section below as to the conflict with the New England Glass Company over this style and the name Amberina.

Reference: Avila, George C. *The Pairpoint Glass Story.* George C. Avila and The New Bedford Glass Society, New Bedford, Massachusetts, 1978.

**Amberina Glass
The New England Glass Company**
c. 1883–1886

The creative accomplishments of Joseph Locke, whose fame as an artist-craftsman in glass began as a cameo artist for the English glasshouse of Hodgetts, Richardson and Company in Wordsley, near Stourbridge, England, and eventually enabled his American employer, the New England Glass Company, to become a leader in the Art Glass period of the last quarter of the 19th century.

Locke was noted for his delicate cameo work in glass in England, and in 1876 he produced a copy of the famous Roman Portland Vase in cameo glass. (His Happy Child and Unhappy Child cameo vases, now in The Chrysler Museum, are discussed in the 19th century European glass section of this volume).

In 1882, Locke came to the United States and began work at the New England Glass Company. An innovator in the field of glass, he was responsible for the creation of a number of Art Glass styles, among which were Amberina, Plated Amberina, Pomona, Wild Rose (Peach Blow), Agata, and Maize glass.

On July 24, 1883, Locke patented the formula and technique for Amberina glass. Amberina is a blown or mold-blown glass made from a gold-ruby, heat-sensitive glass. This glass consisted of a homogeneous single layer of glass whose shading from amber to ruby was accomplished at the time of its creation by a slight cooling of the molten glass and then a reheating. The part of the vessel nearest the intense heat "struck" ruby; the remainder of the glass shaded down to an amber color: thus Amberina, as the glass was named.

In the United States, other glass producers noted for producing amberina art glass were the Mt. Washington Glass Company of New Bedford, Massachusetts, and Hobbs, Brockunier and Company of Wheeling, West Virginia. A patent infringement dispute between the New England Glass Company and the Mt. Washington Glass Company was settled by an agreement which allowed the New England Glass Company to retain the name of Amberina. Therefore, Mt. Washington had to seek a new name for their version of Amberina and they settled on the name of Rose Amber.

214. Amberina Celery Vase, Tumbler, Vases, Bowl
New England Glass Company
Cambridge, Massachusetts
c. 1883–1886

**Plated Amberina
The New England Glass
Company**

Plated Amberina is a glass which was patented for the New England Glass Company in 1886. It is a mold-blown (optic ribbed), luminous, opal glass cased with Amberina, the then popular glass which shades from amber to ruby.

**215. Plated Amberina
Quart Size Pitcher**
c. 1886

**Rose Amber Glass
Mt. Washington Glass Company**

After losing the court battle over the use of the name Amberina (see the introduction to No. 214 above), the Mt. Washington Glass Company used the term Rose Amber for its Amberina-type glass.

**216. Rose Amber Pitcher
(Amberina)**
Mt. Washington Glass Company
New Bedford, Massachusetts
c. 1883

Hobbs, Brockunier Amberina Glass

Hobbs, Brockunier obtained a license from The New England Glass Company to manufacture pressed Amberina.

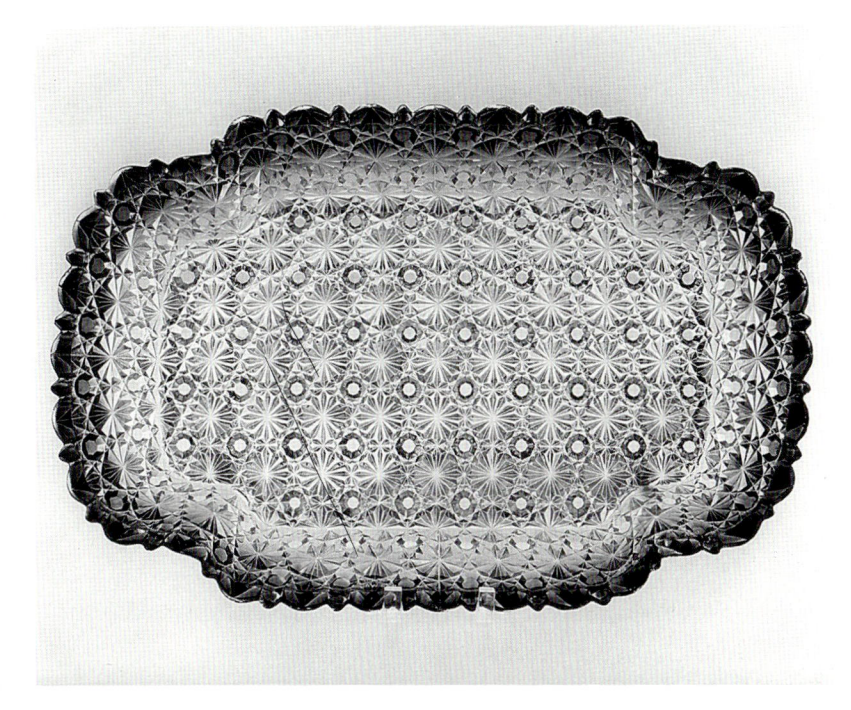

217. Amberina Ice Cream Tray
Hobbs, Brockunier and Company
Wheeling, West Virginia
c. 1886

New England Peach-Blow Glass

Peach Blow glass is a blown or mold-blown glass made from an opaque, gold-ruby, heat-sensitive formula which was patented on March, 2, 1886, by Edward D. Libbey for the New England Glass Company. The shading of the homogeneous single layer glass from cream to opaque rose took place at the time of making by a slight cooling and then reheating. The part of the vessel nearest the intense heat "struck" the rose color. The Wild Rose name came from a patent dispute with the Mt. Washington Glass Company of New Bedford, Massachusetts (see the introduction to No. 214 above). The settlement allowed Mt. Washington the use of the name Peach Blow while the New England Glass Company would call its product Wild Rose. This was part of the Amberina-Rose Amber agreement.

218. New England Peach Blow Pitcher and Tumbler
New England Glass Company
Cambridge, Massachusetts
c. 1886–1888

Hobbs, Brockunier Peach Blow

219. The Morgan Vase
Hobbs, Brockunier and Company
Wheeling, West Virginia
c. 1886

220. Wheeling Peach Blow
Hobbs, Brockunier and Company
Wheeling, West Virginia
c. 1886

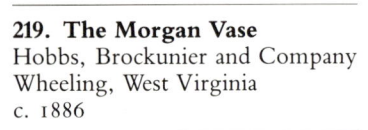

142

**Peach Blow Glass
Mt. Washington Glass
Company**

The Mt. Washington Glass Company version of Peach Blow, patented in 1886, was made from a heat-sensitive glass with additions of prepared gold and cobalt. This Peach Blow resulted in a single layer opaque glass shading from pale blue to soft rose.

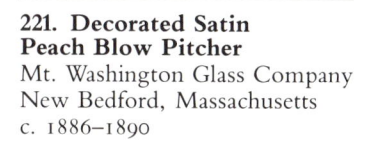

**221. Decorated Satin
Peach Blow Pitcher**
Mt. Washington Glass Company
New Bedford, Massachusetts
c. 1886–1890

**222. Satin Peach Blow
Vase and Bowl**
Mt. Washington Glass Company
New Bedford, Massachusetts
c. 1886–1890

143

Agata Glass
New England Glass Company

Agata glass was created through the addition of a metallic stain to glass which then was mottled by spattering at the furnace with a volatile liquid such as alcohol. The Agata technique was patented for the New England Glass Company on January 18, 1887, by Joseph Locke. Although usually used on Peach Blow glass, some opaque green glass is decorated with stained borders.

223. Agata Glass Vase, Pitcher, and Bowl
New England Glass Company
Cambridge, Massachusetts
c. 1887–1888

Pomona Glass
The New England Glass Company

The "First Ground" Pomona glass was patented for the New England Glass Company by Joseph Locke on April 28, 1885. It was a blown or mold-blown colorless glass decorated with a hand-etched, swirled, Jack Frost-like background and usually had an amber and blue stain decoration. On June 15, 1886, another patent was issued to produce a similar effect but by a less expensive technique. The etching was done using a powder which produced a stipple-like background. Various stain decorations were added. These pieces are known as "Second Ground" Pomona.

224. Pomona Art Glass Cream and Sugar, Pitcher
New England Glass Company
Cambridge, Massachusetts
c. 1885–1886

Burmese Glass
Mt. Washington Glass Company

Burmese is the romantic name given to an opaque glass which shaded from canary yellow to a soft salmon. It is a homogeneous, heat-sensitive glass made from a formula containing small amounts of uranium oxide and prepared gold. The original furnace work produced the canary yellow color, then, after slight cooling and partial reheating, the salmon color "strikes" at the point of most intense heat, making this a single-layer shaded glassware.

The Mt. Washington Glass Company of New Bedford, Massachusetts, was the only U.S. firm to produce Burmese commercially, and it was patented for them on December 15, 1885, by Frederick Shirley. Shortly thereafter, the English rights were acquired by Thomas Webb & Sons of Stourbridge, England, who produced this glass under the name of Queen's Burmese Ware.

225. Burmese Kerosene Lamp
Mt. Washington Glass Company
New Bedford, Massachusetts
c. 1885–1890

**226. Burmese Pitcher
"Fish Swimming in a Net of Gold"**
Mt. Washington Glass Company
New Bedford, Massachusetts
c. 1885–1890

227. Burmese Candlesticks and Vase
Mt. Washington Glass Company
New Bedford, Massachusetts
c. 1885–1890

228. Decorated Satin Burmese Vases
Mt. Washington Glass Company
New Bedford, Massachusetts
c. 1885–1890

**Royal Flemish
Mt. Washington Glass
Company**

Royal Flemish is the name of an enamel design reminiscent of and probably inspired by the then popular Victorian stained glass windows. Colorless glass was lightly enameled in sections which were separated by thick gilt lines intersecting various enameled scenes and designs. Although Royal Flemish was advertised as early as 1889, the trademark of *RF* in a diamond with the *R* reversed was not patented until 1894.

229. Royal Flemish Vase
Mt. Washington Glass Company
New Bedford, Massachusetts
c. 1889–1893

230. Royal Flemish Ewer
Mt. Washington Glass Company
New Bedford, Massachusetts
c. 1889–1894

147

231. Royal Flemish
Mt. Washington Glass Company
New Bedford, Massachusetts
c. 1889–1896

Crown Milano Glass
Mt. Washington Glass Company

Crown Milano is a richly decorated opal satin glass in imitation of porcelain. First it was called Albertine and subsequently Crown Milano. The latter was marked with a patented trade mark of a crown above an entwined *CM*. Glossy Crown Milano is another patented design with a red crown trademark framed with a wreath of leaves.

232. Crown Milano Kerosene Lamp
Mt. Washington Glass Company
New Bedford, Massachusetts
c. 1893

**233. Crown Milano
Pilgrim Flask Style Ewer**
Mt. Washington Glass Company
New Bedford, Massachusetts
c. 1893

**234. Glossy Crown
Milano Covered Jar**
Mt. Washington Glass Company
New Bedford, Massachusetts
c. 1893

235. Napoli Vase
Mt. Washington Glass Company
New Bedford, Massachusetts
c. 1894

236. Cameo Glass Chandelier
Mt. Washington Glass Company
New Bedford, Massachusetts
c. 1890–1895

Napoli Glass

The Napoli decorating design was patented by Albert Steffin, head of the Mt. Washington Glass Company decorating department, on May 22, 1894. The decorating technique is a variant of reverse painting on glass, but it is executed on a three-dimensional object thereby giving the design more depth.

Smith Brothers
New Bedford, Massachusetts
(1874–1899)

The Smith Brothers, whose father had established the decorating department for the Boston & Sandwich Glass Company in the early 1850s, learned glass decorating there. The brothers, Alfred and Harry, opened the Mt. Washington Decorating Department in 1871 and after three years leased the decorating shop from Mt. Washington to operate independently as Smith Brothers until 1885 when they purchased a larger facility of their own.

They advertised "new decorated gas and oil shades, vases, plaques, tiles, salts, peppers, muffiniers," and so forth. The business continued until 1899 when financial reverses forced Smith Brothers into bankruptcy.

237. Vases
Smith Brothers
New Bedford, Massachusetts
c. 1874–1894

237a. Pair of Opal Vases
Cristallerie de Baccarat
France
c. 1875–1885

151

238. Opal Vase
Smith Brothers
New Bedford, Massachusetts
c. 1893

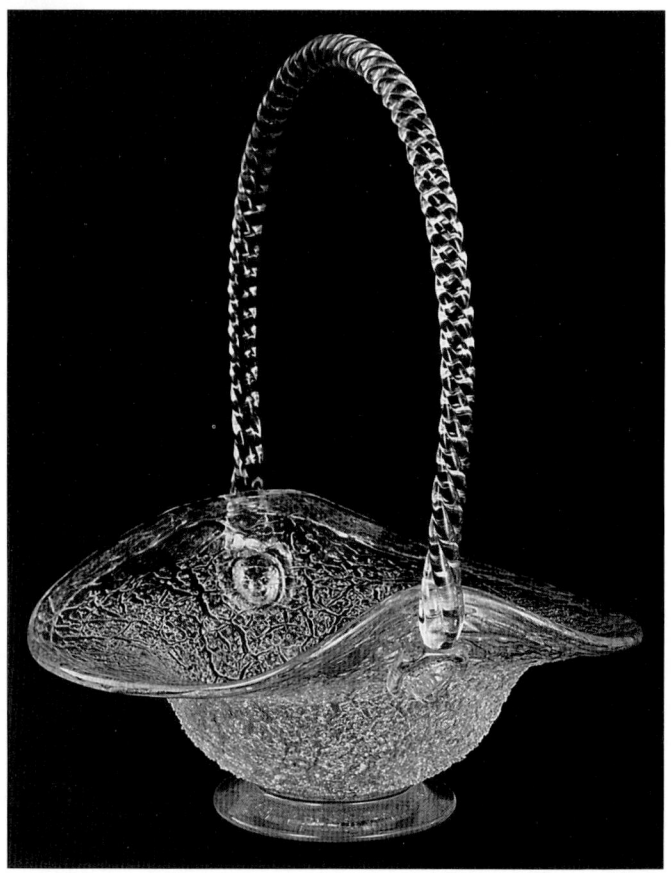

239. Overshot Basket
The Boston & Sandwich
Glass Company
Sandwich, Massachusetts
c. 1874

Other Glass Styles or Companies of the Era:

The Vasa Murrhina Art Glass Company

Vasa Murrhina glass was created from a patented technique and made at the old Cape Cod Glass Company factory building (about a half-mile from The Boston & Sandwich Glass Company) which was leased to Flowers & DeVoy, Vasa Murrhina Art Glass Company of Hartford, Connecticut. Not many examples of Vasa Murrhina survived because of annealing problems.

240. Vasa Murrhina Pitcher
Vasa Murrhina Art Glass Company
Sandwich, Massachusetts
c. 1883

Spangled Glass
Hobbs, Brockunier and Company

The manufacturing technique for this spangled glass was patented by William Leighton, Jr., 1883 and 1884.

241. Pitcher
Hobbs, Brockunier and Company
Wheeling, West Virginia
c. 1884

AMERICAN GLASS OF THE ART NOUVEAU PERIOD:
1895–1920

The Art Nouveau movement began in France in the last quarter of the 19th century, and its influence gradually swept across the artistic world of Europe and America. (A full description of the Art Nouveau movement is given in the introduction to the section on "European Art Nouveau" in this book.) In the United States and England, however, there were other currents which were popular during these last 25 years of the 1800s—the Art Glass movement, the continuing interest in pressed glass, particularly in its pattern mode, and a growing fascination with cut glass. Art Nouveau, nonetheless, was to be the "wave of the future" in America before the century was out.

If there is one name which is associated with Art Nouveau in the United States, it is that of Louis Comfort Tiffany (whose life and work are detailed below). As the new century began, other imitators of Tiffany came to the fore—for imitation is the best way to describe the other artists and firms in the Art Nouveau style who found a place in public taste due to Tiffany's groundbreaking efforts. Quezal Art Glass, Kew Blas glass, the work of the Durand glasshouse, and Frederick Carder's Steuben before the 1930s, among other glass manufacturers, are the other names associated with the American Art Nouveau movement. Few could compete with Tiffany in popularity during the first quarter of the 20th century, however.

While the Art Nouveau movement reached its apogee by the first World War in Europe, in the United States the interest in the style reached well into the 1920s before it too climaxed and began to fade.

Louis Comfort Tiffany
(1848–1933)
Tiffany Glass Company,
1885–1892
Tiffany Glass &
Decorating Company,
1882–1902
Tiffany Studios,
1902–1928

After a successful career as a painter and decorator, Louis Comfort Tiffany focused more on glass. A factory was established in 1892 in Corona, New York, where the first production was glass for the Tiffany Chapel at the 1893 Chicago Columbian Exposition.

In 1894 the trademark Favrile, meaning hand-wrought was registered for decorative glass described as follows:

> . . . *It may therefore be either flat, foliated, convoluted, cylindrical, globular or cubical, of one color or many, laminated, floriated or foliatious.*

The Favrile trademark eventually was used for all products of the Tiffany Studios: glass, metal, pottery, and so forth.

Blown Tiffany vessels were first exhibited in December 1895 at Siegfried Bing's *Maison de l'Art Nouveau*, Paris, and simultaneously at Tiffany's Fourth Avenue showrooms, New York.

The Chrysler collection of blown glass includes all the special techniques: the exotic nature-inspired flower forms, peacock glass with the feather design, *Cypriote* made with a pock-marked surface imitative of the corroded exterior of ancient buried glass, lava glass, heavy irregular shaped rough surfaced dark blue with iridescent decoration, the gooseneck, an old Persian rosewater sprinkler form, the extraordinary Jack-in-the-Pulpit, the paperweight techniques with internal designs and iridescent lining, the solid colored Chinese/Oriental shapes, and carved vessels. All these and more are in the collection. The diversity of Tiffany blown glass and other products is well illustrated in the 1978 catalog, *The Tiffany Collection of The Chrysler Museum at Norfolk* by Paul Doros.

The first portable lamp was made in 1896 and the production of those with metal standards and leaded shades began in *1898* after the bronze foundry was purchased in 1897.

The gifted craftsmen, expert glass blowers, and fine designers, both men and women, working closely under the supervision of Louis C. Tiffany created products which made the Tiffany name internationally famous. The daring, abstract designs and "accidentals" in blown glass previewed abstract expressionism. Tiffany was a pioneer of modern art.

242. Lava Bowl
Tiffany Glass
& Decorating Company
Corona, New York
c. 1895

243. Monumental Plaque
Tiffany Glass
& Decorating Company
Corona, New York
c. 1896

244. Cypriote Vase
Tiffany Glass
& Decorating Company
Corona, New York
c. 1895

245. Wisteria Table Lamp
Tiffany Glass
& Decorating Company
Corona, New York
c. 1901

246. Tiffany Vase
Tiffany Glass
& Decorating Company
Corona, New York
c. 1900

157

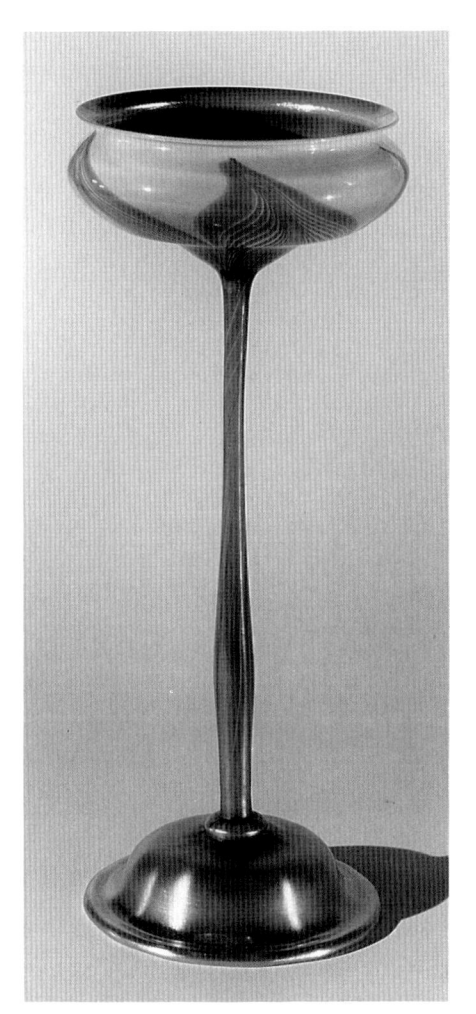

247. Flower Form
Tiffany Glass
& Decorating Company
Corona, New York
c. 1900

248. Vase
Tiffany Furnaces
Corona, New York
c. 1916

249. Plates
Tiffany Furnaces
Corona, New York
c. 1918

250. "Nellie Virginia Sands De Lamar" Stained Glass Portrait Window
Tiffany Studios
Corona, New York
c. 1915

250a. Close-Up

159

251. Table Lamp
Designed by Patricia Gay
Louis C. Tiffany Furnaces, Inc.
Corona, New York
c. 1922–1925

Quezal Art Glass and Decorating Company
Brooklyn, New York
1901–1925

The Quezal Art Glass and Decorating Company, founded by Martin Bach and Thomas Johnson, former Tiffany employees, is a firm which produced fine glass in the Art Nouveau style. It was probably the most successful emulator of Tiffany products. The inspiration for the company's name is described in one of their advertisements as follows:

QUEZAL—THE GLASS NAMED AFTER A BIRD

There is no more beautiful creature in the world than the Quezal bird, a rare feathered denizen of the impenetrable forests of Central America, around which cluster a wealth of strange and beautiful Aztec traditions. Few travelers or even explorers have seen the Quezal, which shuns the haunts of men as does no other living creature. But those who have been fortunate enough to have seen it declare that "matchless" is the only word to describe its beauty. Its back is a brilliant metallic green, so vivid that it shines even in the twilight of the woods. Its breast a crimson so deep and bright as the most brilliant ruby. On its head it wears a jeweled golden crown—a helmet effect of bright yellow and green.

When we were first ready to put on the market our beautiful glass, which exceeds in beauty any other glass on the market, we decided to name it after this glorious forest dweller of Guatemala. The glass is made by a secret process and experts tell us it is the envy and despair of other glass manufacturers and yet it is not exorbitant in price. We show this beautiful glassware in unique and artistic shapes. Our lines include vases, compotes, flower bowls, bud vases, finger bowls, plates, cups, ash trays, indirect light bowls and other lighting glassware, lamp bases, lamp shades, electroliers, etc.

(Ed. note: In fact, the correct spelling of the Central American bird is Quetzal.)

252. Vase
Quezal Art Glass and
Decorating Company
Brooklyn, New York
c. 1904

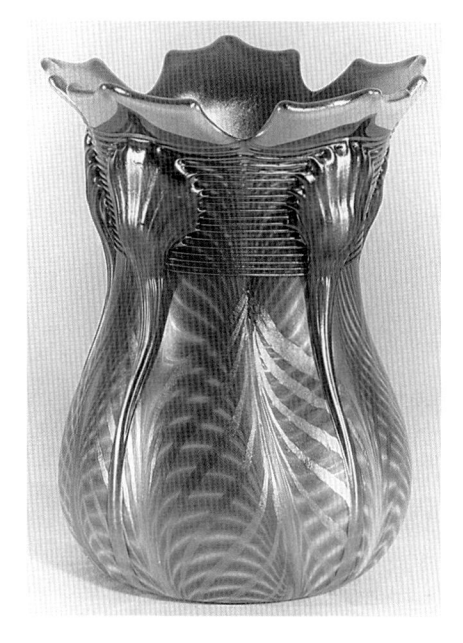

253. Blown, Iridescent Glass
Quezal Art Glass and
Decorating Company
Brooklyn, New York
1903–1925

Kew-Blas Glass
1854–1924

The Union Glass Company was one of the Boston area tableware manufacturers. The firm was particularly noted for pressed glass (including several patented designs), lighting devices, silvered glass, and glass blanks sold for cutting. Around 1900 Union's contribution to American Art Nouveau glass was a Tiffany-type of glass which they called and marked with an engraved KEW-BLAS. The name was an anagram of the name of the Superintendent, W. S. Blake.

254. Kew-Blas Glass
Union Glass Co.
Somerville, Massachusetts
c. 1900–1905

Steuben Glass Works
Corning, New York
(1903–   )

Frederick Carder (1863–1963), a glass artist and designer at the famous Stourbridge, England, glass house of Stevens & Williams, emigrated to Corning in 1903 at the invitation of and with the financial backing of T. G. Hawkes and other stockholders to establish the Steuben Glass Works. The firm was founded mainly to produce crystal blanks for the Hawkes cutting firm but soon Carder was producing colorful table and decorative glass.

In 1917 when wartime restrictions caused Steuben to be declared a nonessential industry, the business was sold to Corning Glass Works for the production of necessary commercial products. Shortly after the war, Steuben, now the art glass division of Corning, reverted to the production of colorful, high-style table and decorative glass.

255. Steuben Aurene
Frederick Carder
Steuben Glass Works
Corning, New York
c. 1904–1925

During the three decades Carder was in charge of the Steuben Glass Works, thousands of styles in hundreds of colors were produced. A mingling of styles was made, some in the classical, some in the Art Nouveau, and some in the Art Deco styles. The popular designs continued in production for many years.

In 1932, as tastes were changing, the Carder era came to an end. A colorless, brilliant, optical-quality glass formula was created for fashionable blown, cut and engraved which is still being produced.

256. Steuben Rosaline
Frederick Carder
Steuben Glass Works
Corning, New York
c. 1925–1930

257. Acid-Etched Cameo Hunting Pattern Vase
Frederick Carder
Steuben Glass Works
Corning, New York
c. 1925–1932

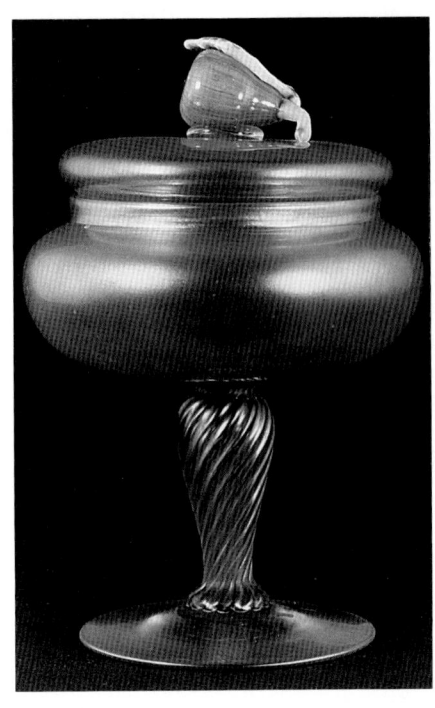

258. Verre de Soie—Covered Compote
Frederick Carder
Steuben Glass Works
Corning, New York
c. 1925

259. Green Jade Vase
Frederick Carder
Steuben Glass Works
Corning, New York
c. 1929–1932

260. Bonbon Dish
Frederick Carder
Steuben Glass Works
Corning, New York
c. 1929

261. Intarsia Vases and Bowl
Frederick Carder
Steuben Glass Works
Corning, New York
c. 1929

The Nash Glass Corporation
Corona, New York
1928–1931

The Nash Corporation, under the direction of A. Douglas Nash, President, was the successor to Tiffany Furnaces. It was he who had been the last manager at Tiffany from 1918 to 1928. The Nash firm ceased operations in 1931.

262. Chintz Vase
A. Douglas Nash Corp.
Corona, New York
c. 1928–1931

T. G. Hawkes & Co.
Corning, New York
1880–1962

In 1880 Thomas G. Hawkes established a glass cutting firm in Corning which grew into Corning's largest cut glass factory. Blanks for cutting were supplied by Corning Glass and Dorflinger among others, and, after its opening in 1903, primarily by Steuben. After World War I "Rich-Cut" glass was no longer fashionable, and lighter blanks and less elaborate cut and engraved designs were offered. The business ceased in 1962.

263. Punch Bowl with Silver-Gilt Stand
T. G. Hawkes & Co.
(for the glass)
Corning, New York
and
Gorham Manufacturing Co.
(for the silver)
Providence, Rhode Island
c. 1904

264. Bright Cut Plate
T. G. Hawkes & Co.
Corning, New York
c. 1909

Henry Clay Fry Glass Company
Rochester, Pennsylvania
1901–1933

Henry Clay Fry had made his name in the glass industry when he founded the H. C. Fry Company in 1901. His experience as president of The Rochester Tumbler Company (1872–1899), the firm which successfully manufactured tumblers exclusively, and, in 1899 as the first president of the short-lived National Glass Company, indicates his importance in the glass field. The superior quality of the early cut glass by the H. C. Fry Company is still recognized. Shortly after World War I, when the taste for brilliant-cut glass was no longer fashionable, Fry produced an art glass line using an ovenware glass formula. Examples of this Pearl Art Glass titled Foval is illustrated in the next entry. Fry also made a reeded line, which is now often confused with Steuben's, and a bubbly glass not dissimilar from Pairpoint's.

265. Pearl Art Glass
H. C. Fry Glass Co.
Rochester, Pennsylvania
c. 1926–1930

167

C. Dorflinger & Sons
1865–1921

Christian Dorflinger, a French glassmaker, came to the United States in 1846, and by 1860 he had acquired three glasshouses. In 1865 he founded the Dorflinger Glass Works in White Mills, Pennsylvania, where he at first made blanks for other glasshouses but then moved into the cutting and engraving of glass. The factory was noted for its excellent table glassware, and the company survived in White Mills until 1921 under the direction of Dorflinger's sons and grandsons.

The Honesdale Decorating Company
Honesdale, Pennsylvania

The Honesdale Decorating Company in Honesdale, Pennsylvania, was a subsidiary of C. Dorflinger & Sons. The decorating division was managed, and, in 1916, purchased by Carl F. Prosch (1901–1932).

266. Bowl
C. Dorflinger & Sons
White Mills, Pennsylvania
c. 1917

267. Vases
Honesdale Decorating Company
Honesdale, Pennsylvania
c. 1910

H. P. Sinclaire & Company
1904–1927

H. P. Sinclaire grew up in Corning, New York, a relative of the Houghton family which had begun the Corning Glass Works. It was only natural that he would follow into the glass industry, and in 1883 he went to work for the T. G. Hawkes & Company of Corning in its financial area.

Developing an interest in engraving, he eventually allied himself with the Dorflingers of White Mills, Pennsylvania, and in 1904, with the aid of the Dorflingers, the H. P. Sinclaire and Company factory opened in Corning. Noted for its engraved tableware, the new company was to flourish throughout the 1920s. Sinclaire's sudden death in 1927 was a blow from which the firm never recovered, and shortly thereafter it went out of business.

268. Vase
H. P. Sinclaire & Co.
Corning, New York
c. 1917

269. Pearl Crystal Vase
H. P. Sinclaire & Co.
Corning, New York
c. 1920–1930

The Libbey Glass Company

In 1888 Edward Drummond Libbey transferred the New England Glass Company from Massachusetts to Toledo, Ohio. There the Libbey Glass Company intended to make rich-cut and artistic glass. It was successful in its intentions, but in time it was forced to make a more commercial and inexpensive line as well, selling tumblers and other such items to hotels. In 1933 it brought Douglas Nash (Tiffany's former associate) to its staff, and that same year the firm purchased the H. C. Fry Company.

270. Vases
The Libbey Glass Co.
Toledo, Ohio
c. 1917

271. Bowl
The Libbey Glass Co.
Toledo, Ohio
c. 1933

272. Vase
The Handel Co., Inc.
Meriden, Connecticut
c. 1910

273. Bright Cut Pitcher
Mt. Washington Company
New Bedford, Massachusetts
c. 1890

The Handel Co., Inc.
Meriden, Connecticut
1885–1936

The Handel Company, although most noted for their lamps, made other products such as this acid-cut stylized design on a cased blank.

The Mt. Washington Glass Company
The Pairpoint Corporation
Gundersen Glassworks

The Mt. Washington Glass Company was begun in 1837 by Deming Jarves, and its earlier importance is detailed in the section on American Art Glass in this book.

In 1894 it merged with the silver-plating firm the Pairpoint Manufacturing Company, and from 1900 to 1938 it was the Pairpoint Corporation. Under successive reorganizations it was the Gun-

274. Puffy Candlestick
Pairpoint Corporation
New Bedford, Massachusetts
c. 1907–1920

171

dersen Glass Works from 1939 to 1952 and then the Gundersen Pairpoint Glass Works until 1957. Its current successor, the Pairpoint Glass Company continues its operations in Sagamore, Massachusetts.

Noted for its Art Glass, the tradition of colored glass, as well as cut and engraved glass, was continued through its various corporate incarnations.

275. Bowl
Pairpoint Corporation
New Bedford, Massachusetts
c. 1924

276. Vase
Pairpoint Corporation
New Bedford, Massachusetts
c. 1924

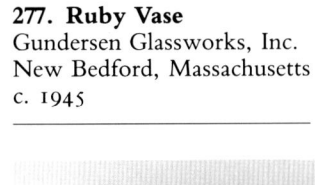

277. Ruby Vase
Gundersen Glassworks, Inc.
New Bedford, Massachusetts
c. 1945

278. Satin Finish Peach Blow
Gundersen Glassworks, Inc.
New Bedford, Massachusetts
c. 1952

279. Table Lamp
Bigelow Kennard & Co.
Boston, Massachusetts
c. 1910

173

Durand Art Glass
1924–1932

The last gasp of good quality Art Nouveau and Tiffany-type glass was made in Vineland, New Jersey, by Durand Art Glass, a subsidiary of the Vineland Flint Glass Works. Victor Durand, Jr., head of Vineland, hired Martin Bach, Jr., in 1924 to establish an art glass division. Bach, who had been associated with his father at the Quezal Art Glass and Decorating Company, gathered many former Quezal workmen and produced glassware in the Quezal style.

Many pieces of Durand were marked in silver script across the polished pontil scar, some with a large "V" and two numbers, one for the design, and one for the height.

The following entries illustrate the interesting glass made by Durand until 1932 when the subsidiary was closed shortly after Victor Durand, Jr., was killed in an automobile accident.

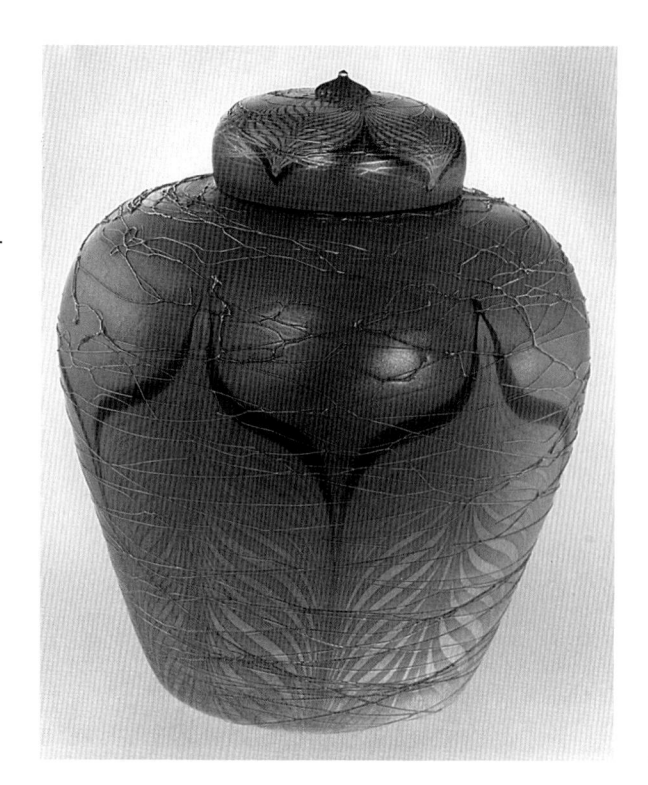

280. Covered Jar
Durand Art Glass
Vineland, New Jersey
c. 1925

281. Iridescent Glass
Durand Art Glass
Vineland, New Jersey
c. 1924–1932

282. Vase
Durand Art Glass
Vineland, New Jersey
c. 1924–1932

283. Crackle Lava Vase
Durand Art Glass
Vineland, New Jersey
c. 1930

284. Feather (Cobweb) Design
Durand Art Glass
Vineland, New Jersey
c. 1924–1932

Consolidated Lamp and Glass Company Art Glass Division
1894–1933/1967

In the 1920s the Art Glass Division of Consolidated Lamp produced several memorable Art Deco designs, some based on the popular Lalique style, and an inventive cubic style which was advertised as "The 'Curve of Beauty' Becomes Angular in Ruba Rombic."

285. Ruba Rombic
Art Glass Division of
Consolidated Lamp
and Glass Co.
Coraopolis, Pennsylvania
c. 1928

AMERICAN GLASS OF THE ART DECO PERIOD:
1920–1939

By the end of the 1920s, the Art Nouveau movement had reached a climax. Before long, a combination of changing public tastes and the results of the financial crash of 1929 were to see a number of the leading glass houses close their doors. Those who remained in operation gradually changed to the Art Deco style, a simpler, sparer, less colorful kind of glass. Some, like Verlys, copied Lalique's approach to modern glass; Steuben, on the other hand, made a clean break with the past and produced glass of a greater clarity as well as designs by leading artists of the world—not necessarily by glass designers alone. Of all these firms, Steuben alone was able to survive as a firm concerned with art in glass production.

286. Orchid Bowl
Verlys of America, Inc.,
a subsidiary of Holphane
Lighting Company
Newark, Ohio
c. 1935–1940

Verlys of America, Inc.
Newark, Ohio
(1935–1951)

The French parent firm (see European 20th century section) Société Anonyme Holophane, Les Andelys Verlys, France, supplied most of the molds used by the Newark, Ohio, subsidiary. Colorful, good quality glassware was made in the popular Lalique style. After World War II both Heisey and Fenton produced a few items using the Verlys molds.

Steuben Glass

In 1932–1933, Arthur A. Houghton, Jr., took over the direction of Steuben Glass. Making a complete break with the past, the colored glass of Frederick Carders Steuben was brought to a halt. Using a new lead glass of great clarity and suitable for engraving, a whole new design approach ensued. In addition to its own staff of glass designers, Steuben invited leading artists from the non-glass world to design for the company. As the "art" branch of the Corning Glass Works, its concern for artistry, craftsmanship, and quality glass made it the leading American art form suitable for gifts to heads of states—as well as an art form which had (and has) great appeal for the general public.

287. David & Goliath Sculpture
Designed by Don Wier
Steuben Glass
Corning, New York
1959

AMERICAN STUDIO GLASS:
1960 TO THE PRESENT DAY

In the 1960s, a period of intellectual and cultural ferment in the United States and elsewhere, young artists began to experiment in the various fields of art. The introduction of new furnaces which could be owned and operated by individual artists (see Labino below) was a boon to the post-World War II art glass movement, and small "studio" glasshouses sprang up, operated by individual artists who desired the freedom such means of creativity offered. Glass as an academic/technical subject became of interest to those of college age, and some 300 colleges in the United States were soon offering classes in glass. The heyday of the movement was the 1960s and 1970s, and although studio artists continued to make glass in the 1980s, a period of originality has been followed by one in which creativity is not as strong as in the initial years of the movement. The work of the artists listed hereafter are all of the Studio Movement.

Dominick Labino
(1910–1987)

Dominick Labino was a founder of the Studio Glass Movement in 1962. His technical advice for appropriate glass formulae and furnace design helped make a success of the first studio glass workshop under the direction of Harvey Littleton at the Toledo Museum of Art. After Labino retired in 1965 as Vice-President and Director of Research and Development for the Johns-Manville Fiber Glass Corporation, he established a hot glass studio on his farm in Grand Rapids, Ohio, where he continued glass research. He was honorary Curator of Glass at Toledo, and, in 1985, he received the Rakow Award for Excellence in the Art of Glass from The Corning Museum of Glass.

288. Dominick Labino
Grand Rapids, Ohio
1910–1987

Thomas J. Patti
Plainfield, Massachusetts

Thomas J. Patti, a studio artist with background in art and industrial design is famous for making small scale architectural-style glass sculpture blown into a semi-vessel, cubic form.

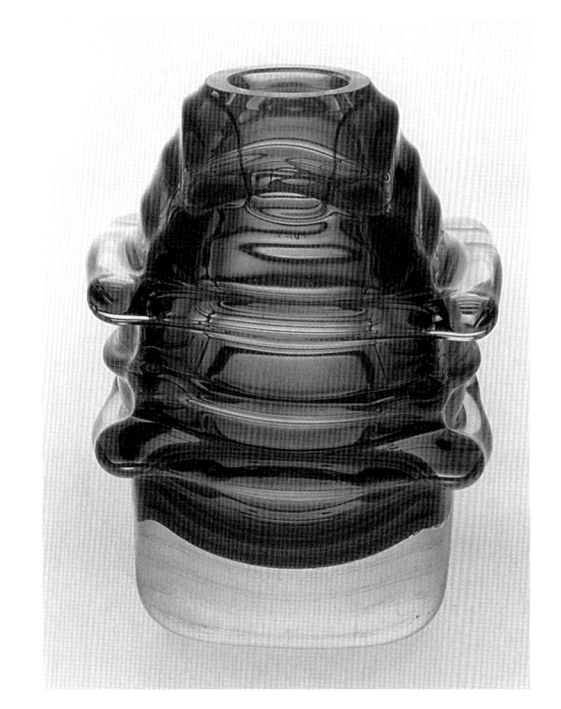

289. Ribbed Compound
Thomas J. Patti
Plainfield, Massachusetts
c. 1977

Harvey K. Littleton
Spruce Pine, North Carolina

Harvey Littleton, artist, ceramicist, hot glass sculptor, researcher, and teacher was the founding father and leader of the Studio Glass Movement. With the scientific collaboration of Dominic Labino, he successfully conducted the first hot glass workshop at the Toledo Museum of Art in 1962 and soon was offering courses in creative glassblowing at the University of Wisconsin. Following his retirement in 1976, he has devoted most of his time to glass sculpture, working in his Spruce Pine, North Carolina, studio.

290. Sculpture
Harvey K. Littleton
Spruce Pine, North Carolina
c. 1978

**291. Sea Form/
Macchia Assemblage**
Dale Chihuly
Tacoma, Washington
1982

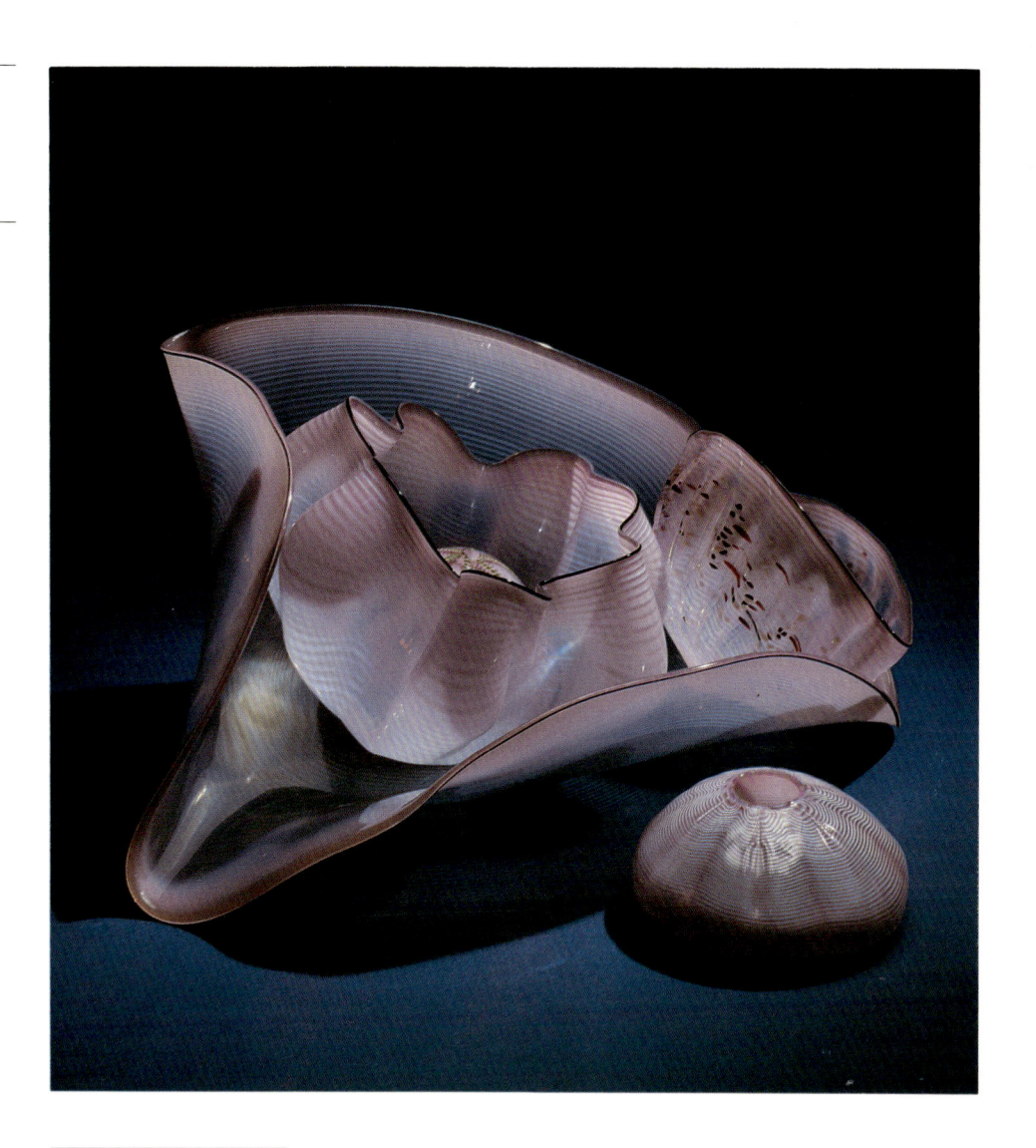

Dale Chihuly
Tacoma, Washington
(1941–   )

From the time Dale Chihuly received a Master's degree from the Rhode Island School of Design in 1968 and then spent a year in Venice on a Fulbright Grant studying glassblowing at the Venini Factory, he was in the vanguard of the Studio Glass Movement. For ten years he was chairman of the Glass Department at Rhode Island and in 1971 was a founder of the glassblowing summer school/workshop at Pilchuck, north of Seattle, Washington. He retired from RISD in 1980 and now devotes full time to his art.

Chihuly is one of, or perhaps, the most widely collected glass artist and is represented in the permanent collections of numerous major art museums both here and abroad.

183

292. "Moon Series #11" Sculpture
Mark Peiser
Penland, North Carolina
1983

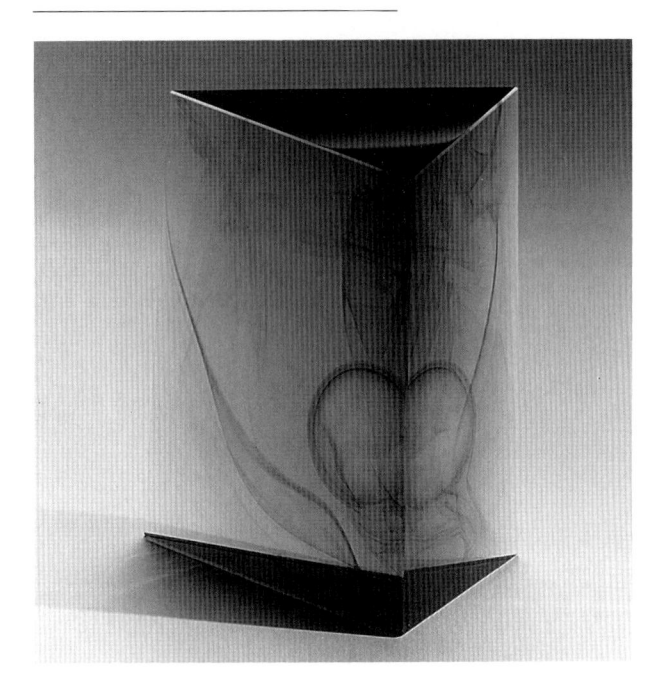

Mark Peiser
Penland, North Carolina

Mark Peiser, an artist with a background in engineering, design, and music, first gained recognition in 1972 with container shapes of colorful opaque glass decorated with semi-realistic, landscape designs. By 1978, he was making his famous and popular wisteria tree vases. These multi-layered, precise glass paintings using glass rods required exact planning and many continuous hours of furnace work.

By 1980, Peiser's vessel designs became more stylized. Two years later, he began making colorful blocks of solid glass by pouring into a mold by well-planned stages. Peiser's art was now the opposite of a vessel form.

Michael M. Glancy
Rehoboth, Massachusetts

Michael M. Glancy is on the faculty of the Metals Program and is a lecturer for the Glass Department of The Rhode Island School of Design. During several summers he has been a faculty member at Pilchuck Glass Center, near Seattle.

293. Golden Triskelion Sculpture
Michael M. Glancy
Rehoboth, Massachusetts
1984

CATALOG
INFORMATION

ANCIENT GLASS:
500 B.C. TO 1000 A.D.

1. Glass Core-Formed Vessels
Eastern Mediterranean
5th–2nd Centuries B.C.

a. Oinochoe
Early 5th Century B.C.
Dark green glass; yellow and light blue thread and zigzag decoration; some weathering and pitting.
H: 3¼" (8.5 cm)
GAnH.66.3 (71.6738)
Gift: Walter P. Chrysler, Jr.

b. Oinochoe
5th Century B.C.
Medium blue glass; yellow and turquoise thread decoration; slight weathering and pitting; some iridescence.
H: 4½" (11.4 cm) (66.34.5)
Museum Purchase.

c. Amphoriskos
2nd Century B.C.
Dark blue glass; red and white combed threading; a pair of applied blue handles; some pitting and iridescence.
H: 6" (15.2 cm)
GAnH.66.2 (71.6746)
Gift: Walter P. Chrysler, Jr.

d. Aryballos
5th Century B.C.
Dark blue glass; decorated with turquoise and yellow zigzags and threads; a pair of yellow double looped handles.
H: 2⅝" (7 cm)
GAnE.66.1 (71.6742)
Gift: Walter P. Chrysler, Jr.

2. Glass Mosaic Inlay—Uraeus (Cobra)
Probably Alexandria (Ptolemaic Egypt)
4th–1st Century B.C.
Multicolor glass mosaic of a rearing cobra; some pitting.
H: 11/16" (1.8 cm) 84.173.GAn
Gift: The Board of Trustees of The Chrysler Museum in honor of Walter P. Chrysler, Jr. for his 75th birthday.

3. Cup
Roman Empire, probably Alexandria, Egypt
Mid-first century A.D.
Mold-pressed; tooled; lathe-cut; polished; blue glass; 17 ribs.
D: 5⅛" (15 cm) GAnR.67.2 (71.6788)
Gift: Walter P. Chrysler, Jr.

4. "Ennion" Bowl
Roman Empire, probably Sidon, Syria
c. A.D. 50
Mold blown; transparent pale blue-green glass: geometric design with central rectangular cartouche in the upper frieze: ENNION/ETTOIE ("ENNION Made Me"); some weathering and iridescence.
H: 2 9/16" (6.5 cm)
GAnR.66.25 (71.6779)
Illustrated in: *The Journal of Glass Studies*, Vol. IV. The Corning Museum of Glass, Corning, New York, 1962. p. 50.
Note: A parallel object exists in the Yale University collection.
Gift: Walter P. Chrysler, Jr.

5. Cameo Fragments (Joining)
Roman Empire, probably Italy
1st Century A.D.
The fragments, from a vessel or plaque, were blown of two blue and two white layers of glass and then cameo carved showing Triton and a Nereid. Triton, the son of Poseidon and Amphitrite, was the trumpeter of the sea (note the shell trumpet); a Nereid was a sea nymph.
a: H: 1¼" (3.2 cm), W: ⅝" (1.6 cm)
85.10 GAnR
Museum Purchase.
b: H: ½" (2.2 cm), W: 11/16" (1.7 cm)
85.10 GAnR
Museum Purchase.

6. Flask and Cups
Roman Empire, probably Eastern Mediterranean or Alexandria, Egypt
Late 1st Century B.C.

a: Mosaic Cup
Cast; pre-formed; brown, yellow, and white glass canes in amethyst glass; some decomposition and reconstruction.
H: 1 9/16" (4 cm) GAnR.66.16 (71.6791)

b: Flask
Blown; mosaic color-band ribbons of blue, amber, white, and brown glass.
H: 3½" (9 cm) GAnR.66.27 (71.6789)

c: Mosaic Cup
Cast; pre-formed; yellow, blue, and red glass canes in green glass; some decomposition; iridescence inside.
H: 1 11/16" (4.3 cm) GAnR.66.15 (71.6790)
Gift: Walter P. Chrysler, Jr.

7. Krater
Roman Empire, Eastern Mediterranean
3rd Century A.D.
Blown; clear green tinted glass; pair of applied handle-like bosses; decorated with a band of thin threading; solid stem with pincered fins and round foot; some weathering, pitting, and iridescence.
H: 5¼" (13.5 cm) GAnR.66.3 (71.6823)
Gift: Walter P. Chrysler, Jr.

8. Rhyton
Roman Empire
3rd Century A.D.
Blown; clear green tinted glass; some iridescence.
L: 10¾" (27.3 cm) GAnR.66.26 (71.6794)
Gift: Walter P. Chrysler, Jr.

9. Roman Diety Beaker
Roman Empire, possibly Syria
Early 2nd Century A.D.
Mold-blown in a five-part mold; amethyst glass; design of Roman deities Neptune, Jupiter, Bacchus, and Mercury; missing areas partly reconstructed; some weathering.
H: 4½" (11.6 cm) GAnR.68.1 (71.6780)
Note: Believed to have been excavated in Asia Minor. A parallel object exists in the collection of the Hermitage Museum, Leningrad. A pale bluish-green one sold at Sotheby's (London), Lot 55 on July 9, 1984. Also see Weinberg, Gladys Davidson. "Mold-Blown Beakers with Mythological Scenes," pp. 39–40, *Journal of Glass Studies*, Vol. XIV. The Corning Museum of Glass, Corning, New York, 1972.
Gift: Walter P. Chrysler, Jr.

10. Mold Blown Glass
Roman Empire, Eastern Mediterranean
2nd–7th Century A.D.

a: Date Flask
Sidon, Syria
1st Century A.D.
Light amber and white glass; some decomposition and iridescence.
H: 2⅞" (7.3 cm) GAnR.66.24 (71.6786)
Gift: Walter P. Chrysler, Jr.

b: Lotus Bud Beaker
Syria
1st Century A.D.
Yellow amber glass; six rows of eight lotus buds in relief.
H: 8¼" (21 cm) GAnR.67.5
(71.6785)
Gift: Walter P. Chrysler, Jr.

c: Jerusalem Pilgrim Vessel
Palestine
580–630 A.D.
Dark amber glass; hexagonal; intaglio design of Jewish symbols; some iridescence and weathering.
H: 5" (12.7 cm) GAnB.67.1
(71.6774)
Gift: Walter P. Chrysler, Jr.

11. Ceremonial Drinking Vessel
Roman
3rd Century A.D.
Blown; clear green tinted glass; shape of a fish with rigaree; some decomposition and iridescence; partly reconstructed.
L: 9¼" (23.5 cm) GAnR.67.1
(71.6839)
Gift: Walter P. Chrysler, Jr.

12. Bowl
Roman Empire
4th–5th Century A.D.
Blown; cut; engraved; clear glass, faintly yellowish; hemispherical vessel; two round cuts above the polished pontil mark; bottom half has three rows of oval (lozenge) cuts then a wide band of seven engraved diamonds whose centers have cross hatching between more pillar cutting and other geometric lines.
Rim D: 5⁷⁄₁₆" (13.8 cm) GAnR.67.3
(71.6792)
Note: Similar to Fig. 3 on page 66 of the *Journal of Glass Studies*, VIII. The Corning Museum of Glass, Corning, New York, 1966. "A Group of Later Roman Glass Goblets from Cologne," Victor H. Elbern, "usually found in the Rhineland or Near East, 3rd or 4th Century A.D."
Gift: Walter P. Chrysler, Jr.

13. Animal "Dromedary" Flask
Syria–Iran
6th Century A.D.
Blown; green tinted glass; ovoid vase in a basket/cage of open zig-zag glass threads of green and amethyst on the back of a four-legged animal with an amethyst colored horn; heavy weathering; some corrosion and iridescence.
H: 4⅜" (11 cm) GAnI.81.1 (81.194)
Gift: Walter P. Chrysler, Jr.

14. Cup
Islamic (Possibly Iran)
c. 9th – 10th Century
Blown; cameo; green glass marquetry bands over clear glass; wheel-cut; stylized lotus design on either side and an intaglio-carved, styled palmette between the lotus designs.
H: 3⅜" (8.7 cm) GAnPe.68.6
(71.6769)
Note: Goldstein, Sidney, L. S. Rakow, and J. K. Rakow. *Cameo Glass: Masterpieces from 2000 Years of Glassmaking*. The Corning Museum of Glass, Corning, New York, 1982. No. 20, illustrated on page 35.
Gift: Walter P. Chrysler, Jr.

15. Flask
Persian (Iran)
c. 9th–10th Century
Blown; cut; colorless glass, yellow tint; bell shape; funnel neck panel; lentiloid and arcade-cut bands; weathering and iridescence.
H: 5⅝" (14.3 cm) 66.34.3
Museum Purchase.
Note: Similar to an object illustrated in the British Museum 1968 catalog: Harden, Donald B., K. S. Painter, R. S. Pindar-Wilson, and Hugh Tait. *Masterpieces of Glass*. Trustees of the British Museum, London, 1968. No. 140, p. 107.

VENETIAN GLASS:
1500–1800

---

16. Footed Bowl
Venice, Italy
c. 1500
Blown; pattern molded; colorless glass; blue rims and threads; enameled and gilded scale design.
H: 7⅜" (8.7 cm) GEV.68.4
(71.6733)
Gift: Walter P. Chrysler, Jr.

17. Bowl
Venice, Italy
16th Century
Mold-blown; colorless glass; hollow, ribbed, blue bulb projecting from the center of the bottom; paired scroll rigaree decorated handles.
H: 4¼" (10.8 cm) GEV.68.6
(71.6735)
Gift: Walter P. Chrysler, Jr.

18. Bowl
Venice, Italy
Early 17th Century
Blown; colorless, cracked ice glass; blue rim; hollow, ribbed, bulb projecting from center of the bottom; paired scroll; rigaree decorated handles.
H: 2¾" (7 cm) 59.37.16
Gift: Dr. Eugen Grabscheid.

19. Façon de Venice Goblet
Holland or Belgium
17th Century
Blown; colorless glass; diamond-engraved; winged stem; funnel bowl engraved with two birds perched among stylized floral foliage; applied wrythen-molded, multi-knopped stem with turquoise wings and colorless pincered decoration; colorless foot with matching foliage; engraved and folded rim, rough pontil mark.
H: 6⅝" (16.8 cm) 86.190.GEH
Museum Purchase.

20. Beaker/Tumbler
Venice, Italy
Second half of
the 18th Century
Blown; clear grey/blue tinted glass; enameled spray of pink flowers on one side; on the reverse, blue flowers divided by banners which read: *Vinum & musica laetificant/cor* and *Modus utendi vino optimus/est corporis necessitas* ("Wine and music delight the heart" and "The optimal use of wine is good for the health."); white enamel circle at the bottom center.
H: 3¹⁵⁄₁₆" (10 cm) 59.37.18.GEV
Gift: Dr. Eugen Grabscheid.
Note: A similar beaker is in the illustrated catalog of the British Museum: Tait, Hugh. *The Golden Age of Venetian Glass*. British Museum, London, 1979. No. 222, and recorded as "Probably painted by a member of the Brussa family."

GERMAN GLASS: BLOWN AND ENAMELED 1500–1750

21. Roemer
The Netherlands
c. 1680

Blown; *waldglas* (forest green) spherical bowl opening into a cylindrical stem with two staggered rows of four raspberry prunts; a 1⅛ inch (3 cm) high coil, wound foot, medium kick; rough pontil mark; applied milled band at the base of bowl.
H: 4⅞" (12.4 cm) 87.317.GEH
Gift: Kathryn K. Porter
Note: Similar to No. 235 illustrated in the British Museum 1968 catalog: Harden, Donald B., K. S. Painter, R. S. Pindar-Wilson, and Hugh Tait. *Masterpieces of Glass*. Trustees of the British Museum, London, 1965, No. 235.

22. Reichsadler Humpen
Saxony, Germany
1679

Blown; light green glass; polychrome enameled design of a crowned double eagle of the Holy Roman Empire with spreading wings covered with 56 armorial shields of city-states, electors, and the apostolic delegates; on the reverse, an enameled green wreath enclosing *IVW 1679* and the statement *Das heilige Römische Reich mit Sampt seiner gliedern* ("The Holy Roman Empire with all its parts."); antique pewter foot repair.
H: 11½" (29.2 cm) GESa.68.2 (71.6840)
Gift: Walter P. Chrysler, Jr.

23. Ochsenkopf Humpen
Franconia, Germany
1729

Blown, colorless glass; polychrome enameled allegorical scene of the Fichtelberg Mountain with a church, oxhead, animals, and the names of four rivers listed around the bottom.
H: 8 15/16" (22.7 cm) 63.37.11
Gift: Dr. Eugen Grabscheid

24. Passglas
Saxony, Germany
1713

Blown; gray tinted glass; enameled polychrome coat-of-arms of a Butchers Guild with inscription: *Martin Jos. Fleck verehret dieses, 1713* ("Martin Joseph Fleck Presents this in 1713") and a statement which reads: *Fritch frolich und macher, veind die, fleitchhaker, Mo fie in fried bey fammer vien, Bev gutten bier oder mein, Da haben fie einen gutter muth, Damit dap glatz nicht fevren Ehut* ("Jolly and merry are the butchers wherever they are together in peace with good beer and wine—there they are in good spirits and see to it that the glass is never empty.")
H: 12¾" (32.4 cm) GESa.68.1 (71.6845)
Gift: Walter P. Chrysler, Jr.

EUROPEAN GLASS: 1700–1880

25. Flask Covered Goblet
Silesia
c. 1725

Blown; colorless, flared oval bowl; canted corners; engraved foliage; floral and scroll work; central medallions on each side, one with two hearts below a sun and other with two hearts on pedestal with burning base; solid paneled and faceted baluster stem; square foot with bracketed corners; alternating oval and cuts on bottom; cover a small flask with matching lobes and engraving, topped with screw joint for solid, faceted, steeple stopper.
H: 8¾" (22.2 cm) GESi 74.7 (0.2361)
Note: Recorded and illustrated in Schmidt, Robert, *Die Gläser der Sammlung Mühsam*. Band I. Verlag für Kunstwissenschaft, Berlin, 1914, No. 126.
Gift: Walter P. Chrysler, Jr.

26. Covered Goblet
Potsdam
c. 1730

Blown; colorless glass; cut; engraved showing Venus and Cupid at Vulcan's forge; after a 1546 engraving by Cornelis Bos (the same scene in a mirror image of a 1536 painting by Maertin van Heemskerck); bubble and facet-cut bowl bottom, stem, and finial.
H: 13⅞" (34.3 cm) overall. GEP.68.2 (71.6860)
Gift: Walter P. Chrysler, Jr.

27. Covered Goblet
Potsdam
c. 1740

Blown; colorless glass; engraved; cut; gilded; profile bust of the Crown Elector of Brandenburg (later Frederick the Great, first king of Prussia); military trophies and battle emblems; facet-cut and gilded bubble stem and cover finial.
H: 14" (35.5 cm) including cover. GEP.68.1 (71.6861 a & b)
Gift: Walter P. Chrysler, Jr.

28. Covered Goblet
Bohemia
Late 17th century

Blown; colorless glass; engraved house and landscape design; gadrooned bowl bottom, and cover; solid multi-knop and merese stem and finial.
H: 12" (20.5 cm) including cover. GEBo.68.13 (71.6867)
Gift: Walter P. Chrysler, Jr.

29. Covered Goblet
Silesia
c. 1773

Blown; gray tinted glass; engraved design showing the First Partition of Poland with figures of Catherine of Russia, Frederick the Great, Joseph II, and Stanislaus II around the map of Poland; engraved on the reverse: *La Situation de La Pologne en MDCCLXXIII* ("The Situation of Poland in 1773"); facet-cut and bubbly stem; floral and scroll engraved cover with solid knop finial with internal red and blue twists. Cover probably a replacement.
H: 12½" (31.7 cm) including cover. GESi.72.1 (72.35a & b)
Note: Recorded and illustrated in Schmidt, Robert, *Die Gläser der Sammlung Mühsam*. Band I. Verlag für Kunstwissenschaft, Berlin, 1914, No. 173.
Gift: Walter P. Chrysler, Jr.

30. Covered Goblet
Saxony
c. 1740
Blown; colorless glass; engraved scrolls and arabesques framing a scene in front of a chateau of a cavalier holding a lady's hand; a reverse engraved inscription: *Unsser freundschaft bestehn soll bis wir mitt der weldt vergehn* ("Our friendship shall last until we leave this world."); facet-cut; reverse baluster stem; double dome cover; engraved floral sprays; facet-cut top and finial.
H: 11⅞" (30.2 cm) including cover. GESa.68.3 (71.6862)
Gift: Walter P. Chrysler, Jr.

31. Zwischengold Tumbler
Bohemia
c. 1730–1740
Blown; colorless glass; precisely fitting, double-walled panel cut so as to sandwich a gold-leaf bear hunting scene; top and bottom have silver foil acanthus leaf bands; the bottom medallion is in gold-leaf and red lacquer with a bear design.
H: 3¼" (8.3 cm) GEBo.68.8 (71.6904)
Gift: Walter P. Chrysler, Jr.

32. Zwischengold Covered Goblet
Bohemia
c. 1730
Blown; colorless glass; precisely fitting, double-walled panel cut so as to sandwich an engraved gold-leaf stag hunt scene on the bowl; solid faceted baluster stem; round foot; faceted lid with a round *zwischengold* medallion of a stylized acanthus design on top; solid octagonal panel cut and pointed finial.
H: 7⅞" (20 cm) including cover. GEBo.72.2 (72.39)
Note: Illustrated and recorded by Schmidt, Robert, *Die Gläser der Sammlung Mühsam*. Band I. Verlag für Kunstwissenschaft, Berlin, 1914, No. 300.
Gift: Walter P. Chrysler, Jr.

33. Tumbler
J. J. Mildner
Gutenbrunn, Austria
1793
Blown; colorless glass; cut; central recessed oval *zwischengold* glass medallion of a saint; a red lacquer background and monogram *FL*; reverse medallion of silver foil; script engraved *Verfertiget/zu Gutenbrunn/im v.Fürnbesghgorossen/Weinspergwald/1793/J. Mildner* ("Handmade in Gutenbrunn, 1793, Mildner.") Oval cuts frame the medallion; half-panel cuts circle the bottom; red and gold *Zwischengold* band at the rim.
H: 4¹¹⁄₁₆" (12 cm) GEA.70.1 (71.6906)
Gift: Walter P. Chrysler, Jr.

34. Goblet
The Netherlands
c. 1780–1785
Blown; colorless glass; facet-cut stem; bowl diamond-stipple engraved showing a girl with a basket embraced by a boy at her side, in a landscape scene.
H: 7⅝" (19.4 cm) GEH.72.1 (72.44)
Note: Illustrated and recorded in Schmidt, Robert. *Die Gläser der Sammlung Mühsam*. Band I, Verlag für Kunstwissenschaft. Berlin, 1914. No. 40; and in the recorded work of engraver David Wolff.
Gift: Walter P. Chrysler, Jr.

35. Goblet
The Netherlands
Wolff-styled diamond-stipple engraving
c. 1785
Blown; colorless glass; cut; solid stem; diamond-stipple engraved crowned coat-of-arms of William V of Orange surrounded by the Order of the Garter flanked by a pair of lions.
H: 7" (17.6 cm) GEH.72.2 (72.47)
Note: Illustrated and recorded by Schmidt, Robert. *Die Gläser der Sammlung Mühsam*. Band II, *neu folge*. Ernst Wassmuth, Berlin, 1926. No. 271; and called "work by D. Wolff, c. 1785."
Gift: Walter P. Chrysler, Jr.

36. Goblet
The Netherlands
Wolff-styled diamond-stippled engraving
c. 1770–1775
Blown; colorless glass; diamond-stippled engraving entitled *Vriendschap* ("Friendship"); below, a scene of a wine peddler with a traveler accepting a glass of wine.
H: 7⅜" (18.7 cm) GEH.68.7 (71.6912)
Gift: Walter P. Chrysler, Jr.

37. Goblets
The Netherlands
Wolff-styled diamond-stipple engraving
c. 1775–1785; 1790
Blown; colorless glass; facet-cut stems; the bowl is diamond-stipple engraved in the Netherlands.

a. Goblet
c. 1790
Portrait bust between banners reading: *MR. E F BERCKEL* and *PENSIONARIS DER STAT AMSTERDAM* and *LUX IN TENEBRIS* and on the reverse *TERRAM PERLUSTRAT & UNDAS* ("Magistrate E. F. Van Berckel, Pensioner of the City of Amsterdam, Illuminates the land and sea"). (Mr. Van Berckel was brother of the first Dutch ambassador to the U.S.A.)
H: 6⅛" (15.5 cm) GEH.72.3 (72.45)
Note: Illustrated and recorded in Schmidt, Robert. *Die Gläser der Sammlung Mühsam*. Band I. Verlag für Kunstwissenschaft, Berlin, 1914, No. 51, pl. 7.
Gift: Walter P. Chrysler, Jr.

b. Goblet
c. 1775–1785
A scene showing two men toasting a woman and, above, a banner with the toast: *VADERLANDIE LIEF EH ALLE MOIE MYSIES* ("My Beloved Country and All Beautiful Women").
H: 6⅙" (15.4 cm) GEH.68.8 (71.6908)
Gift: Walter P. Chrysler, Jr.

38. Goblet
The Netherlands
c. 1775
Blown; colorless glass; diamond-stippled portrait bust with inscription above: *Di Vice Admiraal J. A. Zoutman*; applied stem with white opaque double twist; plain round foot.
H: 5¼" (13.3 cm) GEH.72.4 (72.46)
Note: Illustrated and recorded in Schmidt, Robert. *Die Gläser der Sammlung Mühsam*. Band I. Verlag für Kunstwissenschaft, Berlin, 1914. No. 69.
Gift: Walter P. Chrysler, Jr.

39. Goblet
The Netherlands
c. 1810
Blown; colorless glass; solid/drawn stem; applied foot; diamond-stippled engraving of a boy and a girl with arms entwined; beneath: *Vergeet niet licht/u Broeder Plicht* ("May our fellowship never end.")
H: 4¾" (12 cm) GEH.78.1 (0.444)
Note: Illustrated and recorded in: Schmidt, Robert. *Die Gläser der Sammlung Mühsam*. Band II, *neu folge*. Ernst Wasmuth, Berlin, 1926, No. 273.
Gift: Walter P. Chrysler, Jr.

40. Tumbler
Bohemia
Biedermeier-style
c. 1840
Blown; overlay; blue, colorless, and white glass; cut; enameled in two rows of squares; alternating male figures in hunting scenes; floral design around the punty cuts and at the top of the panel cuts; gilt rim and lines around the squares.
H: 5⁵⁄₁₆" (15 cm) 58.37.34
Gift: Dr. Eugen Grabscheid.

41. Cologne Bottle
Bohemia
c. 1850
Mold-blown; blue opaline glass; four protruding scallops form the foot; the body is in the form of a guitar; enameled gilt and silver floral design; stopper is matching with gilt and silver enameling.
H: 8⅛" (20.5 cm) GECB.74.1 (0.1383)
Note: Illustrated and recorded in Schmidt, Robert. *Die Gläser der Sammlung Mühsam*. Band II, Ernst Wasmuth, Berlin, 1926. No. 299.
Gift: Walter P. Chrysler, Jr.

42. Vase
"Ariadne and the Panther"
Possibly engraved by F. P. Zach
Northern Bohemia
c. 1850
Blown; cameo-cut; blue glass over colorless glass; design after the monument in Leipzig by Thorwaldsen.
H: 12¼" (31 cm) GECB.74.2 (0.1928)
Reference: Klesse, Brigette und Axel von Saldern, *500 Jahre Glaskunst, Sammlung Biemann*. ABC Verlag, Zürich, 1978. No. 241.
Gift: Walter P. Chrysler, Jr.

43. Venetian
19th Century
a. Swan Salt
c. 1880
Blown; filigree design; white, blue, pink, and aventurine glass in colorless glass.
H: 9⅝" (24.5 cm) GEIM.60.2 (71.6717)
Gift: Walter P. Chrysler, Jr.
b. Goblet
Late 19th Century
Blown; filigree design of rose, white and aventurine glass in colorless glass; mold blown, hollow lion mask stem.
H: 6¹³⁄₁₆" (17.4 cm) GEI.78.3 (0.498)
Gift: Walter P. Chrysler, Jr.
c. Ewer
Second Half of the 19th Century
Blown; *vetro di trina* with airtraps; white glass in colorless glass with pink rigaree and rim.
H: 11" including stopper (28 cm) GEIM.59.2 (71.6714a and b)
Gift: Walter P. Chrysler, Jr.

44. Decanter–(one of a pair)
Cork Glass Co.
Cork, Ireland
c. 1783–1818
Mold-blown; colorless glass with a gray tint; a band of 1½ inches (3.8 cm) high; finger fluted at the bottom with a circle of similar flutes around the bottom; inside this circle, molded in relief: *CORK GLASS CO.* around a rough pontil mark; decorated with three double rigaree rings on neck; pressed target or wheel-style stopper.
H: 10⅜" including stopper (26.5 cm). GEEI.72.2 (72.10)
Gift: Walter P. Chrysler, Jr.

45. Bowl
Anglo-Irish,
Early 19th Century
Blown; colorless glass; cut diamond-point; engraved ½ inch (1.3 cm) wide blossom and leaf-engraved band below a trefoil (or Vandyke) cut rim; panel-cut bowl bottom; narrow foot with a star-cut bottom.
H: 6⅛" (15.5 cm) D: 9" (23 cm) M51.1.114
Note: This is a piece of tableware from the Moses Myers House (a Norfolk, Virginia, historic house under the management of The Chrysler Museum). The bowl is a period purchase which was used by the Myers family.

46. Cut Glass
Cork, Ireland
c. 1825 (George IV Period)
a. Pitcher
H: 8⅝" (21.8 cm) GEEI.67.85 (71.7968)
b. Decanter
H: 11½" (29 cm) GEEI.67.82 (71.7971a and b)
c. Cordial
H: 2" (5 cm) GEEI.67.30 (71.7924)
d. Wine Goblet
H: 5⅛" (13 cm) GEEI.67.73 (71.7931)
e. Compote
D: 6¼" (16 cm) GEEI.67.10 (71.4270)
All gifts of Walter P. Chrysler, Jr.

47. English Cameo Vases
Joseph Locke
Hodgetts, Richardson and Son
Stourbridge, England
1877
These vases have cameo engravings after the sculptures with the same titles by the Belgian artist Louis Eugene Simmons. They were exhibited in the 1851 Crystal Palace Exhibition.
Blown; deep blue glass cased with white glass; cameo-carved.
"Happy Child"
Mark: Incised on the right of the pedestal holding the child: *1877*.
H: 8⅞" (22.5 cm) GEER.70.1 (71.4316)
Gift: Walter P. Chrysler, Jr.
"Unhappy Child"
Mark: Incised on the white platform holding the child: *1877*.
H: 8⅞" (22.5 cm) GEER.70.2 (71.4317)
Gift: Walter P. Chrysler, Jr.

47a. Close-up of incised mark on "Unhappy Child"

48. Antarctic Cameo Vase
Designed and carved by
George Woodall
Thomas Webb and Sons
Stourbridge, England
c. 1909–1910
Opaque white glass over citron colored glass; acid- and cameo-carved scene of polar bears, penguins, gulls, ships, and icebergs.
Mark: Engraved around the bottom edge: *Antarctic Vase.*
H: 14″ (35.5 cm) GEEW.68.2 (71.4298)
Gift: Walter P. Chrysler, Jr.
Note: Exhibited in The Corning Museum of Glass exhibition and illustrated in its 1982 catalog: Goldstein, Sidney, L. S. Rakow, and J. K. Rakow. *Cameo Glass: Masterpieces from 2000 Years of Glassmaking.* The Corning Museum of Glass, Corning, New York, 1982. No. 66.

49. Vase
English
Stourbridge Area
c. 1880
Mold-blown; optic ribbed; cylindrical; opalescent, amber glass; applied, crimped rim turned down in four places; four amber root-like feet with tops extending up the vase; decorated with three applied overshot "strawberries" and three white blossoms, amethyst stems and green leaves.
H: 11″ (28 cm) GEE.61.4 (71.4289)
Gift: Walter P. Chrysler, Jr.

50. Vase
Stevens & Williams
Brierley Hill Glass Works
Stourbridge, England
c. 1888–1890
Blown; white and amethyst glass over colorless glass; cameo cut; amber stained interior; swimming fish design.
H: 11¾″ (30 cm) GEES.64.2 (71.4301)
Note: Probably designed by Frederick Carder, later founder of the Steuben Glass Works.
Reference: Exhibited and illustrated in the Corning Museum of Glass exhibition and catalog in 1982: Goldstein, Sidney, L. S. Rakow, and J. K. Rakow. *Cameo Glass: Masterpieces from 2000 Years of Glassmaking.* The Corning Museum of Glass, Corning, New York, 1982. No. 50.
Gift: Walter P. Chrysler, Jr.

51. Vase
Stevens & Williams
Brierley Hill Glass Works
Stourbridge, England
c. 1890–1895
Blown; colorless glass; intaglio engraved Art Nouveau leaf and lily design; an irregular rim follows the blossom edge; star-cut bottom.
Mark: Acid-stamp trademark of *S W* divided by a fleur-de-lis and, below, *England.* Stevens & Williams intaglio engraving was by stone wheel. This may be the work of Joshua Hodgetts from a Frederick Carder (later the founder of the Steuben Glass Works) design.
H: 20⅛″ (51 cm) GEES.66.2 (71.4285)
Gift: Walter P. Chrysler, Jr.

52. Vase
Stourbridge Area, England
Designed and enameled by Jules Barbe
c. 1900
Blown; colorless glass; etched floral design with textured background; enameled stylized bluebell-like design in three frames separated by thick Art Nouveau gilding of a raised glossy design; matt gilt background.
Mark: In blue enamel on the lower side: *J. Barbe.*
H: 11⅛″ (28.5 cm) GEESb.66.1 (71.4296)
Note: Jules Barbe's workshop was associated with Thomas Webb and Richardson and possibly others in the Stourbridge District.
Gift: Walter P. Chrysler, Jr.

EUROPEAN
ART NOUVEAU GLASS:
1878–1920

---

53. Bowl
Emile Gallé
*Cristallerie
d'Emile Gallé*
Nancy, France
c. 1878–1884
Mold-blown; ribbed; pale amber glass; polychrome enameled; Persian design of a medallion of a man on an elephant; on the reverse, a man on a horse; floral leaf overall.
Mark: Red enamel in the center of the polished pontil mark: *E. Gallé à Nancy.*
H: 6⅞″ (17.5 cm) GEFG.70.12 (71.6628)
Gift: The Jean Outland Chrysler Collection.

54. Vase
Emile Gallé
*Cristallerie
d'Emile Gallé*
Nancy, France
c. 1878–1884
Blown; amber glass; inclusions of brown patches and irregular bubbles; enameled with multicolor floral design.
Mark: Gilt script across the polished pontil mark: *Emile Gallé de Nancy in et fecit"* and vertically on the neck in gilt "E ‡ G". The *et fecit* merely indicates an Emile Gallé design.
H. 17½″ (44.5 cm) GEFG.70.26 (71.6406)
Gift: Walter P. Chrysler, Jr.

**55. "Marine" Bowl
in Gilded Bronze Stand**
Emile Gallé
*Cristallerie
d'Emile Gallé*
Nancy, France
c. 1884
Blown; cut and engraved; colorless glass with internal splatters of green, brown, and opalescent; body cut with 16 diagonal panels, intaglio-engraved with sea plants, crabs, and marine life; solid bottom fits into gilt bronze 1⅜″ (3.5 cm) high base.
Mark: Engraved on bottom: *Escalier de Cristal Paris/Emile Gallé* above an engraved pitcher tilted vertically "E ‡ G" and *Nancy 315*; stand incised on bottom edge *ESCALIER DE CRISTAL PARIS.*
H: 5¼″ in stand (13.5 cm) GEFG.70.3 (71.6530)
Gift: Walter P. Chrysler, Jr.

55a. Close-up of Mark.

56. Enameled and Etched Vase
Emile Gallé
*Cristallerie
d'Emile Gallé*
Nancy, France
c. 1885–1900
Each blown; colorless glass: cased opal then golden-yellow glass; lower third brick red with inclusions of metallic patches.
a. Cylindrical with trefoil top; multicolor enamel chrysanthemum design; bottom etched, enameled and gilded in simulation of a pierced metal holder with top rim of three points connected by lower curves and similar half-inch (1.3 cm) wide band just below the rim.

Mark: Script engraved around a chrysanthemum design on the polished pontil mark: *Cristallerie de Gallé à Nancy*.
H: 12¼" (31 cm) GEFG.67.20 (71.6698)
Gift: Walter P. Chrysler, Jr.

b. Oval vase with handles; multi-color enamel and etched lily design with gilded and enamel bottom; band on foot top and near rim and shaped portion extending around one pink and other yellow and gilded handle.
Mark: Script engraved around and through a lily design on the bottom: *Cristallerie de Gallé à Nancy/ modèle et décor déposés*.
H: 9⅜" (24 cm) GEFG.66.11 (71.6652)
Gift: Walter P. Chrysler

c. Oval; mold-blown; etched enameled and gilded chrysanthemum design.
Mark: Gilded script on front right and left near the flat bottom: *Gallé Nancy* and *déposé/GG*.
H: 7⅞" (20 cm) GEFG.63.21 (71.6697)
Note: GG stands for *Gesetzlich Geschützt* meaning "patented" in German. *Déposé* is the French equivalent. Each of these shapes is used by Gallé for various models. No. 57 illustrates two of these using medieval designs.
Gift: Walter P. Chrysler, Jr.

57. Medieval Designs
Emile Gallé
*Cristallerie
d'Emile Gallé*
Nancy, France
c. 1884–1890
Inspired by François Villon's *Ballade des dames du temps jadis"* (Ballad about Ladies of By-Gone Times).

a. Vase
Blown; amber glass; acid-cut; enameled scene of a lady in a forest.
Mark: In relief on the side: *Gallé*.
H: 10½" (26 cm) GEFG.66.23 (71.5535)
Gift: Walter P. Chrysler, Jr.

b. Covered Box
Mold-blown; amber glass; acid-cut cameo; enameled squash vine design; lid with medallion of a peasant scene surrounded by a vine design.
Mark: In relief on the side: *Gallé*.
H: 6" overall (15.2 cm) GEFG.65.2 (71.6631 a&b)
Gift: The Jean Outland Chrysler Collection.

c. Verrerie Parlante Vase
Blown; amber glass; acid-cut cameo; inclusions of green and brown speckles and brown wash to simulate parchment; enameled figure of a queen and, below, *La ballade des dames du temps jadis/François Villon par privil du Roy* including quotation: *Mais ou sont les/ neiges d'anton?* and *Semblablement ou est la Royne/Qui commanda que Buridan/Fust jette en un Sar en Seyne* ("But where are the snows of yesteryear"/and "Similarly where is the Queen/Who ordered Buridan/ To be put in a bag and thrown in the Seine?")
Mark: Engraved across the polished pontil mark: *Redit le Cristal de Nancy, Gallé 1* and in relief on the lower side: *Gallé 1884*.
H: 8½" (21.5 cm) GEFG.66.27 (71.6630)
Gift: The Jean Outland Chrysler Collection

d. Vase
Mold-blown; amber glass; acid-cut; enameled design of a lady in a medieval costume.
Mark: In relief on the lower side: *Gallé*.
H: 9¼" (23.5 cm) GEFG.65.5 (71.6632)
Gift: The Jean Outland Chrysler Collection.

58. Vase
Emile Gallé
*Cristallerie
d'Emile Gallé*
Nancy, France
c. 1889
Mold-blown; ribbed; nautilus shape; amber glass; enameled chrysanthemum design in the Japanese taste with applied glass cabochon blossom centers.
Mark: Engraved on the polished pontil mark around a chrysanthemum leaf: *Cristallerie Emile Gallé modèle et décor déposés*.
H: 11¾" (29.8 cm) GEFG.68.10 (71.6700)
Gift: Walter P. Chrysler, Jr.

59. Dragonfly Bowl
Emile Gallé
*Cristallerie
d'Emile Gallé*
Nancy, France
c. 1889
Blown; dark brown glass; cased with white and colorless glass; carved and enamel dragonfly design in the Japanese taste in green, blue, rust, white, and gilt *martelé* background (hammered look).
Mark: Engraved on the bottom: *E. Gallé Nancy*.
H: 4¾" (12 cm) GEFG.67.10 (71.6654)
Gift: The Jean Outland Chrysler Collection.
Reference: Polak, Ada. *Modern Glass*. Faber and Faber, London. 1962. Color plate A shows a similar style.

60. Arum Lily Flower Form Vase
Emile Gallé
*Cristallerie
d'Emile Gallé*
Nancy, France
c. 1889–1897
Mold-blown; colorless glass; cut into a lily form.
Mark: In relief on the bottom: *Cristallerie d'Emile Gallé à Nancy, Modèle et Décor Déposés*.
H: 10¼" (26 cm) GEFG.67.14 (71.6627)
Gift: The Jean Outland Chrysler Collection
Reference: Garner, Philippe. *Emile Gallé*. Academy Editions, London, 1976. pp. 101–102. A sketch after an original drawing by Gallé illustrates several flower form objects (jug, vases, plate, etc.) based on the "arum lily." This is dated "before 1889."

61. "Marine" Bowl
Emile Gallé
*Cristallerie
d'Emile Gallé*
Nancy, France
c. 1889–1895

Blown; deep red glass with inclusions of dark streaks and metallic flecks; additional surface carving simulating seaweed; applied glass shellfish forms and a starfish.
Mark: In relief vertically down the side: *Gallé.*
H: 2⅞" (7.3 cm) GEFG.70.46 (71.6529)
Gift: Walter P. Chrysler, Jr.
Note: A similar bowl in this series is illustrated in Bloch-Dormant, Janine. *The Art of French Glass: 1860–1914.* The Vendome Press, New York, 1980. No. 174.

62. Vase
Emile Gallé
*Cristallerie
d'Emile Gallé*
Nancy, France
1892

Blown; cameo; opaque blue-green glass; columbine design; internal patches of metallic flecks; *martelé* background.
Mark: Around a blossom carved on the pontil mark: *Emile Gallé fecit 1892.*
H: 21½" (54 cm) GEFG.70.15 (71.6636)
Gift: The Jean Outland Chrysler Collection
Note: Garner, Philippe. *Emile Gallé.* Academy Editions, London, 1976. Color plate page 93, portrait of Emile Gallé by Victor Prouvé, 1892, illustrates this vase, lower left.

63. Bowl
Emile Gallé
*Cristallerie
d'Emile Gallé*
Nancy, France
1892

Blown; internal coloring of red, gray, and blue glass; metallic flecks and several irregular airtraps; engraved scattered blossoms and near rim: *Et maintes fois, plein de langueur/Le souvenir y montre au coeur/Sa fleur melancolique et melancolique et bleue/ Rollinat* ("How many times a languid/ Memory shows the heart/Its blue and melancholy flower.")
Mark: Engraved on the bottom: a snail shell and *Emile Gallé/Nancy/ 1892.*

Illustrated: Catalog for the 1984 Corning Museum of Glass Gallé Exhibition. Warmus, William. *Emile Gallé: Dreams into Glass.* The Corning Museum of Glass, Corning, New York, 1984. pp. 168–171; called "Blue Melancholia Coupe."
H: 5¼" (13.2 cm) GEFG.66.4 (71.6647)
Gift: The Jean Outland Chrysler Collection.

64. Vase
Emile Gallé
*Cristallerie
d'Emile Gallé*
Nancy, France
1895

Blown; acid-cut and carved cameo; rose glass, then lavender over bubbly, colorless glass; garden scene in Japanese taste; from the series *Endormeuses Saisons* designed by Louis Hestaupon, theme from Baudelaire.
Mark: Engraved on the polished pontil mark: *Gallé.*
H: 11½" (29.2 cm) GEFG.70.38 (71.6650)
Gift: The Jean Outland Chrysler Collection.
Reference: Duncan, Alastair & Georges de Bartha. *Glass by Gallé.* Thames and Hudson, London, 1984. p. 183, No. 274.

65. Pitcher
Emile Gallé
*Cristallerie
d'Emile Gallé*
Nancy, France
c. 1898

Blown; cameo; padded green and rose glass then white over colorless glass; wild magnolia design; *martelé* background; applied peach stain on solid colorless handle.
Mark: Engraved across the bottom: *Cristallerie de Gallé à Nancy* and incised vertically on a lower leaf: *Gallé.*
H: 9¾" (24.8 cm) GEFG.67.17 (71.6634)
Gift: The Jean Outland Chrysler Collection.

66. Vase
Emile Gallé
*Cristallerie
d'Emile Gallé*
Nancy, France
c. 1895

Blown; acid-cut cameo; white and amber over colorless glass; grape and vine design in the Japanese taste.
Mark: Engraved across the polished pontil mark: *Gallé.*
H: 5¾" (14.6 cm) GEFG.67.2 (71.6494)
Gift: Walter P. Chrysler, Jr.

67. Nautilus Bowl
Emile Gallé
*Cristallerie
d'Emile Gallé*
Nancy, France
c. 1895

Blown; oval; "nautilus" shape; acid-cut cameo; red over colorless glass; fern and grasshopper design.
Mark: In relief across the bottom, entwined with a fern and moth design: *Cristallerie d'E. Gallé* and around the bottom edge: *Modèle et décor déposés.*
H: 12" (30.5 cm) GEFG.70.48 (71.6659)
Gift: The Jean Outland Chrysler Collection.

68. Vase
Emile Gallé
*Cristallerie
d'Emile Gallé*
Nancy, France
c. 1898

Blown; acid-cut and carved cameo; sunflower and sun design in Oriental taste; amber over colorless glass with internal patches of metallic flecks, amethyst, and green cabochon blossom centers; internal surface etched (frosted).
Mark: Engraved across the polished pontil mark inside of irregular oval lines: *Gallé* and *déposé.*
H: 15½" (39.4 cm) GEFG.66.36 (71.6639)
Reference: A sketch showing this vase is illustrated in Duncan, Alastair & Georges de Bartha. *Glass by Gallé.* Thames and Hudson, London, 1984. p. 24.
Gift: The Jean Outland Chrysler Collection.

69. Vases
Emile Gallé
*Cristallerie
d'Emile Gallé*
Nancy, France
c. 1900–1904

a. Verrerie Parlante Vase
c. 1900–1904
Blown; acid-cut; olive green and amber glass; dahlia and clematis design with the following inscription in relief: *Beni/soit/le coin/sombre/ou s'isolant/nos coeurs"/ "Marceline Valmore"* ("Blessed be the sheltered corner where our hearts find refuge.")
Mark: In relief on the lower side: *Gallé.*
H: 12½" (31 cm) GEFG.67.12 (71.6657)
Gift: The Jean Outland Chrysler Collection.

b. Marine Vase
c. 1900
Blown; acid-cut cameo and intaglio; marine design; rose over green glass with internal colorings of deeper green and rose.
Mark: In relief on the lower side: *Gallé 4.*
H: 7⅝" (19.3 cm) GEFG.70.39 (71.6633)
Gift: The Jean Outland Chrysler Collection.

70. Vase
Emile Gallé
*Cristallerie
d'Emile Gallé*
Nancy, France
c. 1900

Blown; one marquetry-engraved red butterfly and two other engraved ones; deep curved cuts simulating wind; cased lavender glass at top and amber at bottom over irregular, bubbled colorless glass; internal vertical patches of fuschia glass and vertical band of amethyst splatters down the bulb of the glass.
Mark: Engraved on the lower side: *Gallé.*
H: 14" (35.5 cm) GEFG.68.3 (71.6532)
Gift: The Joan Foy French Collection.

71. Seahorse Ewer
Emile Gallé
*Cristallerie
d'Emile Gallé*
Nancy, France
c. 1901

Blown; cased; red and green speckled glass; "satin" finish; two applied "seahorse" figures, one swirled around the bottom and the other swirled up the side with its tail forming a handle.
Mark: Engraved on the bottom edge: *Gallé.*
H: 7" to handle (17.7 cm) GEFG.71.2 (71.6656)
Note: The ewer in the collection of the Musée des Arts Décoratifs, Paris, a presentation to Joseph Reinach dated 1901, is of a similar design, and it includes some cutting. Another in this series is No. 308 illustrated in the catalogue of the Kunstmuseum Düsseldorf: Hilschenz-Mynek, Helga & Helmut Ricke. *Glas: Historismus-Jugendstil-Art Deco.* Band I, Frankreich. Die Sammlung Hentrich in Kunstmuseum Düsseldorf. Prestel Verlag, München, 1985. It is marked *Gallé Etude* ("Gallé Study").
Gift: The Jean Outland Chrysler Collection.

72. Dragonfly Bowl
Emile Gallé
*Cristallerie
d'Emile Gallé*
Nancy, France
c. 1902

Blown; engraved and cameo cut; alabaster glass; internal coloring forming two dragonflies around the bowl, one with a marquetry body in relief and applied cabochon eyes, the other partially carved.
Mark: Incised on the center of the side: *Gallé.*
H: 6⅛" (15 cm) GEFG.70.8 (71.6655)
Gift: The Jean Outland Chrysler Collection.

73. Elephant Vase
Emile Gallé
*Cristallerie
d'Emile Gallé*
Nancy, France
c. 1925

Mold-blown; acid-cut cameo; elephant and palm tree design; pale amber, colorless, green, and brown glass.
Mark: Incised on the lower front: *Gallé.*
H: 15" (38 cm) GEFG.71.1 (71.6640)
Note: An unusual example with panels at the bottom; others in this series are without panels.
Gift: The Jean Outland Chrysler Collection.

74. Vases
Verrerie d'Art de Lorraine,
Burgun, Schverer & Cie.
Meisenthal, Alsace-Lorraine, Germany
c. 1895–1900

a. Vase
Blown; green glass; enameled windy scene of pink and white chrysanthemums painted over green with brick streaks to simulate wind; cased colorless glass; acid- and cameo-cut over enamel design; etched and *martelé* background patches; highlighted with gilt.
Mark: On the bottom in gilt: a Cross of Lorraine entwined with a thistle and *Verrerie d'Art de Lorraine B.S. & Co. déposé.*
H: 9⅛" (23.2 cm) GEFBu.70.3 (71.6615)
Gift: The Jean Outland Chrysler Collection.

b. Vase
Blown; lavender glass; enameled orchid design painted on the lavender; cased colorless glass; acid-cut and cameo-carved over the floral design; etched and *martelé* background patches, highlighted with gilt.
Mark: On the bottom in gilt: a Cross of Lorraine entwined with a thistle and *Verrerie d'Art de Lorraine B.S. & Co. déposé.*
H: 11¾" (30 cm) GEFBu.70.1 (71.6613)

75. Vase
Daum Frères.
Verrerie de Nancy
Nancy, France
c. 1894–1900
Blown; acid-cut intaglio and cameo top half; and from pond down engraved; "Water Lily and Flying Heron" scene in the Japanese taste; black enameled highlights on pale blue glass; upper portion cased with green glass, darker at rim.
Mark: In gilt in the center of the polished pontil mark: *Daum ‡ Nancy*.
H: 10¾" (27.3 cm) GEFD.66.3 (71.6673)
Note: A parallel selection is illustrated in the catalogue *Centenaire de Daum au Japon. (Exhibition à la Musée des Arts Moderne)* Sapporo, Hokkaido, Japan, 1980. [Organized by the Museum of Modern Art, Sapporo, and the Hokkaido *Shimbun* on the third anniversary of the opening of the museum.] It is also illustrated in the book: Daum, Noël. *Daum maîtres verriers*. Editions Denoël, Lausanne, 1980. pp. 12, 13. English Edition 1985.
Gift: The Jean Outland Chrysler Collection.

76. Vase
Daum Frères.
Verrerie de Nancy
Nancy, France
c. 1895
Blown; blue and white glass; cased colorless then opal glass; acid-cut winter pond scene highlighted with black enamel.
Mark: Black script across the polished pontil mark: *Daum/Nancy ‡*.
H: 6¼" (16 cm) GEFD.70.4 (71.6677)
Gift: Walter P. Chrysler, Jr.

77. Compote
Daum Frères.
Verrerie de Nancy
Nancy, France
c. 1900
Blown; acid-cut and carved cameo; floral design of green, pink, and yellow glass.
Mark: Incised on the top foot: *Daum ‡ Nancy*.
H: 9½" (24 cm) GEFD.67.10 (71.6515)
Gift: Walter P. Chrysler, Jr.

78. Pitcher
Daum Frères.
Verrerie de Nancy
Nancy, France
c. 1904
Blown; acid- and cameo-cut; floral and dragonfly design; applied solid green handle twists to form a dragonfly body with marquetry eyes.
Mark: In relief on the lower side: *Daum Nancy ‡* .
H: 13½" (34 cm) GEFD.70.26 (71.6667)
Gift: The Jean Outland Chrysler Collection.

79. Vase
Daum Frères.
Verrerie de Nancy
Nancy, France
c. 1903–1905
Blown; acid-cut cameo; geranium design; internal coloring shading from yellow to lavender glass; cased with rose opalescent and green glass; partly iridized; background etched.
Mark: Engraved on the polished pontil mark: *Daum/Nancy/‡* .
H: 7¼" (18.5 cm) GEFD.67.3 (71.6550)
Gift: Walter P. Chrysler, Jr.

80. Chandelier
Daum Frères.
Verrerie de Nancy
and Louis Majorelle
Nancy, France
c. 1905
Leaded glass; stylized hydrangea design; acid-cut; green over opalescent blossoms; surrounded by enameled leaf outlines on light green-blue "drapery" glass; three vertical, triangular shaped arms hold a matching round, horizontal disc; suspended from arms above the disc are seven light fixtures, two from each arm while a larger one is suspended from the central arm, each with a blown, mottled green and opalescent fluted glass shade.
Mark: Each shade incised and gilded: *Daum ‡ Nancy*.
H: 31½" (80 cm) GEFD.72.6 (72.55)
Note: Illustrated on plate 5 of the catalogue: *Le Salon des Industries du Mobilier Exposition*, Paris, France, 1905.
Gift: Walter P. Chrysler, Jr.

81. Mushroom Vase
Daum Frères.
Verrerie de Nancy
Nancy, France
c. 1907
Blown; acid-cut; enameled orange, brown, and green mushroom designs on mauve glass; textured background.
Mark: Incised on the center of the polished pontil mark: *Daum ‡ Nancy 11*.
H: 8¼" (21 cm) GEFD.70.1 (71.6661)
Gift: The Jean Outland Chrysler Collection.

82. Vase
Daum Frères.
Verrerie de Nancy
Nancy, France
c. 1908
Mold-blown; dark forest scene with black trunks and leaves in relief; carved and polished framing; a yellow and white distant view.
Mark: Incised on the polished pontil mark: *Daum ‡ Nancy*.
H: 16½" (41.3 cm) GEFD.63.4 (71.6555)
Note: There are two smaller versions in the collection: one with opaque pink trees framing a white and yellow scene and one in black framing a red (sunset) scene.
Gift: Walter P. Chrysler, Jr.

83. Vase
Daum Frères.
Verrerie de Nancy
Nancy, France
c. 1912–1913
Blown; acid-cut cameo; autumn landscape scene with falling leaves of multicolored brown and russet.
Mark: In relief on the side: *Daum ‡ Nancy*.
H: 8⅜" (21.3 cm) GEFD.65.3 (71.6560)
Note: A similar design is illustrated in Daum, Noël. *Daum maîtres verriers*. Edition Denoël, Lausanne, 1980. p. 82.
Gift: Walter P. Chrysler, Jr.

84. Vase
Daum Frères.
Verrerie de Nancy
Nancy, France
c. 1910
Blown; cameo; multi-color grape design with purple "berries" applied in high relief.
Mark: Incised on the lower side: *Daum ‡ Nancy*.
H: 20¼" (51.5 cm) GEFD.72.5 (72.30)
Gift: Walter P. Chrysler, Jr.

85. Vase
Daum Frères.
Verrerie de Nancy
and Louis Majorelle
Nancy, France
c. 1921–1922
Blown; colorless glass cased with red-amber glass spattered with green and mica flecks; blown into a wrought iron, brass decorated caged frame with glass bulging through metal.
Mark: Engraved across bottom: *DAUM ‡ NANCY* and *L. MAJORELLE*.
H: 13³⁄₁₆" (33.5 cm) GEFD.69.1 (71.6542)
Gift: Walter P. Chrysler, Jr.

86. Footed Bowl
Daum Frères.
Verrerie de Nancy
Nancy, France
c. 1925–1930
Blown; colorless cased glass, shades of blue; four patches of metallic flecks around the bowl; darker blue stem and foot.
Mark: Incised on the top edge of the foot: *DAUM ‡ NANCY*.
H: 11⅜" (29 cm) GEFD.69.3 (71.7176)
Gift: Walter P. Chrysler, Jr.

87. Vase
Daum Frères.
Verrerie de Nancy
Nancy, France
c. 1925–1930
Blown; straw yellow with metallic flakes; acid-cut; etched geometric design of three bands of squares divided by solid bands.
Mark: Incised on the bottom band: *DAUM ‡ NANCY FRANCE*.
H: 8½" (21.5 cm) GEFD.68.6 (71.6516)
Gift: Walter P. Chrysler, Jr.

88. Vase
Muller Frères
Lunéville, France
c. 1900–1905
Blown; acid-cut and carved cameo; red and dark green glass over a pale multi-colored opaque background; orchid floral design.
Mark: In relief on the lower side: *Muller Frès/Lunéville*.
H: 17" (43 cm) GEFM.67.2 (71.6601)
Gift: Walter P. Chrysler, Jr.

89. Vase
Muller Frères
Lunéville, France
c. 1900–1905
Blown; acid-cut cameo; blackberry vine design of chartreuse, brown, and white glass; flask shape with applied, etched, colorless glass handles.
Mark: In relief on the lower back: *Muller Frès/Lunéville*.
H: 5¼" (13.3 cm) GEFM.70.3 (71.6538)
Gift: Walter P. Chrysler, Jr.

90. Vase
Muller Frères
Lunéville, France
c. 1910
Blown; acid-cut and carved cameo; floral design with marquetry blossoms, one orange and one rose; opalescent glass cased with mottled orange and amethyst glass (more orange in the lower half) and deep green glass; *martelé* background.
Mark: Incised on the lower side: *Muller Frès/Lunéville*.
H: 10⅜" (26.3 cm) GEFM.65.2 (71.6537)
Gift: Walter P. Chrysler, Jr.

91. Vase
Muller Frères
Lunéville, France
c. 1920s
Blown; acid-cut cameo; colorless, yellow, metallic flecks, and green glass; fish bowl design showing nine, various-sized, stylized swimming goldfish; pebbly bottom; all etched textured background.
Mark: In relief on the lower side: *Muller Frès/Lunéville* and scratched across the bottom: *France*.
H: 9" (23 cm) GEFM.68.2 (71.6539)
Gift: Walter P. Chrysler, Jr.

92. Ornament
Philippe-Joseph Brocard & Fils
Paris, France
1884
Blown; colorless glass; multicolor enameled and gilded.
Mark: In gilt script on the center band: *P.J. Brocard & Fils, Paris, 1884*.
H: 7⅛" (18 cm) GEF.81.2 (81.197)
Note: The ornament is enameled in the Islamic Mamluk style which Brocard rediscovered and revived. Another object in The Chrysler Museum collection is similar but is round and is marked with gilt script. It is undated.
Gift: Walter P. Chrysler, Jr.

93. Vase
Eugène Michel
Lunéville, France
c. 1895–1900
Blown; multicolor cased glass; deeply acid-cut and carved tulip design in the Oriental taste; green with purple tulips on the side and dark amber blossom with metallic flecks in the center.
Mark: Script engraved on the lower side: *E. Michel*.
H: 13½" (34.3 cm) GEFMi.68.1 (71.6626)
Gift: Walter P. Chrysler, Jr.

94. Vase
Duc-Amédée de Caranza
Paris, France
c. 1902–1904
Blown; triangular shape; metallic oxide iridescent lustered cyclamen design; shades of tan, mauve, and green oxides.
Mark: Lustered letters on the lower side: *Duc-A.De Caranza*.
H: 5⅝" (14.4 cm) GEFC.68.1 (71.6620)
Gift: Walter P. Chrysler, Jr.

95. Vase
H. A. Copillet & Cie.
Noyon-sur-Seine, France
c. 1903–1906
Blown; colorless glass; metallic oxide iridescent lustered Art Nouveau iris design in green-gold, red-gold, and amber oxides.
Mark: lustered letters near the bottom edge: *H. Copillet*
H: 16¼" (41.3 cm) GEFC.70.1 (71.6624)
Gift: Walter P. Chrysler, Jr.

96. Vase
Cristallerie de Pantin:
Stumpf, Touvier, Viollet & Cie.
Pantin (Seine), France
c. 1901
Blown; acid-cut cameo; iris design; cased teal blue over colorless glass; interior iridized.
Mark: Impressed in a circle on the bottom: *Cristallerie de Pantin* around an intertwined monogram: *S.T.V. & C.*
H: 11⅝" (29.5 cm) GEFP.70.1
(71.6619)
Reference: Illustrated in the 1976 catalog of an exhibition organized by the William Marsh Rice Gallery, Institute for the Arts, Rice University (Houston, Texas), and The Art Institute of Chicago (Chicago, Illinois): Edited by Brunhammer, Yvonne, et al. *Art Nouveau Belgium,/France*. Rice University, Houston, Texas, 1976. p. 279, No. 446.
Note: A similar blue, vase in the Düsseldorf Collection is illustrated in the 1985 catalog by Hilschenz-Mlynek, Helga & Helmut Ricke. *Glas: Historismus-Jugendstil-Art Deco*. Band I, Frankreich. Die Sammlung Hentrich im Kunstmuseum Düsseldorf. Prestel Verlag, München, 1985. p. 357, No. 481.
Gift: The Jean Outland Chrysler Collection

97. Vase
Legras & Cie.
Saint Denis (Seine), France
c. 1912
Blown; yellow and orange body, light blue neck and top; cased with clear etched (satin) finish; enameled blue, red, and green stylized floral design.
Mark: Enameled on the lower side: *Legras*.
H: 11⅛" (28.3 cm) GEFGr.72.1
(72.69)
Gift: Walter P. Chrysler, Jr.

98. Bowl
Legras & Cie.
Saint Denis (Seine), France
c. 1925
Blown; acid-cut; enameled in a cubist design in colorless glass with white splatters; geometric cut enameled yellow, orange, red, and black band; acid finish (etched) inside and out.
Mark: In relief and enameled in black: *Legras*.
H: 5" (12.7 cm) GEFGr.75.1 (0.2514)
Gift: Walter P. Chrysler, Jr.

99. Ewer
Ludwig Moser & Söhne
Karlsbad, Bohemia
c. 1890
Mold-blown; ribbed; pale amberina glass; gilded and multicolored enameled bird and acorn design in high relief with heavily gilded leaves.
H: 14" (35.5 cm) GECM.68.2
(71.6610)
Note: The ewer is said to have been a wedding gift to Mr. and Mrs. Hawkes of the Hawkes Cut Glass Works of Corning, New York.
Gift: The Jean Outland Chrysler Collection.

100. Covered Jar
Ludwig Moser & Söhne
Karlsbad, Bohemia
c. 1925
Blown; deep green reverse baluster shape with 1⅝ inch (4.1 cm) acid-cut and gilded classical figures of fighting centaurs and men; panel-cut; matching dome-shape panel-cut cover with acid-cut and gilded floral leaf band at the rim; solid panel-cut, cone-shaped finial.
Mark: Engraved script on the polished pontil mark: *Made in/CzechoSlovakia/Moser/Karlsbad*.
H: 9⅛" (23 cm) GECM.71.1 (71.6576 a & b)
Gift: Walter P. Chrysler, Jr.

101. Pair of Cordials
Karl Koepping
(Dresden, 1848–Berlin, 1914)
c. 1895–1900
Blown and tooled lampwork; dark fuchsia and bronze color.
Mark: On top foot: *Koepping* (marked while hot).
H: 5¾" (14.5 cm) GEGK.64.1 & .2
(71.6366 a & b)
Gift: Joan Foy French Collection.

102. Vase and Bowl
Johann Loetz Witwe
Klostermühle, Bohemia
c. 1900

a. Vase
Blown; footed tumbler-shape; tooled with four "dimples" above a flaring bottom; copper iridescent glass marbled with some green glass; four applied and marvered blue and copper feather-like designs; narrow swirled brown treading around the "dimples" and extending over the bottom.
Mark: *Loetz/Austria* in engraved script across the polished pontil mark.
H: 9⅝" (24.5 cm) GEAL.65.3
(71.6592)
Gift: Walter P. Chrysler, Jr.

b. Bowl
Blown; blue iridescent glass; hexagonally fluted rim plus an irregular pleat.
Mark: *Loetz/Austria* in engraved script across the the polished pontil mark.
Rim D: 7½" (19 cm) GEAL.70.2
(71.6607)
Gift: Walter P. Chrysler, Jr.

103. Vase
Johann Loetz Witwe
Klostermühle, Bohemia
c. 1905
Blown; cased colorless glass over silvery green and silver glass; polished pontil mark.
H: 5½" (14 cm) GEAL.63.3 (71.6598)
Reference: Neuwirth, Waltraud. *Das Glas des Jugendstils*. Prestel Verlag, München, 1973. pp. 256–257.
Note: This silvery style was purported to be the only type of glass made by Loetz for distribution by Lobmeyr, Vienna, Austria.
Gift: Walter P. Chrysler, Jr.

104. Wine Goblets
Meyr's Neffe Glassworks
Adolf, Bohemia
c. 1906–1914
Designed by Otto Prutscher of the *Wiener Werkstätte*.
a. Blown; cased gold/amber over colorless glass; hemispheric bowl; cut with two rows of ovals near the rim above the panel-cut bottom; tall, solid, cylindrical stem cased and cut with pairs of ovals alternating on four sides; colorless foot.
H. 8⅛" (20.8 cm) GEBC.81.3
(81.46)
Gift: Mrs. Marjory S. Strauss.

b. Blown; cased blue glass over colorless glass; bucket-shape with flaring panel-cut rim and wider panel sides; solid square checkered stem cut with alternating blue and colorless squares; colorless foot.
H: 8¼" (21 cm) GEBC.81.4 (81.47)
Note: Described and illustrated in the article, "Austrian Architecture and Decoration" in the *1912 "Studio" Year Book of Decorative Arts*. Studio, Ltd., London, 1912. p. 223.
Gift: Mrs. Marjory S. Strauss.

EUROPEAN
PÂTE DE VERRE GLASS:
1890–1970

---

105. Vase
George Despret
Jeumont, France
c. 1906
Molded in shades of lavender, blue, and pink glass; decorated with a pair of seahorse forms down the opposite sides simulating handles; surface molded with sea plant forms.
Mark: Lower side incised with script: *Despret* and bottom "★" (gilded) and incised: *831*.
H: 8¼" (21 cm) GEFDs.68.7 (71.6520)
Illustrated in: Daum, Noël. *La pâte de verre*. Editions Denoël, Lausanne, 1984. No. 92.
Gift: The Jean Outland Chrysler Collection.

**106. Statuette/
(Tanagra Style)**
George Despret
Jeumont, France
c. 1906
Molded; shaded from white to lavender to green glass at the bottom.
Mark: On the base incised in script: *Despret* and on the bottom *1110*.
H: 11" (28 cm) GEFDs.68.4 (71.6474)
Note: Tanagra Figures—These *pâte de verre* statuettes are adaptations of the ancient Greek terracotta sculptures discovered by archeologists and named for the Tanagra area in Greece where many were found.

107. Cup
Jules-Paul Brateau
France
c. 1910–1912
Molded; white glass with four stylized pink flowers and green leaves.
Mark: Gold oval paper seal in center of the flat bottom printed: *Brateau*.
H: 2½" (6.3 cm) GEFBr.68.1 (71.6355)
Illustrated in: Daum, Noël. *La pâte de verre*. Editions Denoël, Lausanne, 1984. No. 163.
Reference: Exhibited and in the catalog edited by: Brunhammer, Yvonne. *Art Nouveau: Belgium–France*. Rice University, Houston, Texas, 1976.
The exhibition was organized by the Institute for the Arts, Rice University, Houston, Texas, and the Art Institute of Chicago, Chicago, Illinois.
Gift: The Joan Foy French Collection.

**108. Statuette/
Tanagra Figure**
Amalric Walter
Daum & Cie.
Nancy, France
c. 1905–1906
Molded; brown, shading to buff at the top; classical-style figure of a woman in flowing robes leaning on a pedestal of irregular oblong blocks.
Mark: Incised on flat bottom: *DAUM NANCY*.
H: 9⅞" (25 cm) GEFD.66.14 (71.6562)
Reference: Daum, Noël. *La pâte de verre*. Editions Denoël, Lausanne, 1984. p. 132.
Gift: Walter P. Chrysler, Jr.

108a. A bronze duplicate of this figure
H: 12¾" (32.5 cm) 88.75
Mark: On the side a circular impression: *GART AU TITRE A.L.*

109. "Loïe Fuller" Statuette
Amalric Walter
Nancy, France
c. 1920
Molded; mauve colored glass; Tanagra-like figure.
Mark: Incised on the back of the bottom of the stand: *AWALTER/NANCY*.
H: 9¾" (22.3 cm) GEFW.83.1 (83.101)

Note: Although not marked by the Nancy artist/sculptor, this may be the design of Victor Prouvé. Prouvé was an associate and close friend of Gallé.
Gift: Walter P. Chrysler, Jr.

**110. Vide Poche
or Cendrier**
Amalric Walter
Nancy, France
c. 1920
Molded; hexagonal-shaped design of a dragonfly in high relief on a simulated blue pond; raised leaf-like forms on each corner.
Mark: Incised: *AWALTER NANCY* and *Bergé Sc*.
D: 7⅞" (20 cm) GEFW.70.7 (71.6668)
Illustrated in: Daum, Noël. *La pâte de verre*. Editions Denoël, Lausanne, 1984. No. 196.
Note: *Vide poche* is the French name for a dresser dish designed to hold the contents of a gentleman's pockets.
Gift: The Jean Outland Chrysler Collection.

111. Vide Poche
Amalric Walter
Nancy, France
c. 1920
Molded; multiple shades of green glass; boat-shaped leaf with red/brown berries in relief in the bottom; a deep green chameleon perched on the curved end.
Mark: *AWALTER/NANCY* incised near the pointed end and *BERGÉ SC* near the chameleon end.
Size: 10" long (25.6 cm), 3" wide (7.6 cm) overall GEFW.70.4 (71.6523)
Note: A similar earlier chameleon *vide poche* (before 1914) is illustrated in the *Collection Cristallerie Daum*.
The lizard is not as realistic, and the boat design is ribbed. It is marked on its side: *DAUM/NANCY*.
Illustrated in: Daum, Noël. *La pâte de verre*. Editions Denoël, Lausanne, 1984. No. 127.
Gift: Walter P. Chrysler, Jr.

112. Vide Poche
Amalric Walter
Sculptor: Alfred Finot,
Nancy, 1876–1947
Nancy, France
c. 1920
Molded; a nude lying on a bed of sand and grass.
Mark: Incised on one side: *AWALTER NANCY* and on the other side: *A Finol.*
D: 9" by 6¼" (23 by 16 cm)
GEFW.70.2 (71.6680)
Note: There is a second *vide poche* in the collection, a paler, smaller, less sophisticated design dating about c. 1906–1914, marked: *DAUM/ NANCY:* and *W*
Illustrated in: Daum, Noël. *La pâte de verre.* Editions Denoël, Lausanne, 1984. No. 129.

113. Vase
Amalric Walter
Sculptor: L. E. Jan
Nancy, France
c. 1925
Molded; octagonal; flaring at rim; soft blue-green glass; decorated in relief with thin, horizontal diagonal slashes alternating with stripes of seeds on stem; bottom round with brown ribbed band on a square black foot.
Mark: Incised one side of the foot *AWALTER/NANCY* and on other foot side: *L.E. JAN.*
H: 7⅞" (20 cm) GEFW.70.9 (71.6350)
Gift: Walter P. Chrysler, Jr.

114. Plaque à La Rose
Amalric Walter
Nancy, France
c. 1925
Molded; bas-relief rose design of green glass with slight pink blossom petal tips.
Mark: Incised on the lower right: *AWALTER Nancy* and on the lower left: *Bergé sc.*
Size: 9⅝" by 6½" (24.5 by 16.5 cm)
GEFW.66.6 (71.6480)
Reference: Daum, Noël. *La pâte de verre.* Editions Denoël, Lausanne, 1984. Illustration No. 213.
Gift: Walter P. Chrysler, Jr.

115. Vase
Gabriel Argy-Rousseau
Paris, France
c. 1925
Molded; snow scene of four black wolves against a purple-blue sky.
Mark: Incised on the lower side: *G. Argy-Rousseau* and on the bottom: *France.*
H: 9¼" (23.5 cm) GEFR.70.1 (71.6353)
Gift: The Joan Foy French Collection.

116a. Vase "Nu Couché"
Gabriel Argy-Rousseau
Paris, France
c. 1927
Molded; oval shape; black, white, and gray glass; diamond and nude design.
Mark: Incised vertically on the lower side: *G. Argy-Rousseau* and on the bottom: *France.*
H: 6" (15.2 cm) GEFR.66.1 (71.6344)
Note: A parallel vase is illustrated in the catalog *Verriers Français Contemparies Art et Industrie,* Musée des Arts Décoratifs, Paris, France, 1982.A36.
Gift: Walter P. Chrysler, Jr.

116b. Reverse Medallion— Close Up.

117. "Loïe Fuller"
François-Emile
Décorchemont
Conches, France
c. 1912
Molded sculpture of Loïe Fuller; green glass in a jade-like color.
Mark: Impressed on the top of the base is: *R. Raymond* (sculptor) and on the other side: *Décorchemont* in a horseshoe-shape and *No. 1.*
H: 7" (17.8 cm) GEFDe.66.1 (71.6345)
Loaned to: The Virginia Museum of Fine Arts, Richmond, Virginia, Exhibition, "Loïe Fuller" Magician of Light", 3/13/79 to 4/22/79 and illustrated in the catalog, Item No. 31.
Illustrated in: Daum, Noël. *La pâte de verre.* Editions Denoël, Lausanne, 1984. No. 153.
Gift: The Joan Foy French Collection.

118. Vase
François-Emile
Décorchemont
Conches, France
c. 1919–1920
Molded; pale multicolor vessel with three dark colored Silenus face masques framed with leaves and berries in high relief.
Mark: Impressed: *Décorchemont* in horseshoe-shape on the lower side.
H: 9¼" (23.5 cm) GEFDe.70.2 (71.6459)
Gift: Walter P. Chrysler, Jr. in Honor of Renée Diamonstein.

119. Vase
François-Emile
Décorchemont
Conches, France
c. 1924
Molded; marbleized royal blue and smoke glass; design of females dancing.
Mark: Impressed in a horseshoe shape; *Décorchemont* and in the center of the polished pontil mark: *A-122.*
H: 5¹⁄₁₆" (13 cm) GEFDe.68.1 (71.6347)
Illustrated in: Daum, Noël. *La pâte de verre.* Editions Denoël, Lausanne, 1984. No. 140.
Gift: The Joan Foy French Collection.

120. Porte-Manteau Montre
Salvador Dali
Daum & Cie.
Nancy, France
1970
Molded *pâte de verre;* colorless glass.
Marked: In relief on the back: *DAUM 18/150.* In relief script on the lower front: *DALI 70;* installed on a gilded, textured metal coathanger marked with a facsimile DALI signature.
H: 22" (56 cm) to the coat hanger bar.
GEFD.72.7 (72.001)
Note: This is part of the Daum series "Editeur d'Art," which used designs by noted artists such as the surrealist Salvador Dali.
Gift: Walter P. Chrysler, Jr.

EUROPEAN GLASS:
1920 TO THE PRESENT DAY

121. Flasks
Maurice Marinot
Paris, France
1912–1915

a. Perfume Flask
c. 1914
Blown; colorless glass; enameled inside with red/orange spatters; thick enameled neck band; floral and geometric design; cone-shaped stopper enameled in matching colors.

199

Mark: Signed in dark enameled script at the side near the neck: *marinot*.
H: 5½" (14 cm) including stopper.
83.581.GEFMa
Museum Purchase.

b. Bottle/Flask
c. 1915
Blown; colorless glass made with assorted small brown bubbles and thin brown streaks; enameled multicolor medallion of a female bust in Poiret-style cloche holding a bird; thick, checked, enameled bottle neck; double-stepped stopper decorated with matching colors.
Mark: Signed in dark enameled script near the neck at the side: *marinot*.
H: 7⅛" (18 cm) including stopper.
83.580.GEFMa

c. Bottle
c. 1912
Blown; colorless glass; enameled decoration of a woman in a Paul Poiret-style red dress; neck and stopper of the bottle are enameled to match.
Mark: Signed enameled red script on the lower reverse: *marinot*.
H: 6¼" (16 cm) including stopper.
83.579.GEFMa

122. Decanter
Maurice Marinot
Paris, France
c. 1925
Blown; oval; thick, colorless glass with internal layer of dark brown flecks shading to colorless; small round stopper with internal brown coloring.
Mark: Engraved in script across the flat bottom: *marinot*.
H: 8⅝" (22 cm) GEFMa.66.1 (71.6361a and b)
Gift: The Joan Foy French Collection.

123. Cluny Vase
René Lalique
Wingen-sur-Moder, France
c. 1925
Blown; clear smoke color glass; applied bronze handles simulating hair/snakes holding pressed Medusa-face masque inserts.
Mark: Bottom edge in script: *R. Lalique France No. 961*
H: 10¼" (26 cm) GEFL.65.3 (71.6393)
Gift: The Joan Foy French Collection.

124. Tourbillons Vase
René Lalique
Wingen-sur-Moder, France
c. 1925
Molded; colorless glass; enameled highlights in shiny black.
Mark: Engraved around the bottom edge: *R. Lalique France No. 973*.
H: 7⅞" (20 cm) GEFL.68.4 (71.6384)
Gift: The Joan Foy French Collection.

125. Poissons Vase
René Lalique
Wingen-sur-Moder, France
c. 1930
Mold-blown; green glass; fish design.
Mark: Bottom center in diamond-point script: *Lalique*.
H: 9¼" (23.5 cm) GEFL.70.5 (71.6385)
Note: Listed as No. 925 in the 1932 Lalique Catalogue.
Gift: The Joan Foy French Collection.

126. Aigrettes Vase
René Lalique
Wingen-sur-Moder, France
c. 1930
Molded; smoke colored glass; design of flying birds in waving grass.
Mark: Engraved on the bottom edge: *R. Lalique France No. 988*.
H: 9⅞" (25 cm) 64.108.1
Gift: Selden Grandy.

127. Alicante Vase
René Lalique
Wingen-sur-Moder, France
c. 1930
Mold-blown; opalescent glass; background gray wash; design of three pairs of macaws.
Mark: Engraved on the bottom edge: *R. Lalique France No. 998*.
H: 9¾" (25 cm) GEFL.66.2 (71.6387)
Gift: Walter P. Chrysler, Jr.

128. Druides Vase
René Lalique
Wingen-sur-Moder, France
c. 1930–1932
Mold-blown; opalescent glass; mistletoe design; berries in high relief and with blue-green wash to highlight the design.
Mark: Engraved around the polished pontil mark: *R. Lalique, France No. 937*.
H: 6⅞" (17.5 cm) 86.331 GEFL
Illustrated in: René Lalique et Cie. *Lalique Glass: The Complete Illustrated Catalogue for 1932*. The Corning Museum of Glass in association with Dover Publications, New York, 1981. pl. 9, No. 937.
Gift: Walter P. Chrysler, Jr.

129. Vase
Cristallerie de Schneider
Epinay-sur-Seine, France
c. 1925
Blown; tall cylindrical vase tooled to a square top with pointed corners; round tango color knop stem; frosted dark brown round, ribbed dome foot; colorless bubbly bottom half-etched and with *martelé* surface; decorated at top on either side with an applied brown and colorless pinwheel design with round protruding central tango color glass and wavy tail decorated with various small tango color glass jewels.
Mark: Script engraved on the foot top *Schneider*.
H: 17¼" (43.8 cm) GEFSc.72.2 (72.23)
Gift: Walter P. Chrysler, Jr.

130. Vase
André DeLatte
Nancy, France
c. 1922
Blown; acid-cut cameo; orange, clear, and dark blue glass; design of dancers in the Isadora Duncan style; highlighted with gilt, enameled at the bottom with pink and light blue.
Mark: Enameled on the side: *A DeLatte Nancy*.
H: 12" (30.5 cm) GEFLa.71.1 (71.6364)
Gift: Walter P. Chrysler, Jr.

131. Vase
André DeLatte
Nancy, France
c. 1925
Blown; colorless glass; acid-cut; wide bands above the central cubist-style multicolor landscape band; below, 15 vertical stripes heavily textured between the top and bottom tan wash and black enameled rim.
Mark: Oval design in relief: *ᴁ^{E}Latte/NANCY*.
H: 8⅛" (20.6 cm) GEFLa.72.1 (72.21)
Gift: Walter P. Chrysler, Jr.

132. Vase
Simon Gate (1883–1945)
A. B. Orrefors Glasbruk
Orrefors, Sweden
c. 1928
Blown; pale, smoke-colored glass; octagonally panel cut; one panel engraved with a female nude.
Mark: Engraved on the bottom edge: *Orrefors—Gate—1104 A.L.—Er.*
H: 9½" (24.2 cm) GESO.72.2 (72.26)
Gift: Walter P. Chrysler, Jr.

133. Vase Monart
John Moncrieff, Ltd.
Perth, Scotland
c. 1935
Blown; irregular, jug-shape; inclusions of blue and green glass; irregular bubbles in colorless glass.
Mark: Part of paper *Monart* label attached.
H: 7⅝" (19.5 cm) GEEM.67.1 (71.6371)

134. Vase
André Thuret
Paris, France
c. 1935–1940
Blown; irregular shape; colorless glass with inclusions of red speckles and bubbles.
Mark: Engraved across the polished pontil mark: *André Thuret.*
H: 6¾" (17.2 cm) GEFT.68.1 (71.6362)

135. Vase
Les Andelys, France
c. 1935
Blown; colorless glass; inclusions of browns and tans; ten vertical air traps.
Mark: Engraved across the polished pontil mark: *Verlys 757.*
H: 5⅞" (15 cm) GEFV.68.1 (71.6360)
Gift: The Joan Foy Collection.

136. Vase
Gunnel Nyman (1909–1948)
Notsjö Glassworks
Nuutajarvi, Finland
c. 1945–1947
Blown; bubbly golden-amber glass; cased with thick colorless glass.
Mark: On the bottom: *G. Nyman Nuutajarvi Notsjö or* in diamond-point script.
H: 14" (35.5 cm) GEFi.82.1 (82.11)
Gift: Orva Walker Heissenbuttel, in memory of Jean Outland Chrysler.

137. Vase
Alfredo Barbini
Murano (Venice), Italy
1948
Blown; a thick, irregular cylinder of colorless glass; the interior is silver stained (yellow) with blues and patches of bright yellow enamels embedded in the irregularly textured surface.
Mark: Incised on the flat bottom: *BARBINI/ALFREDO 1948/ MURANO.*
H: 11⅛" (28.3 cm) GEIM.66.1 (71.6212)
Gift: Walter P. Chrysler, Jr.

138. Fazzoletti (Handkerchief) Vase:
Paolo Venini
Venini & Cie.
Murano (Venice), Italy
c. 1950
Blown; gray tinted glass including sixteen groups of three white, spiral, filagree glass canes (known as *vetro a retorti*) which are embedded, flattened, and fused to form a loosely-cupped "linen" version in the handkerchief series.
Mark: Acid-etched across the pontil mark: *VENINI/MURANO/ ITALIA.*
H: 8⅝" (22 cm) 85.58.GEIV
Purchased in memory of Patricia G. Slaasted.

AMERICAN BLOWN AND MOLD-BLOWN GLASS: 1790–1840

---

139. Salt
John Frederick Amelung
New Bremen Glass Manufactory
Frederick County, Maryland
c. 1790
Blown; pattern molded; checkered diamond design.
H: 2⅞" (7.3 cm) 83.582.GAAm
Gift: Walter P. Chrysler, Jr. and Museum Purchase

140. Covered Sugar Bowl
New England Glass Company
Cambridge, Massachusetts
c. 1820

Blown; colorless glass; tooled with an applied guilloche decoration; an 1810 Napoleon franc enclosed in the hollow stem and an 1816 George III penny in the finial.
H: 10⅝" overall (27 cm) 52.18.6
Bequest: The Kate Tyler Smith Collection. The Kate Tyler Smith Collection contains an important group of New England Glass Company heirlooms which were a 1952 gift to the Norfolk Museum by Florence L. Smith, a great-granddaughter of James B. Barnes, an early official of the company. It was accompanied by Miss Smith's annotated copy of *Cambridge Glass* by Lura Woodside Watkins with references marked about Barnes and John and Henry Leighton and noting illustrations of glass similar to the gift. Many of these bequests are illustrated in this catalogue.

141. "Petticoat" Whale Oil Lamp
New England Glass Company
Cambridge, Massachusetts
c. 1820
Blown; colorless glass font; blue glass cone-shape foot with folded rim. The lamp would have had a tin and cork wicker holder.
H: 7" (17.8 cm) GAN.63.3 (71.3745)
Gift: Walter P. Chrysler, Jr.

142. Vase
Pittsburgh Area
c. 1830
Blown; colorless glass; cobalt blue glass bulb; long colorless glass neck; flaring turned rim; solid baluster stem; round foot.
H: 9⅜" (23.8 cm) 86.175.GAPe
Illustrated in: Innes, Lowell. "Pittsburgh Glass," *Antiques Magazine.* December 1948. p. 419.
McKearin, George S. and Helen. *American Glass.* Crown Publishers, New York, 1969. pl. 54.
Innes, Lowell. *Pittsburgh Glass, 1797–1891: A History and Guide for Collectors.* Boston, Houghton Mifflin Co., 1976. fig. 44.
Innes, Lowell. *Early Glass of the Pittsburgh District, 1797–1900.* Carnegie Institute Museum of Art, Pittsburgh, 1949. p. 45.
Note: The above sources indicate that the vase has a history of having been made by Thomas Bovard, a glass blower at a Pittsburgh glass house.
Gift: Walter P. Chrysler, Jr.

143. Bank (Whimsey)
New England Area
Probably The Boston &
Sandwich Glass Company
Sandwich, Massachusetts
c. 1830–1840
Blown; white glass; looping in pale blue glass; blue "chicken" finial; applied, colorless rigaree and basket-like top; hollow stem encloses an 1829 U.S.A. 5 cent coin.
H: 8" (20 cm) GAS.64.1 (71.3951)
Gift: Walter P. Chrysler, Jr. in honor of Kathryn K. Porter.

144. Decanter, Pint Size
Pittsburgh Area
c. 1825–1840
Blown; colorless glass; cut design of star and diamonds, roundels with rays; matching round, hollow-cut stopper.
H: 9⅜" including stopper (23.8 cm) GAPe.78.1 (78.286)
Gift: Kathryn K. Porter.

145. Tumbler
Pittsburgh Area
Perhaps Bakewell
and Company
Pittsburgh, Pennsylvania
c. 1831
Blown; colorless glass; cut; engraved shield design enclosing *TN 1831* (Thomas Norton, Wheeling, West Virginia); opposite, a pair of doves on a pedestal; stylized flowers; leaves and grapes.
H: 3⅜" (8.6 cm) GAPe.79.2
Note: Illustrated in: Innes, Lowell. *Pittsburgh Glass: 1797–1891: A History and Guide for Collectors.* Boston, Houghton Mifflin Co., 1976. Figs. 76 & 77.
Museum Purchase.

146. "Lily Pad" Pitcher
South Jersey or New York Area
c. 1830–1850
Blown; pale aquamarine glass; superimposed "lily pad" decoration on the lower half; applied threading from the rim down the neck; applied solid handle.
H: 6¾" (17 cm) 83.583.GA
Museum Purchase and gift of Walter P. Chrysler, Jr.

147. Compote
Pittsburgh Area
c. 1835–1870
Blown; colorless glass; pillar molded in an eight rib mold; turned rim; solid baluster stem; round foot.
H: 7¼" (18.4 cm) GAPe.74.2 (0.1337)
Gift: Walter P. Chrysler, Jr.

148. Tea-Caddy
New England Area
Probably New England
Glass Company
Cambridge, Massachusetts
c. 1840
Blown; opal glass; green and narrow red looping. Probably used with a metal lid or cork stopper.
H: 6" (15.2 cm) GAN.59.22 (71.3791)
Gift: Walter P. Chrysler, Jr.

149. Sugar and Creamer
New England Area
Probably The Boston &
Sandwich Glass Company
Sandwich, Massachusetts
c. 1840
  a. Sugar Bowl
  c. 1840
  Blown; opal glass with red looping; tooled: galleried rim.
  H: 6" (15.3 cm) GAS.64.39 (71.3948)
  Gift: Walter P. Chrysler, Jr.
  b. Creamer
  c. 1840
  Blown; opal glass with red looping; applied matching solid handle.
  H: 7½" (19 cm) GAS.64.38 (71.3947)
  Gift: Walter P. Chrysler, Jr.

150. Cream Pitcher
Pittsburgh Area
c. 1840
Blown; opal glass; wide red bands marvered into the surface.
H: 6¼" at the handle (15.9 cm) GAPe.79.1 (79.167.1)
Note: Illustrated in: Innes, Lowell. *Pittsburgh Glass, 1797–1891: A History and Guide for Collectors.* Boston, Houghton Mifflin, 1976. figs. 46 and 479. Mr. Innes felt this was a whimsey.
Museum Purchase.

151. Pitcher
New England Area
Probably New England
Glass Company
Cambridge, Massachusetts
c. 1820–1840
Mold-blown; colorless glass; 13 recessed panels; applied double strap handle with curled end; polished pontil mark.
H: 7½" (19 cm) GAN.78.1 (0.453)
Gift: Walter P. Chrysler, Jr.

152. Vase
The Boston &
Sandwich Glass Company
Sandwich, Massachusetts
c. 1830–1840
Mold-blown; amethyst glass; 12 recessed panels.
H: 7¾" (19.7 cm) 84.80.GAS
Note: Similar vases are to be found in blue, green, and colorless glass. Usually they are credited as having been made at Sandwich, although the New England Glass Company could well have produced them. Illustrated in Rose, James. "American Blown Glass in the Seigfred Collection," *Antiques Magazine.* June 1967. p. 747, fig. 10.
Museum Purchase.

153. Vase (Celery)
Pittsburgh Area
Probably Bakewell & Company
Pittsburgh, Pennsylvania
c. 1820–1840
Mold-blown; colorless glass; twelve 2" high recessed panels at the bottom; applied narrow foot; engraved daisy, leaf, and swag design.
H: 6¾" (17.1 cm) 86.179.GABa
Reference: Innes, Lowell. *Pittsburgh Glass, 1797–1891: A History and Guide for Collectors.* Boston, Houghton Mifflin Co., 1976. fig. 127 is similar.
Museum Purchase.

154. Vase (Celery)
Pittsburgh Area
Probably Bakewell & Company
Pittsburgh, Pennsylvania
c. 1820–1840
Mold-blown; colorless glass; 21 deep finger ribs on the bottom third; engraved band of daisy and single leaf design nearer the rim; applied solid knop stem; round foot; rough pontil mark.

H: 8¼" (21 cm) 86.178.GABa
Reference: Innes, Lowell. *Pittsburgh Glass 1797–1891: A History and Guide for Collectors.* Boston, Houghton Mifflin Co., 1976. fig. 123 is similar.
Museum Purchase.

155. Bar Decanter
Midwest or Pittsburgh Area
c. 1850

Pillar molded; colorless glass; eight deeply protruding ribs; thick, heavy outside stripe of bright blue glass; large ring at the shoulder; large bar rim; polished pontil mark.
H: 12½" (31.8 cm) 86.324.GAMw
Reference: Similar to No. 606 in *William Elsholz Collection* (Sale), vol. I. Richard Bourne Auction, No. 606, Hyannis, Massachusetts, December 10, 1986.
Gift: Kathryn K. Porter.

156. Cream Pitcher, Covered Sugar Bowl
New England Area
Believed to be The Boston & Sandwich Glass Company
Sandwich, Massachusetts
c. 1825–1830

Note: The following objects are listed in McKearin, George S. and Helen. *American Glass.* New York, Crown Publishers, 1948, as pattern No. GIII-6. It is unusual to have a matched set.

a. Cream Pitcher
Blown-three-mold; colorless glass; geometric diamond sunburst design.
H: 4½" (11.5 cm) GAS.59.303 (71.3891)
Gift: Walter P. Chrysler, Jr.

b. Covered Sugar Bowl
Blown-three-mold; colorless glass; geometric diamond sunburst design.
H: 5" overall (12.7 cm) GAS.59.302 (71.3890)
Gift: Walter P. Chrysler, Jr.

157. Lamp, Decanters
Probably The Boston & Sandwich Glass Company
Sandwich, Massachusetts
c. 1825–1830

a. Toy or "Sparking" Lamp
Blown-three-mold; colorless glass; made from a decanter stopper; solid applied handle; equipped with a tin and cork single whale-oil wick holder.
H: 2¹⁄₁₆" at handle (5.3 cm) GAS.81.11 (81.150)
Note: Identified as style 16 in McKearin, George S. and Helen. *American Glass.* New York, Crown Publishers, 1948. pl. 114.
Reference: Barlow, Raymond and Joan Kaiser. *The Glass Industry in Sandwich.* Vol. 3. Barlow and Kaiser Publishing Co., Wyndham, N.H., 1987. (In conjunction with Schiffer Publishing, West Chester, Pa.) No. 3303, p. 209; called a "Toy."
Anonymous Gift.

b. Pint Decanter
Blown-three-mold; colorless glass.
H: 9½" (24.2 cm) GAS.59.361 (71.3909)
Note: Identified as a "baroque" style, GV-12, in McKearin, George S. and Helen. *American Glass.* New York, Crown Publishers, 1948, on p. 297; the stopper is identified as style 16 matching the toy/sparking lamp above.
Gift: Walter P. Chrysler, Jr.

c. Half Pint Decanter
Blown-three-mold; colorless glass; geometric with diamond diapering band; one of a pair, pressed, solid wheel stopper.
H: 6⅞" (17.5 cm) 66.129.6b
Note: Identified as style GII-18 in McKearin, George S. and Helen. *American Glass.* New York, Crown Publishers, 1948. p. 294.
Gift: James H. Devereaux, Jr.

158. A Pair of Whale Oil Lamps
The Boston & Sandwich Glass Company
Sandwich, Massachusetts
c. 1830

Blown-three-mold; colorless glass; baroque style Double Horn of Plenty Pattern font on lacy octagonal, pressed acanthus-leaf design foot.
H: 7⅛" (18.1 cm) GAS.59.585 a & b (71.3910 and 71.3911)
Gift: Walter P. Chrysler, Jr.

AMERICAN EARLY PRESSED AND LACY GLASS:
1827–1860

---

159. Cream Pitcher
New England Glass Company
Cambridge, Massachusetts
c. 1827

Pressed; pre-lacy period; colorless glass; an applied, solid handle (similar in style to a Staffordshire pottery version made about the same time).
H: 3⁵⁄₇" (9.3 cm) GAN.83.6 (83.114)
Note: The creamer was pressed before glass craftsmen discovered that a stippled background, now called "lacy pressed glass" disguised many of the imperfections caused by this new technique. A hollow vessel was complicated to make and it may well have been one of the first such objects made successfully. A similar creamer was sold in the first Elsholz sale. See: *The William Elsholz Collection,* Vol. I, Richard Bourne Auction, Hyannis, Massachusetts, December 10, 1986, No. 524.
Gift: Walter P. Chrysler, Jr.

160. Plate
The Boston & Sandwich Glass Company
Sandwich, Massachusetts
c. 1827–1830

Pressed; pre-lacy period; colorless glass; "Heart, Lyre and Strawberry Diamond" design—inspired by Anglo-Irish cut glass. This plate is almost flat; another in the collection is a shallow bowl.
D: 9⅜" (23.8 cm) GAS.59.284 (71.3864)
Note: A similar plate was sold in the first Elsholz sale. See: *The William Elsholz Collection,* Vol. I, Richard Bourne Auction, Hyannis, Massachusetts, December 10, 1986, No. 677.
Gift: Walter P. Chrysler, Jr.

161. Lacy Period Cup Plates
The Boston & Sandwich
Glass Company
Sandwich, Massachusetts
c. 1827–1955

a. Cup Plate
c. 1835
Pressed; lacy period; violet-blue glass; heart design.
D: 3½" (9 cm) GAS.59.259 (71.4197)
Reference: Lee, Ruth Webb and James Rose. *American Glass Cup Plates*. R. W. Lee, Northboro, Mass., 1948. No. 459-D.
Gift: Walter P. Chrysler, Jr.

b. Cup Plate
c. 1835–1840
Pressed: lacy period; colorless glass; Henry Clay design, facing right.
D: 3⅜" (8.7 cm) GAS.64.32 (71.4159)
Reference: Lee, Ruth Webb and James Rose. *American Glass Cup Plates*. R. W. Lee, Northboro, Mass., 1948. No. 562-A.
Gift: Walter P. Chrysler, Jr.

c. Cup Plate
c. 1827
Pressed; lacy period; colorless glass; heart & sheaf of wheat design.
D: 3⅜" (8.7 cm) GAS.59.135 (71.4174)
Reference: Lee, Ruth Webb and James Rose. *American Glass Cup Plates*. R. W. Lee, Northboro, Mass., 1948. No. 425.
Gift: Walter P. Chrysler, Jr.

d. Cup Plate
c. 1830–1835
Pressed; lacy period; colorless glass; hairpin design.
D: 3⅝" (9.2 cm) GAS.59.139 (71.4177)
Reference: Lee, Ruth Webb and James Rose. *American Glass Cup Plates*. R. W. Lee, Northboro, Mass., 1948. No. 285.
Gift: Walter P. Chrysler, Jr.

e. Cup Plate
c. 1840–1852
Pressed; lacy period; blue glass; Henry Clay design.
D: 3⁹⁄₁₆" (9 cm) GAS.59.256 (71.4189)
Reference: Lee, Ruth Webb and James Rose. *American Glass Cup Plates*. R. W. Lee, Northboro, Mass., 1948. No. 565-B.
Gift: Walter P. Chrysler, Jr.

162. Bowl/Plate
New England
Probably The Boston & Sandwich Glass Company
Sandwich, Massachusetts
c. 1830
Pressed; lacy period; colorless glass; variety of diamond and strawberry-diamond design of cross.
D: 12" (30.5 cm) 83.348.GAS
Museum Purchase.

163. Lacy Candlesticks
Probably The Boston & Sandwich Glass Company
Sandwich, Massachusetts
c. 1830

a. Lacy Candlestick
c. 1830
Pressed; colorless glass; "Horn of Plenty Socket" with grape design on top attached by multiple mereses to a hollow, tripodal base with C-scroll sides and three paw feet.
H: 7" (17.8 cm) GAS.59.231 (71.3985)
Note: The tripodal base is also seen on lamps, compotes, and other candlesticks. The grape design appears on the rim of a lacy dish.
Gift: Walter P. Chrysler, Jr.

b. Lacy Candlestick
c. 1830
Pressed; colorless glass; trefoil floral design socket attached by multiple mereses to an octagonal, hollow, three-stepped base.
H: 5⅛" (13 cm) GAS.59.215 (71.3964)
Note: This socket appears on a Corning Museum of Glass candlestick with the tripodal base.
Gift: Walter P. Chrysler, Jr.

164. Lamp
Pittsburgh Area
Probably Bakewell & Company
Pittsburgh, Pennsylvania
c. 1835–1840
Blown; font engraved with *Bakewell*-type three leaf daisy band; applied with mereses to pressed, hollow, ribbed stem; quatrefoil foot.
H: 10¾" (27.3 cm) 86.180.GABa
Illustrated in: Innes, Lowell. *Pittsburgh Glass 1797–1891: A History and Guide for Collectors*. Boston, Houghton Mifflin, 1976. fig. 119; also, the cover illustration on the *National Early American Glass Club Bulletin*, March, 1977.
Gift: The Chrysler Museum Glass Club.

165. Oval Bowl
The Boston & Sandwich
Glass Company
Sandwich, Massachusetts
c. 1830
Pressed; lacy period; colorless glass; Eagle and Constitution design. (Known as the "Cadmus-Eagle" Bowl.)
D: 6¾" x 3⅞" (15.9 cm x 9.8 cm) GAS.59.296 (71.3852)
Note: The design is believed to have been inspired by the public outcry to save the frigate *Constitution* which had been condemned as unseaworthy. (See also No. 166.)
Illustrated: McKearin, George S. and Helen. *American Glass*. Crown Publishers, New York, 1948. pl. 128.
Gift: Walter P. Chrysler, Jr.

166. U.S.F. Constitution Tray
The Boston & Sandwich
Glass Company
Sandwich, Massachusetts
c. 1830–1835
Pressed; lacy period; colorless glass. Primitive design of the famous ship with the title and stars above; rim has alternating hearts and stars.
D: 4½ x 7" (11.5 cm x 17.8 cm) 83.347.GAS
Note: The design was inspired by the public outcry to save the frigate *Constitution* which had been condemned as unseaworthy. (An identical rim is seen on the tray for the Gothic Arch design covered casket.)
Reference: Rose, James H. *The Story of American Pressed Glass of The Lacy Period, 1825–1850*. The Corning Museum of Glass, Corning, New York, 1954. Catalogue No. 127.
Museum Purchase.

167. Union Plate
Midwestern
c. 1830–1845
Pressed; lacy period; colorless glass; design of three masted vessels titled at bottom *UNION* and with thirteen stars above; four sprigs of oak leaves on the shoulder; octagonal cap ring with eight large bull's-eyes on rim corners with three smaller ones between.
D: 6⅛" (15.5 cm) (side to side) 87.421.GAMw
Illustrated: *The William Elsholz Collection*, Vol. I, Richard Bourne Auction, Hyannis, Massachusetts, December 10, 1986, No. 513.
Gift: Kathryn K. Porter.

168. Lacy Dish
The Boston & Sandwich
Glass Company
Sandwich, Massachusetts
c. 1830–1835
Pressed; lacy period; colorless glass; open handle; eyelet-style edge; scroll and stylized floral design center.
D: 11¾" x 8⅜" (30 cm x 21.3 cm)
GAS.59.96 (71.4093)
Gift: Walter P. Chrysler, Jr.

169a. Lacy Covered Bowl
New England Area
Probably The Boston &
Sandwich Glass Company
Sandwich, Massachusetts
c. 1830–1840
Pressed: lacy period; colorless glass; arch and thistle design; peacock eye design cover. See No. 169b for medallion design cover.
H: 5⅛" (13 cm) 83.349.GAS
Reference: The 1954 "American Pressed Glass Exhibition" at The Corning Museum of Glass: see plate No. 99 in: Rose, James H. *The Story of American Pressed Glass of the Lacy Period 1825–1850.* The Corning Museum of Glass, Corning, New York, 1954.
Museum Purchase.

169b. Lacy Bowl
Same item as above but with a cover design of three medallions.
This type of cover is more often used with this bowl although both fit properly. (Cover 87.185.GAS)
Cover: Gift of the Henry Ford Museum, Dearborn, Michigan.

170. Whale Oil Peg Lamp
The Boston & Sandwich
Glass Company
Sandwich, Massachusetts
c. 1825–1830
Blown-three-mold; opal glass; ribbed design; central leaf band; metal whale oil wick holder.
H: 4½" (10.8 cm) GAS.77.14 (0.1346)
Note: The font is similar to a light blue opaque "Lion's Head Basket of Flowers" lamp at The Sandwich Glass Museum. (See No. 171 and a pair in *The William Elsholz Catalog.* Vol. I, Richard Bourne Auction, Hyannis, Massachusetts, December 10, 1986, No. 439.)
Gift: Walter P. Chrysler, Jr.

171. Lamp
New England Area
Probably The Boston &
Sandwich Glass Company
Sandwich, Massachusetts
c. 1830
Pressed; opal glass; hollow square base; each side with a design of a basket of flowers and a lion's head top of each corner attached with triple mereses to the blown globular font.
H: 7⅝" (19.3 cm) 83.352.GAS
Note: Similar lamps made by the New England Glass Company, Cambridge, Massachusetts, were marked on the inside hollow base with "NEGCo," and it is believed that those made by Sandwich were unmarked, as is this one.
Gift: Walter P. Chrysler, Jr.

172. Lacy Period Salts
The Boston & Sandwich
Glass Company
Sandwich, Massachusetts
c. 1830–1845
Top Row: (left to right)
a. Salt
Pressed; lacy period; blue opalescent glass; rectangular shape; wide horizontal rib design.
H: 2" (5 cm) GAS.77.15 (0.1377)
Illustrated: Spillman, Jane. *American and European Pressed Glass in the Corning Museum of Glass*, The Corning Museum of Glass, Corning, New York, 1981. No. 944 has a similar shape.
Gift: Walter P. Chrysler, Jr.

b. Salt
Pressed; lacy period; fiery blue opalescent glass; rectangular shape; Gothic arch and heart design.
H: 1¾" (4.4 cm) GAS.70.40 (71.4134)
Reference: Neal, Logan W. and Dorothy B. *Pressed Glass Salt Dishes of the Lacy Period: 1825–1850.* L. W. and D. B. Neal, Philadelphia, 1962. *GA-4.* Rare.
Gift: Walter P. Chrysler, Jr.

Center:
c. Salt
Pressed; lacy period; fiery blue opalescent glass; rectangular shape; basket of flowers motif.
H: 2 1/16" (5.2 cm) GAS.70.30 (71.4098)
Reference: Neal, Logan W. and Dorothy B. *Pressed Glass Salt Dishes of the Lacy Period: 1825–1850.* L. W. and D. B. Neal, Philadelphia, 1962. *BF-1d.* Unlisted in this color.
Gift: Walter P. Chrysler, Jr.

Bottom Row: (left to right)
d. Salt
Pressed; lacy period; opaque, silvery blue glass; rectangular shape; chariot motif.
H: 2⅛" (5.4 cm) GAS.70.35 (71.4098)
Reference: Neal, Logan W. and Dorothy B. *Pressed Glass Salt Dishes of the Lacy Period: 1825–1850.* L. W. and D. B. Neal, Philadelphia, 1962. *CT-1.* Very rare.
Gift: Walter P. Chrysler, Jr.

e. Salt
Pressed; lacy period; opaque, silvery blue glass, "Lafayet" boat shape.
Mark: *Sandwich* inside the bottom and base and stern; marked in relief: *B & S Glass Co.* and on the paddle wheel *Lafayet.*
H: 1½" (4 cm) GAS.60.76 (71.4116)
Note: There was insufficient room on the glass to print the complete word "Lafayette."
Reference: Neal, Logan W. and Dorothy B. *Pressed Glass Salt Dishes of the Lacy Period: 1825–1850.* L. W. and D. B. Neal, Philadelphia, 1962. *BT8.* Very rare.
Gift: Walter P. Chrysler, Jr.

f. Salt
Pressed; lacy period; opaque, purple-blue mottled glass; oval shape; checkered diamond design.
H: 1¾" (4.5 cm) GAS.59.345 (71.4052)
Reference: Neal, Logan W. and Dorothy B. *Pressed Glass Salt Dishes of the Lacy Period: 1825–1850.* L. W. and D. B. Neal, Philadelphia, 1962. *OL15.* Very rare or unique, as the color is not listed.
Gift: Walter P. Chrysler, Jr.

173. Window Pane
J. & C. Ritchie
Wheeling, West Virginia
c. 1833–1835
Pressed; lacy period; colorless glass; urns, floral and thistle design surround a central medallion of an Ohio River paddlewheel steamboat entitled: *J. & C. Ritchie.*
Size: 7″ x 5″ (17.8 cm x 12.7 cm)
86.72.GARt
Illustrated: Innes, Lowell. *Pittsburgh Glass, 1797–1891: A History and Guide for Collectors.* Boston, Houghton Mifflin Co., 1976. fig. 306.
Museum Purchase.

174. Lacy Window Pane
Midwestern, probably
Pittsburgh, Pennsylvania
c. 1835–1840
Pressed; lacy period; colorless glass; design of diamond center and fan end.
Size: 6⅞″ x 4¹⁵⁄₁₆″ (17.5 cm x 12.5 cm)
86.188.GAMw
Illustrated: Innes, Lowell. *Pittsburgh Glass, 1797–1891: A History and Guide for Collectors.* Boston, Houghton Mifflin Co., 1976. fig. 303 (a).
Museum Purchase.

175. Lacy Window Pane
Pittsburgh Area
c. 1835–1845
Pressed; lacy period; amethyst glass; blossom design.
Size: 6⅞″ x 5″ (17.5 cm x 12.7 cm)
83.345.GAPe
Note: This pane was one of the sidelights from a doorway of a home in Franklin County, Indiana. Although the home was built in 1850, family tradition recorded that the glass was bought many years earlier somewhere in the Ohio River Valley. The doorway panes were of alternating colorless and amethyst glass. This is one of two known surviving amethyst glass panes.
Reference: Spillman, Jane. *American and European Pressed Glass in the Corning Museum of Glass.* The Corning Museum of Glass, Corning, New York, 1981, No. 134.
Museum Purchase.

176. Gothic Style Lacy Window Pane
Bakewell & Company
Pittsburgh, Pennsylvania
c. 1836–1839
Pressed; lacy period; colorless glass; gothic revival style.
Marked: In relief on the center of the smooth side, in reverse, to be read from the front: BAKEWELL.
Size: 6⅞″ x 4⅞″ (17.5 cm x 12.4 cm)
86.187.GABa
Illustrated: Innes, Lowell. *Pittsburgh Glass, 1797–1891: A History and Guide for Collectors.* Boston, Houghton Mifflin Co., 1976, fig. 303 (g).
Museum Purchase.

177. "Industry" Bowl
New England Glass Company
Cambridge, Massachusetts
c. 1840
Pressed; lacy period; colorless glass; design of a log cabin and a cider barrel, the emblems of Whig Presidential candidate, William Henry Harrison. The surrounding shoulder design shows a factory building from an etching of the New England Glass Company, a sailing schooner *The Cincinnatus of the West*, and two scenes of a man with a horse-drawn plow, emblems for American industry and Presidential candidate Harrison, who was known as the "Farmer of North Bend."
D: 6⁵⁄₁₆″ (16 cm) GAN.59.5 (71.3746)
Illustrated: McKearin, George S. and Helen. *American Glass.* Crown Publishers, New York, 1969. pl. 141, fig. 6.
Gift: Walter P. Chrysler, Jr.

178. Lacy Compote
The Boston & Sandwich
Glass Company
Sandwich, Massachusetts
c. 1840
Pressed; lacy period; electric blue glass; princess feather and basket of flowers design; top attached with a glass wafer to the matching hollow, hexagonal stem and foot.
H: 6⅜″ (16.2 cm) 86.394.GAS
Note: The compote is rare and perhaps unique in this color, and, with the unusual hexagonal foot, it is similar to that seen on the Leaf Vase (No. 186) and the "Four Printie Block" Lamp (No. 184).

Reference: *The William J. Elsholz Collection*, Vol. I., Richard Bourne Auction, Hyannis, Mass., December 10, 1986. No. 507.
Museum Purchase with help from The Chrysler Glass Club and Kathryn K. Porter.

179. Dish
The Boston & Sandwich
Glass Company
Sandwich, Massachusetts
c. 1835–1840
Pressed; lacy period; colorless glass; princess feather medallion and basket of fruit/flowers design; same as the top of the Electric Blue Compote No. 178.
Rim: 10½″ x 8¾″ (26.6 cm x 22.2 cm)
GAS.59.586 (71.3879)
Gift: Walter P. Chrysler, Jr.

180. Fruit Bowl
The Boston & Sandwich
Glass Company
Sandwich, Massachusetts
c. 1845
Pressed; amethyst glass; design of 22 open ribs; flaring scalloped rim; narrow round foot; the inside is enameled tan; primitive floral design.
D: 5¾″ (14.5 cm) GAS.59.565 (71.4349)
Note: There is a similar enameled opalescent fruit bowl in The Sandwich Glass Museum collection.
Gift: Walter P. Chrysler, Jr.

181. Compote
The Boston & Sandwich
Glass Company
Sandwich, Massachusetts
c. 1845–1855
Pressed; blue tint opalescent; lattice (ribbon or openwork); 16 ribs tooled and fire polished top attached with wafer to hexagonal knop stem and hollow foot.
H: 7″ to 7¾″ (17.8 to 19.7 cm)
87.504.GAS
Reference: *The William Elsholz Collection*, Vol. III, Richard Bourne Auction, Hyannis, Massachusetts, November 17, 1987. No. 1487.
Museum Purchase.

182. Dish
The Boston & Sandwich
Glass Company
Sandwich, Massachusetts
c. 1840
Pressed; deep amber glass; waffle bottom; rectangular shape; curved wide slightly flaring rim with simulated handles at the ends.
Rim: 11 1/8" x 9 1/4" (28.5 cm x 23.5 cm)
84.250.GAS
Museum Purchase.

183. Pressed Glass Selections
The Boston & Sandwich
Glass Company
Sandwich, Massachusetts
c. 1850–1860
These objects were made at the time when the technique for pressing had not progressed sufficiently to produce such complicated objects in a single mold. They were therefore made by pressing the tops and the stem with the foot made separately but simultaneously. These separate parts were then immediately joined with a wafer of hot glass.
a. **Vase**
  Pressed; amethyst glass; hexagonal loop pattern and rim; attached by wafer to hexagonal baluster stem and round foot.
  H: 8 7/8" (22.5 cm) GAS.59.617 (71.4462)
  Note: Rim left plain, not stretched or gauffered.
  Gift: Walter P. Chrysler, Jr.
b. **Vase**
  Pressed; electric blue glass, swirled hexagonal loop pattern tooled to a plain rim with a turned edge; attached by a wafer to a solid round knop and octagonally paneled baluster stem on 1" high square foot with chamfered corners.
  H: 9 1/2" (24.2 cm) GAS.59.610 (71.4458)
  Gift: Walter P. Chrysler, Jr.
c. **Candlestick**
  Pressed, green glass; hexagonal socket and extension; attached by a wafer to a hexagonally paneled baluster stem and round foot (stem and foot like [a]); one of a pair.
  H: 6 3/4" (17.2 cm) GAS.59.471a (71.4471)

Reference: McKearin, George S. and Helen. *American Glass.* Crown Publishers, New York, 1969; (a) pl. 199, No. 19; (b) pl. 197, No. 1; (c) pl. 199, No. 20, pp. 384–393.
Gift: Walter P. Chrysler, Jr.

AMERICAN PATTERN (PRESSED) GLASS:
1850–1875

---

184. Lamp
The Boston & Sandwich
Glass Company
Sandwich, Massachusetts
c. 1850–1860
Pressed; purple/blue glass; "Four Printie Block" pattern; font attached by a wafer to the hollow hexagonal foot; one of a pair.
H: 11" including metal cap (28 cm)
GAS.59.407a (71.3903)
Note: This style of lamp, with a tall font, probably originally was designed for burning fuel/camphene, the highly volatile combination of alcohol and turpentine.
Gift: Walter P. Chrysler, Jr.

185. Sugar Bowl and Creamer— Ashburton Pattern
New England Glass Company
Cambridge, Massachusetts
c. 1850–1860
a. **Covered Sugar Bowl**
  Pressed; gold (canary) glass; Ashburton Pattern.
  H: 7 1/4" overall (18.4 cm)
b. **Creamer**
  Pressed; gold (canary) glass; Ashburton Pattern.
  H: 5 5/8" (14.2 cm) 52.18.7
  Note: An 1849 invoice for a New England Glass shipment to San Francisco recorded in Wilson, Kenneth. *New England Glass and Glassmaking.* Thomas Y. Crowell Co., New York, 1972, pp. 294-295, lists "gold color Ashburton." No doubt gold was substituted for the usual canary color descriptions because of the California Gold Rush craze.
  Bequest: The Kate Tyler Smith Collection (see No. 140).

186. Vases, Compote, Bowl —Leaf Design
The Boston & Sandwich
Glass Company
Sandwich, Massachusetts
c. 1840–1850
Pressed; leaf pattern vases, compote, and bowl.
Note: The common design of each of the following objects is the leaf top. The bowl and compote are as they come from the mold. The vase starts the same way, but, while still hot and pliable, it is manipulated into four compartments. At the same time, by a separate operation, the desired foot is pressed and, while still hot, the foot is attached to make a compote or vase. One vase has the plain hexagonal foot like electric blue compote No. 178. The canary vase and the compote No. b and No. c are made with an octagonally paneled leaf foot. Such a foot is usually found on lacy compotes with the princess feather design top, see No. 178.
a. **Vase**
  Pressed; colorless glass; trefoil bowl; contracted into four compartments; applied, pressed, hexagonal dome base; one of a pair.
  H: 10 3/4" (27.3 cm) GAS.60.11 (71.4371)
  Gift: Walter P. Chrysler, Jr.
b. **Vase**
  Pressed; canary colored glass; trefoil; applied leaf-design octagonal paneled foot.
  H: 10 1/8" (25.7 cm) GAS.81.4 (81.13)
  Note: McKearin, George S. and Helen. *American Glass.* New York, Crown Publishers, 1969. pl. 195, fig. No. 5 and pp. 383–384.
  Museum Purchase.
c. **Compote**
  Pressed; colorless glass; leaf bowl; applied octagonally paneled leaf-design foot.
  H: 6" (15.2 cm) GAS.78.32 (78.577)
  Museum Purchase.
d. **Bowl**
  Pressed; colorless glass; leaf design; polished pontil mark.
  D: 8" (20.3 cm) GAS.81.2 (81.10)
  Anonymous Gift.

**187. Covered Butter Dish—
Comet Pattern**
The Boston & Sandwich
Glass Company
Sandwich, Massachusetts
c. 1850–1870

Pressed; colorless glass; "Comet Pattern"; the cover finial has a representation of George Washington's head; one of a pair.
H: 5" (12.7 cm) GAS.59.730 (71.4725)
Note: Today the "Comet Pattern" is popularly known as the "Horn-of-Plenty" pattern. This pattern was manufactured by The Boston & Sandwich Glass Company of Sandwich, Massachusetts; by McKee and Brothers of Pittsburgh, Pennsylvania; and probably by other East and Midwest factories. "Comet," a fashionable mid-19th century pressed glass pattern, was made in a wide variety of tableware items from the tiny, round, so-called "honey" dishes, goblets, and other drinking vessels, to a round covered butter dish adorned with a finial in the form of George Washington's head. Decanters, bar bottles, lamps, many sizes of bowls, some with covers and several on stems, were a part of the items offered. The surviving Sandwich wooden pattern models include a "Comet" goblet.
Gift: Walter P. Chrysler, Jr.

**188. Compote, Covered Sugar
Bowl, Decanter—Sharp
Diamond Pattern**
New England Glass Company
Cambridge, Massachusetts
c. 1850–1870

Note: One hundred and thirty pieces of pressed Sharp Diamond pattern glass were displayed by the New England Glass Company at the New York City Crystal Palace Exhibition 1853–1854 as listed in an excerpt from the C. R. Goodrich report of the exhibition in Fauster, Carl. *Libbey Glass*. Len Beach Press, Toledo, Ohio, 1979. p. 17. The surviving 1870 New England Glass Catalog shows this pattern was still being made at that date.

a. Compote
Pressed; fire polished; colorless glass; Sharp diamond bowl; applied with a glass wafer to the hollow octagonal stem; round foot; a scalloped rim.
(23.8 cm) GAN.59.32 (71.5958)
Gift: Walter P. Chrysler, Jr.

b. Covered Sugar Bowl
Pressed; fire polished; colorless glass; short, hexagonal stem; round foot; star design on the bottom; polished pontil mark; matching dome cover with a solid pointed finial.
H: 8½" including cover (21.5 cm) GAN.73.29 (0.1285)
Gift: Walter P. Chrysler, Jr.

c. Decanter
Pressed; fire polished; colorless glass; hexagonally scalloped base; polished pontil mark; matching hollow stopper.
H: 13⅝" (34.5 cm) GAN.73.24 a & b (0.1288)
Gift: Walter P. Chrysler, Jr.

**189. Compote—
Sandwich Star Pattern**
The Boston & Sandwich
Glass Company
Sandwich, Massachusetts
c. 1860

Pressed; colorless glass; "Sandwich Star" pattern; triple dolphin stem; round dome foot.
H: 9½" (24.2 cm) GAS.59.447 (71.4205)
Note: Only a few of these with dolphin stem are known. The same stem and foot are found on Sandwich lamps and at least one pair of candlesticks.
Reference: Barlow, Raymond and Joan Kaiser. *The Glass Industry in Sandwich*. Vol. 4., Barlow & Kaiser Publishing Co., Wyndham, N.H., 1983. No. 4, No. 4049, p. 63.
Gift: Walter P. Chrysler, Jr.

190. Dolphin Candlesticks
The Boston & Sandwich
Glass Company
Sandwich, Massachusetts
c. 1855–1870

Note: The smaller dolphin candlestick is often not recognized as Sandwich, but it can be identified by the quantities of fragments excavated from the factory site, fragments of which are in the collection of The Sandwich Glass Museum.

**a. White and Blue Dolphin
Candlestick**
c. 1855–1870
Pressed; white glass, double-stepped, square base; dolphin stem attached by a wafer to the blue hexagonal petal socket and extension.
H: 10" (25.5 cm) GAS.59.555 (71.4516)
Reference: McKearin, George S. & Helen. *American Glass*. Crown Publishers, New York, 1969. pl. 204, No. 67.
Gift: Walter P. Chrysler, Jr.

**b. Blue and White Dolphin
Candlestick**
c. 1855–1870
Pressed; blue glass; square base; dolphin stem attached by a wafer to a white hexagonal petal socket extension; one of a pair.
H: 10¼" (26 cm) GAS.59.552b (71.4517)
Reference: McKearin, George S. & Helen. *American Glass*. Crown Publishers, New York, 1969. pl. 204, No. 66.
Gift: Walter P. Chrysler, Jr.

**c. White Opaline Dolphin
Candlestick**
c. 1855–1870
Pressed; hexagonal base; small dolphin stem attached by wafer to hexagonal socket; one of a pair.
H: 6⅞" (17.5 cm) GAS.77.12b (0.1440)
Gift: Walter P. Chrysler, Jr.

**191. Bar Decanter—
Washington Pattern**
New England Glass Company
Cambridge, Massachusetts
c. 1865

Pressed; colorless glass; "Washington Pattern"; moveable metal, cork, and glass pouring stopper; polished pontil mark.
H: 11" including stopper (28 cm) GAN.73.21 (0.1294)
Reference: "Pressed Glass of the New England Glass Company," *Journal of Glass Studies*. Vol. XII, 1970, The Corning Museum of Glass, Corning, New York; fig. 1, pl. 2, pp. 151-152.
Gift: Walter P. Chrysler, Jr.

192. Pitcher, Sugar Bowl, Covered Butter — Paneled Wheat Pattern
Hobbs, Brockunier & Company
Wheeling, West Virginia
c. 1870–1880

a. Pitcher
Pressed; opaque white glass; "Paneled Wheat Pattern."
H: 6" (15.2 cm) GAW.64.8 (71.4813)
Gift: Walter P. Chrysler, Jr.

b. Sugar Bowl with Wide Rim
Pressed; opaque white glass; "Paneled Wheat Pattern"; made with 9 slots for spoons; a matching cover with a sheaf of wheat finial.
H: 7½" (19 cm) including cover. GAW.64.9 (71.4814)
Gift: Walter P. Chrysler, Jr.

c. Covered Butter
Pressed; opaque white glass; "Paneled Wheat Pattern"; sheaf of wheat finial on the cover.
H: 4" (10.1 cm) including cover. GAW.64.10 (71.4812)
Gift: Walter P. Chrysler, Jr.
Reference: Peterson, Arthur G., *Glass Patents and Patterns*. Celery City Printing Co., Sanford, Florida. pp. 84–85. Design patented February 28, 1871, by John H. Hobbs of Wheeling, West Virginia. The white glass was probably called "hot-cast porcelain" like the "Grape with Overlapping Foliage," also p. 84.

193. Tumbler, Candlestick
Pittsburgh Area
c. 1860

a. Footed Tumbler
McKee and Brothers
Pittsburgh, Pennsylvania
c. 1860
Pressed; opalescent glass; Excelsior variant pattern.
H: 4⅜" (11.1 cm) GAMc.70.1 (71.3996)
Gift: Walter P. Chrysler, Jr.

b. Candlestick
c. 1860
Pressed; opalescent glass; "Tulip Pattern."
H: 9⅝" (24.4 cm) GAPe.77.6 (71.3997)
Note: Illustrated in: Innes, Lowell. *Pittsburgh Glass, 1797–1891: A History and Guide for Collectors*. Boston, Houghton Mifflin Co., 1976. pl. 331; Ringwalt Sales Catalog.
Gift: Walter P. Chrysler, Jr.

194. Perfume Bottle
New England Glass Company
Cambridge, Massachusetts
c. 1865–1875
Pressed; opal glass; hexagonally paneled with a raised oval on each panel; six solid protruding bracket-like galleries near the bottom.
H: 4¼" (10.8 cm) GAN.63.24 (71.3813)
Note: An illustration of this bottle appears on page 25 of the 1869 New England Glass Company catalogue recorded on page 107 of Watkins, Lura W. *Cambridge Glass 1818 to 1888: The Story of the New England Glass Company*. Marshall Jones Company, Boston, 1930. The Chrysler collection contains a similar canary color pair with steeple stoppers made about the same time, probably by The Boston & Sandwich Glass Company, as well as a better impression of an amber one, highlighted by floral gilt with a panel cut neck and a taller steeple stopper. This latter seems a match to one illustrated in *L'Opaline Française* by Amic, pl. XLIV, from the 1865 Cristallerie de Baccarat catalogue. Recently (1984), a contemporary French perfume maker reproduced this exact same design in two sizes of bottles for a perfume named "Scheherazade." Four examples (see small photograph No. 194a) left to right are:

194a. Perfume Bottles
1865–1875

a. Perfume Bottle
1865–1875
Pressed; amber glass; gilt decorated Baccarat bottle.
H: 6⅞" (17.5 cm) including stopper GEFB.76.1 (0.2338)
Gift: Walter P. Chrysler, Jr.

b. Perfume Bottle
1865–1875
Pressed; canary color glass; The Boston & Sandwich Glass Company.
Gift: Walter P. Chrysler, Jr.

c. Perfume Bottle
1865–1875
Pressed; colorless glass; 1984 French.
H: 3½" (9 cm) including stopper 85.14.GEF
Gift: Walter P. Chrysler, Jr.

d. Perfume Bottle
1865–1875
Pressed; opal glass; New England Glass Company (see No. 56)
Gift: Walter P. Chrysler, Jr.

195. Inkwell
New England Glass Company
Cambridge, Massachusetts
c. 1870
Pressed; opal glass; in the shape of a dory in a stand; white metal cap with an anchor in relief on the opal glass central cylinder; both sides enameled floral spray; gilt rim; brown enameled stand to simulate wood. Marked in relief inside: *PAT'D Aug. 9 1870* (patent issued to Henry Whitney, Jr. for the New England Glass Co.).
L: 5½" (14 cm) GAN.64.36 (71.3812)
Gift: Walter P. Chrysler, Jr.

196. Vase
Pittsburgh Area
c. 1860
Blown; opal glass with raspberry and thin blue glass loopings; applied blue glass rim; plain opal glass reverse baluster stem; round foot.
H: 9¾" (24.8 cm) GAPe.79.3 (79.167.3)
Museum Purchase.

AMERICAN CUT, ENGRAVED, AND ENAMELED GLASS: 1850–1880

197. Enameled Opal Glass
The Boston & Sandwich Glass Company
Sandwich, Massachusetts
c. 1874

a. Tumble-Up (Water Bottle and Tumbler)
c. 1874
Blown; opal glass; enameled and gilded; bug and fern design.
H: 6½" with tumbler top (16.5 cm) GAS.65.11 (71.4765)
Note: Illustrated in the reprint of the 1874 *Boston & Sandwich Glass Co. Catalogue*. Lee Publications, Wellesley Hills, Mass., 1968. pl. 58.
Gift: Walter P. Chrysler, Jr.

b. Ring Vase
c. 1874
Mold-blown; opal glass; enameled and gilded; design of white bird, yellow blossoms; beige background; flat bottom.
H: 4⅝″ (11.8 cm) GAS.77.9 (0.1881)
Note: Ring vases are illustrated in the reprint of the 1874 *Boston & Sandwich Glass Co. Catalogue.* Lee Publications, Wellesley Hills, Mass., 1968, pl. 59. This is the smallest size. Mount Washington Glass and Smith Brothers also produced similar ring vases. Reference: Revi, Albert C. *Nineteenth Century Glass.* Revised Edition. Gallahad Books, New York City, 1967, pp. 81–86.
Gift: Walter P. Chrysler, Jr.

c. Vase
c. 1874
Mold-blown; opal glass; raised flower design; background enameled rose with two gilt bands; one at the rim and the other above the raised leaf-like top fringe.
H: 10″ (25.5 cm) GAS.66.5 (71.4766)
Note: Illustrated in the reprint of the 1874 *Boston & Sandwich Glass Co. Catalogue.* Lee Publications, Wellesley Hills, Mass., 1968. pl. 60. The Chrysler collection includes a similar plain blue opaline one.
Gift: Walter P. Chrysler, Jr.

198. Engraved Glass
New England Glass Company
Cambridge, Massachusetts
c. 1850–1860

a. Goblet
c. 1850–1860
Blown; colorless glass; cut; engraved; five floral and vintage medallions; one "Aunt Julia" medallion framed by floral and vine swags.
H: 6⅛″ (15.5 cm) 52.18.41.GAN
Bequest: The Kate Tyler Smith Collection (see No. 140).

b. Goblet
Blown; colorless glass; engraved fern design.
H: 8″ (20.3 cm) 52.18.82.GAN
Note: This engraving design is illustrated on pl. 51 and pp. 116 and 122 of Watkins, Lura. *Cambridge Glass, 1818 to 1888: The Story of the New England Glass Company.* Marshall Jones Company, Boston, 1930. Henry S. Fillebrown designs from *Engraver's Pattern Book.*
Bequest: The Kate Tyler Smith Collection (see No. 140).

c. Cologne Bottle
c. 1850–1860
Blown; colorless glass; cut; engraved floral basket; hanging basket of fern and ivy, a hunting dog in the landscape; the fourth side has a curtain design.
H: 5¾″ including stopper (14.6 cm) 52.18.67.GAN
Bequest: The Kate Tyler Smith Collection (see No. 140).

199. Decanter and Spoon Holder
New England Glass Company
Cambridge, Massachusetts
c. 1850–1870

a. Decanter
c. 1850–1870
Blown; colorless glass; panel-cut neck; engraved Greek key band; monogrammed *T* (Tyler); star-cut bottom; matching hollow flat top stopper.
H: 12⅞″ (32.7 cm) including stopper 52.18.95.GAN
Bequest: The Kate Tyler Smith Collection (see No. 140).

b. Spoon Holder
c. 1850–1870
Blown; colorless glass; hexagonal shape; panel-cut stem; engraved Greek key band; star-cut bottom; gilt rim band.
H: 5¾″ (14.6 cm) 52.18.17.GAN
Bequest: The Kate Tyler Smith Collection (see No. 140).
The Smith Collection also includes six matching sauce dishes.

200. Oil Lamp
The Boston & Sandwich
Glass Company
Sandwich, Massachusetts
c. 1860
Blown; colorless glass; font with four yellow-stained medallions engraved to clear glass; two medallions have floral designs, one with a deer in a landscape and one with *R.F. Fish 1860;* additional floral engravings between the medallions; metal stem; marble base.
H: 8″ (20.3 cm) GAS.64.46 (71.4862)
Gift: Walter P. Chrysler, Jr.

201. Celery Vase, Compote, Covered Sugar Bowl
New England Area
Probably The Boston & Sandwich Glass Company
Sandwich, Massachusetts
c. 1855

a. Celery Vase
c. 1855
Blown; colorless glass; cut; checkered diamond bowl; a vintage engraved top band; monogram *B. McC.* in a floral cartouche; panel-cut hollow stem enclosing an 1852 U.S. half dime.
H: 9⅝″ (24.5 cm) GAS.63.97 (71.4873)
Gift: Walter P. Chrysler, Jr.

b. & c. Compote and Covered Sugar Bowl
c. 1855
Blown; colorless glass; cut checkered diamond below a row of "punty" cuts; top band of leaf and floral engraving; the monogram "C" in a leaf cartouche; panel-cut hollow stem.
H: (Compote) 9¼″ (23.5 cm) GAS.59.45 (71.4875)
H: (Covered sugar bowl) 8⅝″ with cover (21.9 cm) GAS.59.10
Gift: Walter P. Chrysler, Jr.

202. Decanter and Two Goblets
The Boston & Sandwich
Glass Company
Sandwich, Massachusetts
c. 1870–1880
Blown; colorless glass; cut; engraved scrolled ivy design; monogrammed *R.*
Note: These are all illustrated in the reprint of the 1874 *Boston Sandwich Glass Co. Catalogue.* Lee Publications, Wellesley, Mass., 1968. See pp. 73, 24, 35 for various shapes and engraved styles. A descriptive price guide at The Sandwich Glass Museum describes these shapes and the engraving.

a. Decanter
c. 1870–1880
Clark shape; lace-cut neck; star-cut bottom; solid facet-cut stopper.
H: 10½" (26.7 cm) including stopper. GAS.59.764 (71.4581)
Gift: Walter P. Chrysler, Jr.

b. & c. Two Goblets
c. 1870–1880
Barrel shape; panel-cut bowl bottom; applied straw stem; polished pontil mark.
H: 4⅞" (12.4 cm) GAS.59.550 (71.4585)
H: 3¾" (9.5 cm) GAS.60.52 (71.4580)
Gift: Walter P. Chrysler, Jr.

203. Pitcher, Tumbler, Jar
The Boston & Sandwich
Glass Company
Sandwich, Massachusetts
c. 1870–1886

a. Pitcher
c. 1870–1886
Blown colorless glass; applied clear handle; pink threading; engraved pond lilies, cattails, and a stork.
H: 7¼" (18.5 cm) GAS.59.930 (71.4630)
Gift: Walter P. Chrysler, Jr.

b. Handled Tumbler
c. 1870–1886
Blown; colorless glass; with pink threading; engraved pond lilies and cattails. (matching pitcher).
H: 5¾" (14.5 cm) GAS.59.938 (71.7055)
Gift: Walter P. Chrysler, Jr.

c. Covered Jar
c. 1870–1886
Blown; colorless glass; pink threading on jar; blue threading on the hollow stopper; engraved with a spray of leaves framing an engraved *Musk*.
H: 6¾" overall (15.9 cm) GAS.59.902 (71.4633)
Reference: Barlow, Raymond and Joan Kaiser, *The Glass Industry in Sandwich*. Vol. 4. Barlow and Kaiser Publishing Co., Wyndham, N.H., 1983. p. 253, No. 4262.
Gift: Walter P. Chrysler, Jr.

204. Finger Bowl and Wine
The Boston & Sandwich
Glass Company
Sandwich, Massachusetts
c. 1874
Blown; pale canary colored glass; engraved geometric band called "Ionic"; monogrammed P.
H: Bowl–3" (7.5 cm) GAS.65.32 (71.4895)
H: Wine–4⅝" (11.8 cm) GAS.65.32
Note: The engraved style is illustrated on p. 74 of the reprint of the 1874 *Boston and Sandwich Glass Co. Boston Catalogue*. Lee Publications, Wellesley, Mass., 1968. A matching wine goblet is in the collection of The Sandwich Glass Museum, Sandwich, Massachusetts.
Reference: Barlow, Raymond and Joan Kaiser, *The Glass Industry in Sandwich*. Vol. 4. Barlow and Kaiser Publishing, Co., Wyndham, N.H., 1983. fig. 22, p. 239.
Gift: Walter P. Chrysler, Jr.

205. Newel Post Finial
New England Glass Company
Cambridge, Massachusetts
c. 1850–1860
Silvered glass cased with colorless and ruby glass; cut with four rows of punties; star top; panel-cut stem installed with plaster on the screw-end metal socket.
H: 6" (15.2 cm) 85.72.GAN
Note: This style of glass, silvered, cased, and cut was a part of the New England Glass display at The New York Crystal Palace Exhibition of 1853–1854 by The New England Glass Company.
Gift: Kathryn K. Porter.

206. Compote
New England Glass Company
Cambridge, Massachusetts
c. 1855
Blown; cased with gold ruby over colorless glass; punty and panel-cut design, a technique now known as "overlay."
D: 10⅜" (26.3 cm) 52.18.43.GAN
Bequest: The Kate Tyler Smith Collection (see No. 140).

207. Celery Vase
M. & R. H. Sweeney
North Wheeling Flint Glass Works
Wheeling, West Virginia
c. 1844–1860
Blown; colorless glass; thick, heavy and hexagonally cut design.
H: 9¾" (24.8 cm) 84.98.GAWe
Note: This matches a vase in the collection of the Mansion Museum, Wheeling, West Virginia. Illustrated in Spillman, Jane and Estelle Farrar. *The Cut and Engraved Glass of Corning: 1868–1940*. The Corning Museum of Glass, Corning, New York, 1977. fig. 8, p. 17–19.
Museum Purchase.

208. Castor Set
New England Glass Company
Cambridge, Massachusetts
c. 1857–1862
Blown; colorless glass; cut diamond design; two bottles with steeple stoppers (for oil and vinegar), a mustard pot, and a pepper shaker each with silver tops; in a four part basket-style holder.
Mark: In relief on a shield applied to the holder bottom: *Rogers Smith/& Co/Hartford/Con.*
Reference: Rainwater, Dorothy T. *Encyclopedia of American Silver Manufacturers*. Third Edition Revised, Schiffer Publishing, Ltd., West Chester, Pennsylvania, 1986. An entry on p. 168 dates this mark 1857–1862.
H: 8½" (21.5 cm) to silver handle top 52.18.15.GAN
Bequest: The Kate Tyler Smith Collection (see No. 140).

209. Spoonholder
New England Glass Company
Cambridge, Massachusetts
c. 1860
Blown; colorless glass; cut block pattern; hollow waisted; panel-cut stem; round foot; star-cut bottom.
H: 7¼" (8.4 cm) 52.18.66.GAN
Bequest: The Kate Tyler Smith Collection (see No. 140).

210. Paperweights
New England Glass Company
Cambridge, Massachusetts
c. 1852–1880
Clockwise from top:
a. Paperweight
c. 1852–1880
Five evenly arranged yellow and pink pears and green leaves on a *latticino* ground.
D: 3″ (7.6 cm) GAN.64.38 (71.4040)
Gift: Walter P. Chrysler, Jr.
b. Paperweight
c. 1852–1880
Blown apple in colors of red and light green on a clear glass wafer.
D: 3″ (7.6 cm) GAN.64.37 (71.4042)
Gift: Walter P. Chrysler, Jr.
c. Paperweight
c. 1852–1880
Blown pear in colors of rose, pink, and light green on a clear glass wafer.
D: 2⅞″ (7.3 cm) GAN.64.4 (71.4043)
Gift: Walter P. Chrysler, Jr.
d. Paperweight
c. 1852–1880
Zachary Taylor sulphide on a blue ground.
D: 2¾″ (7 cm) GAN.64.6 (71.3789)
Gift: Walter P. Chrysler, Jr.
e. Paperweight
c. 1852–1880
Red poinsettia with green leaves on a white *latticino* ground.
D: 2¾″ (7 cm) GAN.64.55 (71.4037)
Gift: Walter P. Chrysler, Jr.
f. Paperweight (Center)
c. 1852–1880
Blown; hollow crown-style; multi-colored ribbons from central blue, pink, and white cane.
D: 2¼″ (5.7 cm) 52.18.86
Bequest: The Kate Tyler Smith Collection (see No. 140).

211. Bohemian Style Tumble-Up
New England Glass Company
Cambridge, Massachusetts
c. 1850–1860
Blown; cased with green cut through to colorless glass; oval designs; decorated gilt floral and leaf bands.
H: 7½″ overall (19 cm) 52.18.20.GAN
Note: The records of The New York Crystal Palace Exhibition of 1853–1854 list: "One set plated, cut and gilded toilette water-bottle, tumbler and stand."
Bequest: The Kate Tyler Smith Collection (see No. 140).

212. Kerosene Lamp
The Boston & Sandwich Glass Company
Sandwich, Massachusetts
c. 1865–1875
Blown; double overlay of blue glass over white glass cut through to colorless; triple-stepped ormolu decorated marble base (known as a "banquet size").
H: 32″ (81.2 cm) GAS.59.977 (71.4868)
Note: Catalogue illustration of petroleum or kerosene oil lamps and chandeliers: Crane, "The Boston and Sandwich Glass Company," *Antiques Magazine*, April 1925. p. 188.
Gift: Walter P. Chrysler, Jr.

AMERICAN ART GLASS:
1878–1900

---

213. Lava Glass Vases
Mt. Washington Glass Company
New Bedford, Massachusetts
c. 1878
a. Lava Glass Vase
c. 1878
Blown; black/brown glass; multi-color patches.
H: 5¾″ (14.6 cm) GAM.78.3 (0.465)
Gift: Walter P. Chrysler, Jr.
b. Lava Glass Vase
c. 1878
Blown; black/brown glass; multi-color patches.
H: 10″ (25.4 cm) GAM.75.4 (0.1938)
Gift: Walter P. Chrysler, Jr.
c. Lava Glass Vase
c. 1878
Blown; black/brown glass; multi-color patches; etched (matte or satin) finish.
H: 6⅞″ (17.4 cm) GAM.68.6 (71.5741)
Gift: Walter P. Chrysler, Jr.

214. Amberina Celery Vase, Tumbler, Vases, Bowl
New England Glass Company
Cambridge, Massachusetts
c. 1883–1886
a. Amberina Celery Vase
c. 1883–1886
Mold-blown; Amberina glass; diamond quilted design; tooled, square, scalloped rim.
H: 6¾″ (17.1 cm) GAN.64.12 (71.3818)
Gift: Walter P. Chrysler
b. Amberina Tumbler
c. 1883–1886
Mold-blown; optic ribbed; Amberina glass; engraved central floral leaf band.
H: 3¾″ (9.5 cm) GAN.64.14 (71.3827)
Gift: Walter P. Chrysler, Jr.
c. Amberina Trumpet Vase
c. 1883–1886
Mold-blown; optic ribbed; Amberina glass; triangular fluted rim.
H: 11″ (28 cm) GAN.59.7 (71.3833)
Gift: Walter P. Chrysler, Jr.
d. Amberina Rose Bowl
c. 1883–1886
Mold-blown; Amberina glass; inverted thumbprint design; applied amber rigaree neck band.
H: 4⅛″ (10.5 cm) GAN.59.44 (71.3838)
Gift: Walter P. Chrysler, Jr.

215. Plated Amberina Quart Size Pitcher
c. 1886
Mold-blown; optic ribbed, opal glass; cased with Amberina glass; applied amber handle.
H: 7″ (17.8 cm) GAN.65.13 (71.3849)
Gift: Walter P. Chrysler, Jr.

216. Rose Amber Pitcher (Amberina)
Mt. Washington Glass Company
New Bedford, Massachusetts
c. 1883
Blown; optic ribbed glass; engraved fern design.
H: 6" (15.2 cm) GAM.64.3 (71.5738)
Gift: Walter P. Chrysler, Jr.

217. Amberina Ice Cream Tray
Hobbs, Brockunier and Company
Wheeling, West Virginia
c. 1886
Pressed Amberina glass; Hobnail Diamond Pattern*; corners curved inward.
D: 14¼ x 9¼" (36 cm x 23.5 cm) GAW.65.1 (71.4914)
Gift: Walter P. Chrysler, Jr.
*Note: Now known as "Daisy and Button."

218. New England Peach Blow Pitcher and Tumbler
New England Glass Company
Cambridge, Massachusetts
c. 1886–1888

a. Peach Blow Pitcher
c. 1886
Blown; opaque "Wild Rose" (gold-ruby, heat-sensitive) glass (New England "Peach Blow" glass); applied, solid ribbed handle.
H: 12" (30.5 cm) GAN.66.5 (71.3811)
Gift: Walter P. Chrysler, Jr.

b. Peach Blow Tumbler
c. 1886
Blown; opaque "Wild Rose" (gold-ruby, heat-sensitive glass (New England "Peach Blow" glass).
H: (b) 3¼" (8.3 cm) GAN.66.6 (71.3801)
Note: The pitcher and tumbler are part of a lemonade set.
Gift: Walter P. Chrysler, Jr.

219. The Morgan Vase
Hobbs, Brockunier and Company
Wheeling, West Virginia
c. 1886
Blown; opal glass; cased with dark Amberina glass; separate pressed amber glass; etched (satin finish); holder of five griffins surrounding a hollow cup.
H: 10⅛" (25.7 cm) with stand. GAW.68.3 (71.4926)
Note: This is a glass replica of a Chinese porcelain vase, from the collection of Mrs. Mary J. Morgan, which sold at a New York City auction on March 8, 1886, for the then astounding price of $18,000. The price caused great excitement and the story was fully covered by the press.
Hobbs, Brockunier took advantage of their decorative glass called "Coral" which was appropriate for a replica of the Chinese porcelain. "Peachbloom" was incorrectly called "Peach Blow" in the auction catalog. The Mt. Washington Glass Company and the New England Glass Company also produced their own versions of "Peach Blow"—see above.
Reference: Revi, Albert C. *Nineteenth Century Glass*. Revised Edition, Gallahad Books, New York City, 1967. pp. 44–53.

220. Wheeling Peach Blow
Hobbs, Brockunier and Company
Wheeling, West Virginia
c. 1886

a. Peach Blow Ewer
c. 1886
Blown; opal glass; cased with Amberina; decorated with an amber glass rigaree neck band; a ribbed handle.
H: 10¼" (26 cm) GAW.75.5 (0.1541)
Gift: Walter P. Chrysler, Jr.

b. Peach Blow Vase
c. 1886
Blown; opal glass; cased with Amberina; gourd-shape.
H: 7½" (18 cm) GAW.71.1 (71.4933)
Gift: Walter P. Chrysler, Jr.

221. Decorated Satin Peach Blow Pitcher
Mt. Washington Glass Company
New Bedford, Massachusetts
c. 1886–1890
Blown; opaque pale blue glass shading to rose; enameled design of a daisy, a butterfly, a bee, and a poem by James Montgomery.
   On waste and woodland, rock
      and plain,
   Its humble buds unheaded rise;
   The rose has but a summer reign;
   The Daisy never Dies!
H: 8⅝" (21.9 cm) GAM.80.1 (80.122)
Gift: Walter P. Chrysler, Jr.

222. Satin Peach Blow Vase and Bowl
Mt. Washington Glass Company
New Bedford, Massachusetts
c. 1886–1890

a. Satin Peach Blow Vase
c. 1886–1890
Blown; heat-sensitive, opaque glass shading from rose to pale blue; enameled, thick gilt and floral design; Jack-in-the-Pulpit shape; crimped rim.
H: 10½" (26.6 cm) GAM.69.3 (71.5074)
Gift: Walter P. Chrysler, Jr.

b. Satin Peach Blow Bowl
c. 1886–1890
Mold-blown; heat-sensitive, opaque glass shading from rose to pale blue; octagonally ribbed.
H: 4½" (11.4 cm) GAM.69.5 (71.5064)
Gift: Walter P. Chrysler, Jr.

223. Agata Glass Vase, Pitcher, and Bowl
New England Glass Company
Cambridge, Massachusetts
c. 1887–1888

a. Agata Glass Vase
c. 1887–1888
Blown; "Wild Rose"/"Peach Blow" glass; tooled with four impressed "dimples" near the bottom.
H: 9⅞" (25 cm) GAN.65.23 (71.3760)
Gift: Walter P. Chrysler, Jr.

b. Agata Glass Tankard Pitcher
c. 1887–1888
Blown; "Wild Rose"/"Peach Blow" glass; cylindrical shape.
H: 11 11/16" (29.7 cm) GAN.66.1 (71.3754)
Gift: Walter P. Chrysler, Jr.

c. Agata Glass Bowl
c. 1887–1888
Blown; "Wild Rose"/"Peach Blow" glass; hemispheric shape.
H: 2¾" (7 cm) GAN.65.5 (71.3765)
Gift: Walter P. Chrysler, Jr.

224. Pomona Art Glass Cream and Sugar, Pitcher
New England Glass Company
Cambridge, Massachusetts
c. 1885–1886

a. Pomona Tankard Pitcher
c. 1885–1886
Mold-blown; diamond-quilted pattern; "First Ground" Pomona glass; amber stained top band and leaves; blue stained butterfly.
H: 9¼" (23.5 cm) GAN.67.3 (71.3732)
Gift: Walter P. Chrysler, Jr.

b. & c. Pomona Cream and Sugar
c. 1885–1886
Mold-blown; inverted thumbprint pattern; "Second Ground" Pomona glass; enameled blueberry design with red stems and gilt leaves; amber stained band around the rim and the bottom.
H: 4¼" creamer (10.8 cm) GAN.75.8 (0.1299)
H: 4" sugar (10.2 cm) GAN.75.5 (0.1298)
Gift: Walter P. Chrysler, Jr.

225. Burmese Kerosene Lamp
Mt. Washington Glass Company
New Bedford, Massachusetts
c. 1885–1890

Blown; heat-sensitive glass; satin finish (etched); enameled blue and white flowers; a metal base and a kerosene well; the inside of the shade and the chimney below the shade were left glossy.
H: 19¼" overall (49 cm) GAM.64.36 (71.5035)
Gift: Walter P. Chrysler, Jr.

226. Burmese Pitcher "Fish Swimming in a Net of Gold"*
Mt. Washington Glass Company
New Bedford, Massachusetts
c. 1885–1890

Blown; heat-sensitive glass; satin finish; enameled and gilded fish design.
H: 8 15/16" (25.2 cm) GAM.70.3
Gift: Walter P. Chrysler, Jr.
*Note: Mt. Washington's title for this decoration.

227. Burmese Candlesticks and Vase
Mt. Washington Glass Company
New Bedford, Massachusetts
c. 1885–1890

a. & b. Burmese Candlesticks
c. 1885–1890
Mold-blown; optic ribbed and diamond quilted glossy Burmese glass shading from opaque yellow to rose.
H: 7¾" (19.7 cm) GAM.79.10 (0.573) & GAM.79.11 (0.574)
Gift: Walter P. Chrysler, Jr.

c. Burmese Vase
c. 1885–1890
Blown; glossy Burmese glass; wide "Jack-in-the-Pulpit" type of rim.
H: 5⅛" (13 cm) GAM.79.12 (0.575)
Gift: Walter P. Chrysler, Jr.

228. Decorated Satin Burmese Vases
Mt. Washington Glass Company
New Bedford, Massachusetts
c. 1885–1890

a. Burmese Vase
c. 1885–1890
Blown; heat-sensitive glass; stick style; triangularly fluted rim; heavily enameled stylized floral design; on the reverse, two dragons; patches of gilt highlights on the neck.
H: 10¾" (27.3 cm) GAM.68.12 (71.4994)
Gift: Walter P. Chrysler, Jr.

b. Burmese Vase
c. 1885–1890
Blown; heat-sensitive glass; "Jack-in-the-Pulpit" shape; finely crimped rim; enameled with a daisy design in semi-pointerly style. (This was called "Queen's" pattern since samples of Burmese with this decoration were sent to Queen Victoria.)
H: 14" (35.5 cm) GAM.65.12 (71.5004)
Gift: Walter P. Chrysler, Jr.

c. Burmese Vase
c. 1885–1890
Blown; heat-sensitive glass; ovoid shape with slightly flaring neck; enameled in a stylized floral design of a rather pointerly style. The original oval, paper label remains on the polished pontil mark: *Mt. W.G. Co./BURMESE/Pat. Applied for.*
H: 6¼" (16 cm) GAM.64.14 (71.4996)
Note: Two vases (a. & c.) are enameled in a style credited to Albert Steffin, head of the decorating department, of the Mt. Washington Glass Company.
Gift: Walter P. Chrysler, Jr.

229. Royal Flemish Vase
Mt. Washington Glass Company
New Bedford, Massachusetts
c. 1889–1893

Blown; enameled with an Arabian scene.
H: 12¾" (32.5 cm) GAM.71.4 (71.5060)
Gift: Walter P. Chrysler, Jr.

230. Royal Flemish Ewer
Mt. Washington Glass Company
New Bedford, Massachusetts
c. 1889–1894

Blown; enameled mauve, blue, tan, and gilt.
H: 11⅞" (30.2 cm) GAM.79.6 (83.110)
Gift: Walter P. Chrysler, Jr.

231. Royal Flemish
Mt. Washington Glass Company
New Bedford, Massachusetts
c. 1889–1896

a. Royal Flemish Stick Vase
c. 1889–1896
Blown; enameled; peacock design; blue and lavender background.
Mark: In red enamel on polished pontil ⊕ *594*.
H: 12¾" (32.4 cm) GAM.65.52 (71.5061)

Note: Exhibited from October 20, 1986, to January 11, 1987, in the exhibition: "In Pursuit of Beauty: America and the Aesthetic Movement" at the Metropolitan Museum of Art, New York City. The object is illustrated in the catalogue of the exhibition.
Gift: Walter P. Chrysler, Jr.

b. Royal Flemish Vase
c. 1889–1896
Blown; enamel blue, violet and green sections; gilt stars and large gilt moon and white ducks flying across moon.
H: 7¾" (19.7 cm) GAM.71.3 (71.5056)
Gift: Walter P. Chrysler, Jr.
Note: Known as the Guba Duck vase as it may have been painted or designed by the New Bedford artist, Frank Guba.

232. Crown Milano Kerosene Lamp
Mt. Washington Glass Company
New Bedford, Massachusetts
c. 1893
Blown; opal satin glass; enameled scene with elephants; metal mount and kerosene well; matching shade; enameled Arabian desert.
H: 16¾" not including the chimney (42.5 cm) GAM.76.4 (0.1548)
Gift: Walter P. Chrysler, Jr.

233. Crown Milano Pilgrim Flask Style Ewer
Mt. Washington Glass Company
New Bedford, Massachusetts
c. 1893
Blown; opal satin glass; enameled shepherdess scene; smoky blue and gilt; on the reverse, birds on a flowering rose branch.
Mark: Crown Milano trademark and *504* on the polished pontil mark.
H: 10⅜" (26.3 cm) GAM.71.10 (71.5042)
Gift: Walter P. Chrysler, Jr.

234. Glossy Crown Milano Covered Jar
Mt. Washington Glass Company
New Bedford, Massachusetts
c. 1893
Blown; opal satin glass; multi-colored enameled floral design; gilded curled handles.
Mark: Red Crown Milano trademark and *1031* on polished pontil mark.
H: 5¼" including cover (13.3 cm) GAM.69.2 (71.5043)
Gift: Walter P. Chrysler, Jr.

235. Napoli Vase
Mt. Washington Glass Company
New Bedford, Massachusetts
c. 1894
Blown; colorless glass; an enameled yellow chrysanthemum design inside; thick gilt webbing outside.
Mark: Yellow script with the trademark: *Napoli/829*.
H: 15½" (39.4 cm) GAM.64.50 (71.5093)
Gift: Walter P. Chrysler, Jr.
Note: Exhibited from October 20, 1986, to January 11, 1987, in the exhibition: "In Pursuit of Beauty: America and the Aesthetic Movement" at the Metropolitan Museum of Art, New York City. The object is illustrated in the catalogue of the exhibition.

236. Cameo Glass Chandelier
Mt. Washington Glass Company
New Bedford, Massachusetts
c. 1890–1895
Blown; opal glass cased with rose glass; etched (acid-cut) cameo design; griffin design shade; bird design font holder; colorless prisms from a metal ring holding the shade.
H: 48" (122 cm) GAM.65.62 (71.6929)
Gift: Walter P. Chrysler, Jr.

237a. Vases
Smith Brothers
New Bedford, Massachusetts
c. 1874–1894

a. Opal Vase
Blown; opal glass; enameled multi-colored bird design.
Mark: Marked in script on the lower front: *Smith Bros*.
H: 7⅞" (19.6 cm) GASm.66.2 (71.5760)
Gift: Walter P. Chrysler, Jr.

b. Opal Vase
c. 1874–1894
Blown; opal glass; enameled multi-colored bird design.
Mark: Marked in script on the lower front: *Smith Bros*.
H: 5⅞" (15 cm) GASm.67.1 (71.5755)
Gift: Walter P. Chrysler, Jr.

c. Opal Vase
c. 1874–1894
Blown; opal glass; enameled multi-colored bird design.
Mark: Marked in script on the lower front: *Smith Bros*.
H: 5¾" (14.6 cm) GASm.65.1 (71.5761)
Note: Exhibited from October 20, 1986, to January 11, 1987, in the exhibition: "In Pursuit of Beauty: America and the Aesthetic Movement" at The Metropolitan Museum of Art, New York City. Illustrated in the exhibition catalogue.
Gift: Walter P. Chrysler, Jr.

237b. Pair of Opal Vases
Cristallerie de Baccarat
France
c. 1875–1885
Blown; opal glass; enameled in the Aesthetic-Japanese taste with a pink background and white *prunus*-like blossoming branches extending over and around two overlapping round medallions, one vase a blue bird, the other a robin; lower medallions faint/faded Oriental landscape scene.
Mark: In black script on the lower front left: *Baccarat*.
H: 7⅞" (20 cm) 88.99 a & b GEFB
Note: The enamel design is almost identical to The Smith Brothers vases, "a" and "c" except that the birds are illustrated in the top medallions.
Gift: Kathryn K. Porter

238. Opal Vase
Smith Brothers
New Bedford, Massachusetts
c. 1893
Blown; opal glass; pilgrim flask shape; enameled multi-color vessel "Santa Maria."
Mark: In script on the lower side: *Copyrighted by/A. E. Smith*.
H: 8½" (21.5 cm) GASm.66.1 (71.5757)
Gift: Walter P. Chrysler, Jr.

215

239. Overshot Basket
The Boston & Sandwich
Glass Company
Sandwich, Massachusetts
c. 1874
Blown; colorless glass with colorless glass "overshot"; applied solid, colorless twisted glass handle attached to the bowl with a glass wafer; decorated with an impressed masque at the handle ends; applied plain narrow foot; polished pontil mark; turned rim.
H: 12" to top of the handle (30.5 cm)
GAS.59.914 (71.4598)
Note: Illustrated on p. 2 of the reprint of the 1874 *The Boston & Sandwich Glass Co. Catalogue*. Lee Publications, Wellesley Hills, Mass., 1968. Sandwich called this type of glass "frosted," and Hobbs Brockunier, Wheeling, called theirs *Cracquelle*. Today it is known as "overshot." A hot, partly shaped bubble of glass is marvered over crushed crumbs of glass then expanded and finished.
Gift: Walter P. Chrysler, Jr.

240. Vasa Murrhina Pitcher
Vasa Murrhina Art Glass Company
Sandwich, Massachusetts
c. 1883
Mold-blown; optic ribbed glass; blue spattered white, green, spangled copper flecks; cased with colorless glass; applied solid matching handle.
H: 6⅞" (17.5 cm) GA.65.1 (71.4781)
Gift: Walter P. Chrysler, Jr.

241. Pitcher
Hobbs, Brockunier and Company
Wheeling, West Virginia
c. 1884
Mold-blown; blue spangled glass with mica flecks; cased light blue and applied blue glass handle with mica inclusions.
H: 7¾" (19.7 cm) GAW.59.4 (71.4932)
Gift: Walter P. Chrysler, Jr.

AMERICAN GLASS OF
THE ART NOUVEAU PERIOD:
1895–1920

---

242. Lava Bowl
Tiffany Glass
& Decorating Company
Corona, New York
c. 1895
Blown; blue/black textured *lava* glass over pale amber glass; an irregular spiral, gold iridescent glass band from the round bottom; the top two inches have plain gold iridescent glass, partially stretched; the interior has cased gold/rainbow iridescent glass and fits at an angle into a three legged brass stand with two prong feet.
Mark: Paper label.
H: 8½" (21.5 cm) at the highest in the stand. GAT.63.8 (71.6196)
Gift: Walter P. Chrysler, Jr.

243. Monumental Plaque
Tiffany Glass
& Decorating Company
Corona, New York
c. 1896
Blown; heavy, thick, opaque, green iridescent glass with gold, copper, and rainbow iridescence; feather outlines radiating from the center of the pontil mark/wafer; the back of the glass is a mottled blue-purple and is slightly iridescent.
Mark: Around the center of the back: *L.C.T. F894*; and a paper label.
D: 21⅞" (55.5 cm) GAT.65.26 (71.6205)
Note: This plaque may be the item in the Tiffany Favrile Glass display of the United States Pavillion at the *Exposition Universelle* in Paris in 1900, as illustrated in the period photograph reproduced in: Koch, Robert. *Louis C. Tiffany's Art Glass*. Crown Publishers, New York, 1977. No. 87 in the upper right of the first case at the left. The Chrysler Museum acquired this from a dealer who bought it from an English collection; thus, it could well have been in France or England since 1900.
Gift: Walter P. Chrysler, Jr.

244. Cypriote Vase
Tiffany Glass
& Decorating Company
Corona, New York
c. 1895
Blown; irregular, bulbous, colorless glass; spattered white glass; surface gold-rainbow iridized, faintly stretched and pock-marked in imitation of ancient excavation glass.
Mark: Engraved around polished pontil mark *Louis C. Tiffany L.C.T. D 1884*.
H: 4½" (11.5 cm) GAT.63.27 (71.6265)
Gift: Walter P. Chrysler, Jr.

245. Wisteria Table Lamp
Tiffany Glass
& Decorating Company
Corona, New York
c. 1901
Bronze tree trunk base with leaded wisteria shade of blues, amethyst, green for leaves and open lattice top which fits into the base with a central stem.
Mark: Trunk base: *Tiffany Studios New York 1073*
Shade: Bottom center stem *W*.
H: 25" (63.5 cm) GAT.66.40 (71.6932 a & b)
Gift: Walter P. Chrysler, Jr.
Note: The shade was designed by Mrs. Curtis Freshel of Boston for her home. The base was a Louis C. Tiffany design.

246. Tiffany Vase
Tiffany Glass
& Decorating Company
Corona, New York
c. 1900
Blown; ovoid shape; green iridescent glass; diagonal band of gold-green iridescence from the rim to the base.
Mark: Engraved around the polished pontil mark: *L.C.T. N2937*.
H: 5" (12.7 cm) GAT.83.2 (83.97)
Gift: Walter P. Chrysler, Jr.

247. Flower Form
Tiffany Glass
& Decorating Company
Corona, New York
c. 1900

Blown; wide, even, bowl-shape blossom with a plain, narrow, slightly flaring rim; opalescent glass; six green leaf outlines; gold iridescent glass inside; 10" long, green stem; applied gold; iridescent; ribbed dome foot.
Mark: Engraved on the turned under edge: *L.C.T.*
H: 14" to 14⅜" (35.5 cm to 36.6 cm) 84.199.GAT
Note: The Tiffany Flower Form adds an unusual uniform floral style to The Chrysler collection which includes pieces as different as the dramatic jack-in-the-pulpits and the cool white tulip.
Samuel Bing whose Parisian Gallery, *Maison de l'Art Nouveau*, gave the name to Art Nouveau, wrote the following catalog description for a 1899 London exhibition:

> ... Everything should have the ease and softness and spontaneity of nature herself. He showed us the delightfully soft effect produced by semi-opaque tints which were found, amalgamated with the vitreous material, fine veins and filaments, and blushes of colour similar to the delicate shades observable in the skins of fruit, the petal of the flower, and in the "sere and yellow leafe." And in the artist's hands there grew vegetable fruit, and flower forms, all which, while not copied from nature in a servile manner, gave one the expression of real growth and life.

Gift: Walter P. Chrysler, Jr., in honor of Dr. T. Lane Stokes for his tireless and successful leadership of The Chrysler Museum.

248. Vase
Tiffany Furnaces
Corona, New York
c. 1916

Blown; opal glass; cased with bronze iridescent glass; applied narrow blue iridescent foot and lighter blue iridescent glass neck decorated with an Egyptian "Tel el Amarna" zigzag band of light green and tan-cream glass; tan-cream band at the rim.
Mark: Engraved around the polished pontil mark: *904K L.C. Tiffany—Favrile*; a green and gold Tiffany paper label.
H: 6⅝" (16.8 cm) GAT.80.2 (80.229)
Gift: Walter P. Chrysler, Jr.

249. Plates
Tiffany Furnaces
Corona, New York
c. 1918

a. Blown; cream opal iridized glass; ¼ inch wide green iridescent rim with edges of gold iridescent; entire plate iridized.
Mark: Engraved "X299 2217M L.C. Tiffany Favrile."
D: 7" (17.8 cm) 87.478.GAT
Gift: Walter P. Chrysler, Jr.

b. Blown; cream opal mottled gold iridized glass; ¼ inch wide bright blue rim with gold edges; entire plate iridized.
Mark: Engraved on bottom "X299 L.C. Tiffany—Favrile."
D: 7" (17.8 cm) 87.479.GAT
Note: The X number indicates experimental. The technique is similar to vases called "Tel el Amarna" decorated with different color tops. Similar plates are illustrated in McKean, H.F. *The "Lost" Treasures of Louis Comfort Tiffany*. Doubleday & Company, Inc. Garden City, New York, 1980. pp. 167, fig. 164, also with X numbers. The same number on each plate may indicate this may be two of a set of eight or twelve.
Gift: Walter P. Chrysler, Jr.

250. "Nellie Virginia Sands De Lamar" Stained Glass Portrait Window
Tiffany Studios
Corona, New York
c. 1915

A triptych; side panel of wisteria draped pillars using mottled and fractured glass and some plating (two or more layers); the middle portrait panel also includes drapery glass of deep folds for the Near Eastern-style costume and painting of arms and face.
H: (a & c) 92½" (235 cm) including frames.
H: (b) 76¾" (195 cm)
H: The 3 pieces together: 86 x 106½" (218.5 cm x 275 cm) 78.477 a, b, c. GAT
Note: The window was commissioned by Joseph Raphael de Lamar in honor of his young wife, the celebrated beauty Nellie Virginia Sands for "Pembroke," his $15 million Glen Cove, Long Island, estate. It was installed above the front entrance. De Lamar, one of Tiffany's major patrons, had built a vast fortune by investing in conglomerates such as International Nickel, Dome, and Nippissing, and speculating in gold and lead ore mines in Canada and the western United States.
Gift: Walter P. Chrysler, Jr.

250a. Close-Up

251. Table Lamp
Designed by Patricia Gay
Louis C. Tiffany Furnaces, Inc.
Corona, New York
c. 1922–1925

Lamp shade: bronze; green patina; double-stepped; straight sides decorated with copper mesh; enamel band of rectangles and squares on each of the two sides.
Mark: Incised on a small, attached, rectangular metal tab *Louis C. Tiffany Furnaces, Inc/L/852.*
D: 13¼" (33.6 cm) 86.135 GAT (a)
Lamp base: matching bronze; green patina; foot shaped with five prongs, each decorated with three graduated-sized, enameled, pagoda-shaped finials topped with a gold iridescent textured glass ball.
Mark: Incised on the bottom: *Louis C. Tiffany Furnaces Inc./L/755.*
H: 22" (56 cm) overall. 86.135 GAT (b)
Note: Robert Koch, in his volume *Louis C. Tiffany's Glass—Bronzes—Lamps*. Crown Publisher, New York, 1971. p. 113, records that Patricia Gay is known to have designed a few enameled lamps when she returned to Tiffany for A. Douglas Nash. The photograph, No. 53 in the book shows a similar lamp half way up on the extreme right in the picture.
Gift: Walter P. Chrysler, Jr.

252. Vase
Quezal Art Glass and
Decorating Company
Brooklyn, New York
c. 1904
Blown; green and gold leaf design over opal glass; applied gold threading and plant forms; inside cased with gold glass.
Mark: Engraved on the polished pontil mark: *Quezal P 286*.
H: 6" (15.3 cm) GAQ.67.4 (71.6121)
Gift: Walter P. Chrysler, Jr.

253. Blown, Iridescent Glass
Quezal Art Glass and
Decorating Company
Brooklyn, New York
1903–1925

a. Jack-in-the-Pulpit Vase
c. 1903–1906
Green and gold leaf design over opal glass; the back of the "blossom" has a green and "chain-link" design; the inside is cased gold glass.
Mark: Engraved on the polished pontil mark: *Quezal 10*.
H: 13½" (34.3 cm) GAQ.66.2 (71.6120)
Gift: Walter P. Chrysler, Jr.

b. Vase
c. 1910
Green and gold glass; swirled feather outlines on mottled white glass.
Mark: Engraved on the polished pontil mark: *Quezal E444*.
H: 3¾" (9.5 cm) GAQ.63.4 (71.6138)
Gift: Walter P. Chrysler, Jr.

c. Gourd-Shape Vase
c. 1915
Red-purple and gold glass; checkered design on mottled white.
Mark: Engraved on the polished pontil mark: *Quezal 125*.
H: 4¼" (10.8 cm) GAQ.67.6 (71.6124)
Gift: Walter P. Chrysler, Jr.

254. Kew-Blas Glass
Union Glass Co.
Somerville, Massachusetts
c. 1900–1905

a. Bowl
c. 1900–1905
Blown; mottled white glass; cased with gold glass with green and gold leafing.
Mark: Engraved across the polished pontil mark: *Kew-Blas*.
H: 4¾" (12 cm) GAU.63.19 (71.6098)
Gift: Walter P. Chrysler, Jr.

b. Vase
c. 1900–1905
Blown; mottled white glass; cased with gold glass with green and gold leafing.
Mark: Engraved across the polished pontil mark *Kew-Blas*.
H: 5¼" (13.3 cm) GAU.65.4 (71.6097)
Gift: Walter P. Chrysler, Jr.

255. Steuben Aurene
Frederick Carder
Steuben Glass Works
Corning, New York
c. 1904–1925

a. Footed Bowl
Blown; calcite lined with gold aurene.
H: 5⅞" (15 cm) GASt.63.3 (71.5852)
Gift: Walter P. Chrysler, Jr.

b. Vase
Blown; cone shape blue aurene decorated with a tan iridescent leaf and vine band near the rim.
Mark: Script on bottom edge *Steuben Aurene 6298*
H: 10" (25.5 cm) GASt.65.42 (71.5717)
Gift: Walter P. Chrysler, Jr.

c. Bowl
Blown; blue/red aurene; squat with flaring rim; amber color base.
Mark: Near the polished pontil mark in engraved script: *Aurene*
H: 2⅛" (5.5 cm) GASt.63.37 (71.5716)
Gift: Walter P. Chrysler, Jr.
Note: "Aurene" is the name for Steuben's iridescent glass. The title derived from *Au*, the chemical symbol for gold and from the Latin word *aurum*, meaning gold, plus the middle English *schene* which later became "sheen." Gold Aurene was first produced and the name "Aurene" patented in 1904. About a year later blue Aurene was made. Other iridescent glass followed: brown, red, and green. White and colorless iridescent glass were called Ivrene and *Verre de Soie*.

256. Steuben Rosaline
Frederick Carder
Steuben Glass Works
Corning, New York
c. 1925–1930

a. Candlesticks
c. 1925–1930
Blown; rosaline over alabaster glass; engraved with a grape design.
H: 2⅛" (30.8 cm) GASt.64.31 & .32 (71.5881 a & b)
Gift: Walter P. Chrysler, Jr.

b. Vase
c. 1925–1930
Blown; rosaline over alabaster glass; double-etched fir cone design.
H: 6¾" (17.2 cm) GASt.65.50 (71.6015)
Gift: Walter P. Chrysler, Jr.

c. Vase
c. 1925–1930
Blown; acid-cut-back; alabaster over rose Cintra glass; "Marlene" pattern.
H: 11¾" (29.8 cm) GASt.68.5 (71.5997)
Gift: Walter P. Chrysler, Jr.

257. Acid-Etched Cameo Hunting Pattern Vase
Frederick Carder
Steuben Glass Works
Corning, New York
c. 1925–1932
Blown; alabaster and colorless glass over red glass; etched, stylized deer hunting scene.
H: 12¼" (33.6 cm) GASt.63.16 (71.6012)
Gift: Walter P. Chrysler, Jr.

258. Verre de Soie—Covered Compote
Frederick Carder
Steuben Glass Works
Corning, New York
c. 1925
Blown; applied diagonally ribbed blue iridescent glass stem; plain round *verre de soie* foot and lid; pear-shaped and colorful finial.
H: 6⅜" (16.2 cm) GASt.67.13 (71.5862)
Gift: Walter P. Chrysler, Jr.

259. Green Jade Vase
Frederick Carder
Steuben Glass Works
Corning, New York
c. 1929–1932
Mold-blown; twelve vertical ribs on flaring alabaster foot.
Mark: Acid-stamp script *Steuben* on the bottom center.
H: 9¼" (23.5 cm) 86.11.GASt.
Gift: Walter P. Chrysler, Jr.
Note: This design is similar to an earlier Joseph Hoffmann, Wiener Werkstätte gold glass vase, metal bowls, etc. illustrated on pp. 190–197, in Neuwirth, W. *Wiener Werkstätte*.

260. Bonbon Dish
Frederick Carder
Steuben Glass Works
Corning, New York
c. 1929
Pattern molded and pressed; colorless glass with mica flecks; oval shape; curved leaf design of four pressed leaves on either side; one inch wide diagonally ribbed stem; ribbed cone-shape foot.
Mark: Acid-stamp bottom side *Steuben*.
H: 5¼" (13.3 cm) 87.24.GASt.
Gift: Walter P. Chrysler, Jr.

261. Intarsia Vases and Bowl
Frederick Carder
Steuben Glass Works
Corning, New York
c. 1929
Blown; colorless glass; internal blue design.
Mark: Each with facsimile *Fred'k Carder* engraved on the lower side; vases acid-stamped with the Steuben *fleur de lis* mark on the bottom.
H: (left to right)
7¼" (18.4 cm) GASt.67.19 (71.5994)
9" (22.5 cm) GASt.71.1 (71.5993)
2½" (6.5 cm) GASt.79.2 (0.552)
Note: "Intarsia" glass is a technique similar to Orrefors' "Graal" and Daum's "Intercalary." It is difficult to finish successfully. In its creation, a two-layer vessel was blown. Then, following annealing (cooling), the piece was etched, leaving a colored design on the colorless glass. Next it was reheated, cased with another layer of colorless glass, and then it was finally worked to its desired shape.
Gift: Walter P. Chrysler, Jr.

262. Chintz Vase
A. Douglas Nash Corp.
Corona, New York
c. 1928–1931
Mold-blown; colorless glass; mottled vertical green, bubbly glass; textured panels separated by thin, bright blue, dotted lines; attached pale green foot; polished pontil mark.
H: 17½" (44.5 cm) GANa.65.5 (71.6079)
Gift: Walter P. Chrysler, Jr.

263. Punch Bowl with Silver-Gilt Stand
T. G. Hawkes & Co.
(for the glass)
Corning, New York
and
Gorham Manufacturing Co.
(for the silver)
Providence, Rhode Island
c. 1904
Bowl: blown; colorless glass; rock crystal style; engraved Art Nouveau poppy design; rim of alternating small and large scallops; plain, round peg bottom marked with the Hawkes etched trademark.
Stand: matching poppy design; silver-gilt die stamp and engraved saucer; short stem and reposé effect; die-stamped hexagonal protruding feet.
Mark: Impressed Gorham trademark and date mark on bottom.
H: 10¾" (27.3 cm) with stand.
D: 13¾" (34.9 cm) 85.133GAH
Gift: Walter P. Chrysler, Jr.

264. Bright Cut Plate
T. G. Hawkes & Co.
Corning, New York
c. 1909
Blown; colorless glass; brilliant-cut panel pattern.
Mark: Acid-stamp *Hawkes* trademark in the center.
D: 11" (28 cm) GAH.80.1 (80.5)
Note: The panel pattern design was patented on August 3, 1909.
Museum Purchase.

265. Pearl Art Glass
H. C. Fry Glass Co.
Rochester, Pennsylvania
c. 1926–1930

a. Teapot
c. 1926–1930
Blown; opalescent (Foval) glass; jade glass handle, spout, and lid finial.
H: 6¼" (16 cm) GAF.65.5 (71.5931 a & b)
Gift: Walter P. Chrysler, Jr.

b. Trivet
c. 1926–1930
Pressed opalescent (Foval) glass; three feet.
D: 6" (15 cm) GAF.65.6 (71.5931 c)
Gift: Walter P. Chrysler, Jr.

c. Bud Vase
c. 1926–1930
Blown; opalescent (Foval) glass; Jack-in-the-Pulpit style; jade glass rim.
H: 10¼" (26 cm) GAF.64.1 (71.5927)
Gift: Walter P. Chrysler, Jr.

d. Sherbet Goblet
c. 1926–1930
Blown; opalescent (Foval) glass; jade glass stem.
H: 4¾" (12 cm) GAF.65.15 (71.5960)
Gift: Walter P. Chrysler, Jr.

266. Bowl
C. Dorflinger & Sons
White Mills, Pennsylvania
c. 1917
Blown; colorless glass; brilliant cut; etched; cut panels; hammered; "Kelana Poppy"; called *No. 896*.
D: 9¼" (23.5 cm) GADr.78.1 (0.497)
Gift: Walter P. Chrysler, Jr.

267. Vases
Honesdale Decorating Company
Honesdale, Pennsylvania
c. 1910
a. Blown; amethyst over colorless glass; acid-cut cameo; stylized tulip design; enameled gilt highlights.
Mark: In gilt script across the polished pontil mark: *Honesdale*.
H: 11⅞″ (30.2 cm) GAHd.69.1 (71.5940)
Gift: Walter P. Chrysler, Jr.
b. Blown; green over colorless glass acid-cut cameo; daisy design; enameled gilt highlights.
Mark: In gilt script across the polished pontil mark: *Honesdale*.
H: 10½″ (26.7 cm) GAHd.64.2 (71.5924)
Gift: Walter P. Chrysler, Jr.

268. Vase
H. P. Sinclaire & Co.
Corning, New York
c. 1917
Mold-blown; colorless glass; optic ribbed; polished rock crystal-style; engraved daisy, scroll and leaf design; cylindrical shape; contracted at foot; slightly flaring scalloped rim.
Mark: Acid stamped on the top of the foot: *SINCLAIRE* below the trademark *S* in a wreath.
H: 14¾″ (37.5 cm) GASi.63.1 (71.5905)
Gift: Walter P. Chrysler, Jr.

269. Pearl Crystal Vase
H. P. Sinclaire & Co.
Corning, New York
c. 1920–1930
Blown; colorless glass; flaring top and bottom; Pearl Crystal; iridized inside; etched; stained Art Nouveau purple, tan, and brown glass; poppy design; gilt band at the rim and the bottom.
H: 10⅜″ (26.3 cm) 83.607.GASi.
Museum Purchase.

270. Vases
The Libbey Glass Co.
Toledo, Ohio
c. 1917
Blown; amberina glass; shading from amber to ruby.
Mark: Each with an acid-stamp *Amberina Libbey* trademark in the center of the polished pontil mark.

a. **Bud Vase**
c. 1917
Blown; amberina glass; shading from amber to ruby.
Mark: An acid-stamp *Amberina Libbey* trademark in the center of the polished pontil mark.
H: 11⅛″ (28.2 cm) GAL.75.3 (0.1955)
Gift: Walter P. Chrysler, Jr.
b. **Jack-in-the-Pulpit Style Vase**
c. 1917
Blown; amberina glass; shading from amber to ruby.
Mark: An acid-stamp *Amberina Libbey* trademark in the center of the polished pontil mark.
H: 5⅛″ (13 cm) GAL.78.3 (0.450)
Gift: Walter P. Chrysler, Jr.
c. **Bud Vase**
c. 1917
Blown; amberina glass; shading from amber to ruby.
Mark: An acid-stamp *Amberina Libbey* trademark in the center of the polished pontil mark.
H: 10⅞″ (27.5 cm) GAL.71.1 (71.5920)
Gift: Walter P. Chrysler, Jr.

271. Bowl
The Libbey Glass Co.
Toledo, Ohio
c. 1933
Blown; colorless glass; diagonally pattern-molded; aqua outlined air traps; oval shape; flaring rim; applied plain round foot.
Mark: Acid-stamped *Libbey* in a circle in the center of the polished pontil mark.
H: 4″ (10.2 cm) GAL.78.18 (0.513)
Gift: Walter P. Chrysler, Jr.
Note: This is the A. Douglas Nash design.

272. Vase
The Handel Co., Inc.
Meriden, Connecticut
c. 1910
Blown; acid-cut cameo; cased gold glass over colorless glass; stylized lotus design; chipped background.
Mark: In relief on the lower side *PALME*, and in relief on the bottom *HANDEL 4246* (George Palme, a decorator/designer).
H: 8″ (20.3 cm) GAHa.63.1 (71.5939)
Gift: Walter P. Chrysler, Jr.

273. Bright Cut Pitcher
Mt. Washington Company
New Bedford, Massachusetts
c. 1890
Blown; colorless glass; brilliant cut; star design; central raised medallion engraved; entwined monogram *C.R.A.*
H: 11 9/16″ (29 cm) GAM.69.9 (71.5769)
Gift: Walter P. Chrysler, Jr.

274. Puffy Candlestick
Pairpoint Corporation
New Bedford, Massachusetts
c. 1907–1920
Mold-blown; "Blow out" called "Puffy"; the shade is floral enameled inside; for a silver plated candle holder.
Mark: The bottom is impressed *PAIRPOINT MFG CO.*
H: 7¾″ (19.7 cm) GAP.77.5 (0.411)
Gift: Walter P. Chrysler, Jr.

275. Bowl
Pairpoint Corporation
New Bedford, Massachusetts
c. 1924
Blown; colorless glass; engraved in the Buckingham pattern in a silver plate frame.
Mark: The frame is impressed by a diamond Pairpoint " ◇ "
D: 12″ (30.5 cm) GAP.65.1 (71.5792)
Note: This was part of the Fine Arts Line of best plate with plain or "Butler Oxidized" finish.
Gift: Walter P. Chrysler, Jr.

276. Vase
Pairpoint Corporation
New Bedford, Massachusetts
c. 1924
Blown; blue glass; engraved in the Osiris pattern (stylized Egyptian motifs).
H: 10¼″ (24 cm) GAP.59.5 (71.5788)
Note: This vase is illustrated in: Wilson, Kenneth. *New England Glass and Glassmaking*. Thomas Y. Crowell Company, New York, 1972. p. 372, fig. 361 (catalog print).
Gift: Walter P. Chrysler, Jr.

277. Ruby Vase
Gundersen Glassworks, Inc.
New Bedford, Massachusetts
c. 1945
Blown; selenium ruby glass; hollow ribbed stem; round foot; one of a pair.
Mark: Silver paper Gundersen label on top of the foot: *Gundersen Masterpiece.*
H: 11¾" (30 cm) GAG.63.45 (71.5844 b)
Gift: Walter P. Chrysler, Jr.

278. Satin Finish Peach Blow
Gundersen Glassworks, Inc.
New Bedford, Massachusetts
c. 1952

a. Vase
c. 1952
Blown; shading from opaque rose glass to cream glass.
H: 12½" (30.8 cm) GAG.63.27 (71.5837)
Gift: Walter P. Chrysler, Jr.

a. Compote
c. 1952
Blown; shading from opaque rose glass to cream glass.
H: 4⅝" (11.7 cm) GAG.63.36 (71.5840)
Gift: Walter P. Chrysler, Jr.

c. Cup and Saucer
c. 1952
Blown; shading from rose glass to pale blue glass.
H: 2⅞" (7.3 cm) GAG.67.1 (71.5841 a & b)
Gift: Walter P. Chrysler, Jr.

279. Table Lamp
Bigelow Kennard & Co.
Boston, Massachusetts
c. 1910
Bronze foot and stem; three bulb sockets; round top shade holder for a red glass floral shade with green leaves on an opal background.
Mark: Incised on the bottom of the base and on a pair of metal bands attached to the shade rim: *BIGELOW STUDIOS/BIGELOW KENNARD & CO/BOSTON.*
H: 21" (53 cm) GA.63.3 (71.4913)
Note: Bigelow Kennard was a high-style Boston jewelry firm whose design studio was known to order exclusive designs, especially, silver from manufacturers such as Gorham, Tiffany & Co. and others; therefore, it is reasonable to believe a Bigelow Studio design lamp could be ordered from Tiffany Studios, New York. The bronze lamp and leaded shade are of the quality of Tiffany, and the marks are rendered in exactly the same manner as the marks on the Tiffany lamps. The floral design is more of a conventional one, and the bronze base reflects the then popular Mission style furniture.
Gift: Walter P. Chrysler, Jr.

280. Covered Jar
Durand Art Glass
Vineland, New Jersey
c. 1925
Blown; opal glass; cased gold leaf designs outlined with green glass; iridescent gold glass lid; applied gold iridescent spider webbing overall.
H: 11" (23 cm) including lid
GAD.65.6 (71.6069 a & b)
Gift: Walter P. Chrysler, Jr.

281. Iridescent Glass
Durand Art Glass
Vineland, New Jersey
c. 1924–1932

a. Vase
c. 1924–1932
Blown; iridescent rose glass with green swirls; interior neck iridescent gold.
Mark: In silver script on the polished pontil mark: *Durand 1977-8.*
H: 5⅝" (14.3 cm) GAD.65.18 (71.6060)
Gift: Walter P. Chrysler, Jr.

b. Vase
c. 1924–1932
Blown; orange-gold iridescent glass; blue-green iridescent swirls; interior swirls; interior neck and rim gold iridescent.
Mark: In silver script on the polished pontil mark: *Durand 1735.*
H: 5⅝" (14.3 cm) GAD.63.1 (71.6058)
Gift: Walter P. Chrysler, Jr.

c. Covered Jar
c. 1924–1932
Blown; yellow-gold iridescent glass; decorated with gold swirls.
Mark: In silver script on the polished pontil mark: *Durand 1991-8*; inside, a large V.
H: 11¼" overall with lid (28.5 cm) GAD.65.21 (71.6051 a & b)
Gift: Walter P. Chrysler, Jr.

282. Vase
Durand Art Glass
Vineland, New Jersey
c. 1924–1932
Blown; blue iridescent glass; beehive-shape top.
Mark: Silver script across the polished pontil mark: *Durand* and *1978-10* and a large V.
H: 10¼" (26 cm) GAD.64.3 (71.6071)
Gift: Walter P. Chrysler, Jr.

283. Crackle Lava Vase
Durand Art Glass
Vineland, New Jersey
c. 1930
Mold-blown; heavy, optic ribbed glass; cased with green glass over white; crackled decorated with gold rim and up from the bottom; interior rim and neck gold iridescent.
H: 10" (25.4 cm) GAD.74.3 (0.2283)
Gift: Walter P. Chrysler, Jr.

284. Feather (Cobweb) Design
Durand Art Glass
Vineland, New Jersey
c. 1924–1932

a. Bowl
c. 1924–1932
Blown; blue and white glass; feather outlines below the blue top; engraved rose design; iridescent amber stained foot.
Mark: Silver script across the polished pontil mark: *Durand.*
H: 5⅝" (14.4 cm) GAD.64.12 (71.6049)
Gift: Walter P. Chrysler, Jr.

b. Trumpet Vase
c. 1924–1932
Blown; red and white glass feathers in colorless glass; red glass cased rim and foot.
H: 13¾" (35 cm) GAD.63.2 (71.6037)
Gift: Walter P. Chrysler, Jr.

c. Vase
c. 1924–1932
Blown; amber glass; white feathers outlined with green glass; silver iridescent top.
H: 12" (30.5 cm) GAD.65.9 (71.6032)
Gift: Walter P. Chrysler, Jr.

285. Ruba Rombic
Art Glass Division of
Consolidated Lamp
and Glass Co.
Coraopolis, Pennsylvania
c. 1928
a. Perfume Bottle
c. 1928
Mold-blown; colorless glass with lavender wash; original label (but now lost) read: *Ruba Rombic—An Epic in Modern Art.*
H: 4¾" (12 cm) 63.114.1
Gift: Lela M. Hine.
b. Vase
c. 1928
Mold-blown; cubist design; cased "honey" glass; etched surface (frosted).
H: 6" (15.3 cm) GACs.66.1 (71.6378)
Note: A 1928 ad states "The 'Curve of Beauty' Becomes Angular in Ruba Rombic" and called it "an epic of Modern Art."
Gift: Walter P. Chrysler, Jr.

AMERICAN GLASS OF THE ART DECO PERIOD: 1920–1939

286. Orchid Bowl
Verlys of America, Inc.,
a subsidiary of Holphane
Lighting Company
Newark, Ohio
c. 1935–1940
Pressed; "*Directoire* Blue" glass; three raised orchids in a swirled design; *Verlys* script engraved on the center of the inside.
D: 14⅛" (36.2 cm) GAVe.63.1 (71.5943)
Gift: Walter P. Chrysler, Jr.
Reference: McPeek, C. and W., *Verlys of America Decorative Glass.*

287. David & Goliath Sculpture
Designed by Don Wier
Steuben Glass
Corning, New York
1959
Blown; colorless glass; mound/rock shape; engraved with a figure of a giant (Goliath) seen from behind, armed in mail with a helmet, shield, and sword; beyond, on the reverse and seen through the giant's legs, is the figure of a lightly clad boy (David) approaching, holding a sling.
H: 9¾" with a wooden stand (24.7 cm) GASt.79.7 (79.251)
Gift: Jerome L. Simon.

AMERICAN STUDIO GLASS: 1960 TO THE PRESENT DAY

288. Dominick Labino
Grand Rapids, Ohio
1910–1987
Blown; "silver schmeltz" glass; dichroic, showing green in reflected light and deep red in transmitted light.
a. Bowl
c. 1968
H: 4¾" (12 cm) GALb.68.6 (71.6923)
Mark: Engraved on the polished pontil mark: *Labino 1968.*
Gift of the artist.
b. Vase
c. 1966
H: 14" (35.5 cm) GALb.68.3 (71.7914)
Mark: Engraved on the polished pontil mark: *Labino 1966.*
Gift of the artist.

289. Ribbed Compound
Thomas J. Patti
Plainfield, Massachusetts
c. 1977
Inflated cube of horizontal, laminated layers of glass; pale gray, green, and smoke colored glass; three rust threads at the bottom and one across the top beneath a slightly iridescent layer.
Mark: Engraved on the lower side: *Patti '77.*
H: 4⅜" (11 cm) GA.80.19 (80.251)
Museum Purchase with funds provided from the Paramount Industrial Companies Contemporary Glass Purchase Fund.

290. Sculpture
Harvey K. Littleton
Spruce Pine, North Carolina
c. 1978
Blown; solid loop; clear glass; cased with gray-green glass with white lines and then clear, polished ends.
Mark: At one end with a diamond point: *Harvey K. Littleton 1978 ©.*
H: 13½" (34.3 cm) GALH.79.1 (79.144)
Museum Purchase with grants from the Virginia Commission of the Arts and Humanities and the National Endowment of the Arts.

291. Sea Form/ Macchia Assemblage
Dale Chihuly
Tacoma, Washington
1982
The assemblage of objects below was produced by a highly skilled team of glassblowers orchestrated by the artist-glassblower-designer, Dale Chihuly. They used innovative molding, threading, twisting, and glassblowing techniques.
Museum Purchases with funds from the Paramount Industrial Companies Contemporary Glass Purchase Fund.
a. Clam
1982
Blown; shades of pink and opalescent glass trailings; irregular shapes.
Rim: 19¾ x 15¾" (50.5 cm x 40 cm) GA.82.1a (82.17 a)
Note: The large "clam" holds most of the pieces, but the arrangement need not be static. The assemblage can be changed in the same way that on the beach shells are moved by the tides.
b. Ripple Shell
1982
Blown; shades of pink and opalescent glass trailings; irregular shapes.
Rim: 9½ x 7½" (24 cm x 19 cm) GA.82.1b (82.17 b)
c. Macchia Form
1982
Blown; shades of pink and opalescent glass trailings; irregular shapes. As above, but it also includes dark red spots.
Rim: 8½ x 4⅜" (21.5 cm x 11 cm) GA.82.1c (82.17 c)

d. Sea Urchin Form
1982
Blown; shades of pink and opalescent glass trailings; irregular shapes.
H: 2¹/₁₆" (5.4 cm) GA.82.1d
(82.17 d)

e. Sea-Form/Jelly Fish Form
1982
Blown; shades of pink and opalescent glass trailings; irregular shapes; dome shape; green-brown spots radiating from the polished pontil mark top.
Rim: 4 x 3½" (10.2 cm x 9 cm) GA.82.1e
(82.17 e)

292. Moon Series #11 Sculpture
Mark Peiser
Penland, North Carolina
1983
Cast; flat bottom; slanted top; triangular shape; colorless glass; included swirls; streaks and veils of glass of tans, blue, and a gold "full moon."
Mark: Engraved on the bottom edge: *PEISER 15065 83 ©*.
H: 7¹/₁₆" (18.2 cm) GA.83.17 (83.179)
Museum Purchase with funds from the Paramount Industrial Companies Contemporary Glass Purchase Fund.

293. Golden Triskelion Sculpture
Michael M. Glancy
Rehoboth, Massachusetts
1984
Blown; cased, colorless glass over opaque golden/yellow glass; sandblasted with triangular graduated projections (larger at middle); electroplated with copper, leaving the outer triangular surface uncoated.
Mark: Diamond point engraved on the bottom edge: *MICHAEL M. GLANCY 1984, GOLDEN TRISKELLION* and impressed (sandblasted) on the bottom: *Glancy* in script.
H: 5⅛" (13 cm) 84.422.GA
Note: The techniques used to make this diminutive sculpture are complicated and time-consuming. First a two-layer glass vase was blown of opaque yellow cased with colorless glass. Carving by sandblasting followed, with a design cut into a rubber resist adhered to the vase. Next, the powdery sandblasted surface was polished with hydrofluoric acid. The copper electroplating was last. The body of the vessel was copper plated leaving only the glass of the triangular projections showing. Golden color glass now glows through pale blue iridescent metal. The copper surface will oxidize, slowly changing the patina.
Museum Purchase with funds from the Paramount Industrial Companies Contemporary Glass Purchase Fund.

BIBLIOGRAPHY

BIBLIOGRAPHY

A combination of references included in the text and suggested background readings.

Amic, Yolande. *L'Opaline Française au XIX Siècle.* Librairie Gründ. Paris. 1952.

Arwas, Victor. *Glass: Art Nouveau to Art Deco.* Harry N. Abrams, Inc. New York, New York. 1987.

"Austrian Architecture and Decoration." *1912 Studio Yearbook of Decorative Arts.* Studio, Ltd. London. 1912.

Auth, Susan H. *Ancient Glass at the Newark Museum.* The Newark Museum. Newark, New Jersey. 1976.

Avila, George C. *The Pairpoint Glass Story.* George C. Avila and the New Bedford Glass Society. New Bedford, Massachusetts. 1978.

Barlow, Raymond and Joan Kaiser. *The Glass Industry in Sandwich.* Vol. 3. Barlow and Kaiser Publishing Company. Wyndham, New Hampshire. 1987.

Barlow, Raymond and Joan Kaiser. *The Glass Industry in Sandwich.* Vol. 4. Barlow and Kaiser Publishing Company. Wyndham, New Hampshire. 1983.

Bloch-Dormant, Janine. *The Art of French Glass: 1860–1914.* The Vendome Press. New York, New York. 1980.

Boston and Sandwich Glass Company Catalogue (1874). Lee Publications. Wellesley Hills, Massachusetts. 1968.

Brunhammer, Yvonne, *et al.*, ed. *Art Nouveau Belgium-France.* Rice University. Houston, Texas. 1976.

Centenaire de Daum au Japon. Exhibition du Musée d'Art Moderne de Hokkaido. Sapporo, Japan. 1980.

Charles Schneider, Maître Verrier. Exposition. Le Louvre des Antiquaires. Paris. 1984.

Crane, Priscilla C. "The Boston and Sandwich Glass Company." *Antiques Magazine.* Vol. 7. April 1925. p. 188.

Darr, Patrick T. *A Guide to Art and Pattern Glass.* Pilgrim House Publication Company. Springfield, Massachusetts. 1960.

Daum, Noël. *Daum maîtres verriers.* Editions Denoël. Lausanne. 1980. (English edition 1985)

Daum, Noël. *La pâte de verre.* Editions Denoël. Lausanne. 1984.

Doros, Paul. *The Tiffany Collection of The Chrysler Museum at Norfolk.* The Chrysler Museum. Norfolk, Virginia. 1978.

Duncan, Alistair and Georges de Bartha. *Glass by Gallé.* Thames and Hudson. London. 1984.

Elbern, Victor H. "A Group of Later Roman Glass Goblets from Cologne." *Journal of Glass Studies.* Vol. VIII. The Corning Museum of Glass. Corning, New York. 1966. p. 66.

Elsholz Collection, The William. Vol. 1. Richard Bourne Auction. Hyannis, Massachusetts. December 10, 1986.

Elsholz Collection, The William. Vol. 3. Richard Bourne Auction. Hyannis, Massachusetts. November 17, 1987.

Fauster, Carl. *Libbey Glass.* Len Beach Press. Toledo, Ohio. 1979.

Gardner, Paul V. *The Glass of Frederick Carder.* Crown Publishers. New York, New York. 1971.

Garner, Philippe. *Emile Gallé.* Academy Editions. London. 1976.

Goldstein, Sidney M. *Pre-Roman and Early Roman Glass in the Corning Museum of Glass.* The Corning Museum of Glass. Corning, New York. 1979.

Goldstein, Sidney, L. S. Rakow and J. K. Rakow. *Cameo Glass: Masterpieces from 2,000 Years of Glassmaking.* The Corning Museum of Glass. Corning, New York. 1982.

Harden, Donald B., J. S. Painter, R. S. Pinder-Wilson, and Hugh Tait. *Masterpieces of Glass*. The Trustees of the British Museum. British Museum Publications, Ltd. London. 1968.

Hayward, Jane. "Roman Mold-Blown Glass at Yale University." *Journal of Glass Studies*. Vol. IV. The Corning Museum of Glass. Corning, New York. 1962. p. 50.

Hilschenz-Mynek, Helga und Helmut Ricke. *Glas: Historismus-Jugendstil-Art Deco*. Band I, Frankreich. Die Sammlung Hentrich im Kunstmuseum Düsseldorf. Prestel Verlag. München. 1985.

In Pursuit of Beauty: America and the Aesthetic Movement. The Metropolitan Museum of Art. New York, New York. 1987.

Innes, Lowell. *Early Glass of the Pittsburgh District 1797–1900*. Carnegie Institute Museum of Art. Pittsburgh, Pennsylvania. 1949.

Innes, Lowell. "Pittsburgh Glass." *Antiques Magazine*. Vol. 54. December 1948. p. 419.

Innes, Lowell. *Pittsburgh Glass, 1797–1891: A History and Guide for Collectors*. Houghton Mifflin Company. Boston. 1976.

Journal of Glass Studies. Volumes 1ff. The Corning Museum of Glass. Corning, New York. 1959–. An annual publication with articles about a wide variety of glass subjects.

Klesse, Brigette und Gisela Reineking-von Brock. *Glas*. Kunstgewerbe Museum der Stadt Köln. Köln. 1973.

Klesse, Brigette und Axel von Saldern. *500 Jahre Glaskunst, Sammlung Bieman*. ABC Verlag. Zürich. 1978.

Koch, Robert. *Louis C. Tiffany's Art Glass*. Crown Publishers. New York City, New York. 1977.

Koch, Robert. *Louis C. Tiffany's Glass—Bronzes—Lamps*. Crown Publishers. New York City, New York, 1971.

Koch, Robert. *Louis C. Tiffany, Rebel in Glass*. Updated, Third Edition. Crown Publishers. New York City, New York. 1982.

Lalique et Cie, René. *Lalique Glass: The Complete Illustrated Catalogue for 1932*. The Corning Museum of Glass in association with Dover Publications. New York City, New York. 1981.

Lee, Ruth Webb. *Early American Pressed Glass*. Ruth Webb Lee. Northboro, Massachusetts. 29th edition, 1946.

Lee, Ruth Webb. *Sandwich Glass*. Lee Publications. Wellesley Hills, Massachusetts. 10th edition, 1966.

Lee, Ruth Webb. *Victorian Glass*. Ruth Lee Webb. Northboro, Massachusetts. 1944.

Lee, Ruth Webb and James Rose. *American Glass Cup Plates*. R. W. Lee. Northboro, Massachusetts. 1948.

McKean, H. F. *The "Lost" Treasures of Louis Comfort Tiffany*. Doubleday and Company. New York City, New York. 1980.

McKearin, George and Helen McKearin. *American Glass*. Crown Publishers. New York City, New York. 1969.

McPeek, C. and W. *Verlys of America Decorative Glass: 1935–1957*. Carole and Wayne McPeek. Newark, Ohio. 1972.

Neal, Logan W. and Dorothy B. Neal. *Pressed Glass Salt Dishes of the Lacy Period: 1825–1850*. L. W. and D. B. Neal. Philadelphia, Pennsylvania. 1962.

Neuwirth, Waltraud. *Das Glas des Jugendstils*. Prestel Verlag. München. 1973.

Neuwirth, Waltraud. *Wiener Werkstätte*. Vol. I. Selbstverlag. Dr. Waltruad Neuwirth. Wien. 1985. (German/English text)

Neuwirth, Waltraud. *Glass: 1905–1925, Volume 1, from Art Nouveau to Art Deco*. (German/English text) Selbstverlag. Dr. Waltraud Neuwirth. Wien. 1985.

Neuwirth, Waltraud. *Wiener Werkstätte: Avantgarde, Art Deco, Industrial Design.* Selbstverlag. Dr. Waltraud Neuwirth. Wien. 1984.

Newman, Harold. *An Illustrated Dictionary of Glass.* Thames and Hudson, Ltd. London. 1977.

Peterson, Arthur. *Glass Patents and Patterns.* Celery City Printing Company. Sanford, Florida. 1973.

Polak, Ada. *Modern Glass.* Faber and Faber. London. 1962.

Rainwater, Dorothy T. *Encyclopedia of American Silver Manufacturers.* 3rd Edition Revised. Schiffer Publishing, Ltd. West Chester, Pennsylvania. 1986.

Revi, Albert C. *American Art Nouveau Glass.* Schiffer Publishing Ltd. Exton, Pennsylvania. Fifth Printing, 1981.

Revi, Albert C. *Nineteenth Century Glass.* Revised Edition. Gallahad Books. New York City, New York. 1967.

Rose, James. "American Blown Glass in the Seigfred Collection." *Antiques Magazine.* Vol. 91. June 1967. p. 747.

Rose, James H. *The Story of American Pressed Glass of the Lacy Period, 1825–1850.* The Corning Museum of Glass. Corning, New York. 1954.

Saldern, Axel von. *German Enameled Glass.* Crown Publishers. New York City, New York. 1971.

Salon des Industries du Moblier Exposition. Librairie d'Art Décoratif Armand Guérinet, 140, Faubourg Saint-Martin, 140, Paris. 1905.

Schmidt, Robert. *Die Gläser der Sammlung Mühsam.* Band I. Verlag für Kunstwissenschaft. Berlin. 1914.

Schmidt, Robert. *Die Gläser der Sammlung Mühsam.* Band II, *neu folge.* Ernst Wassmuth. Berlin. 1926.

Spillman, Jane. *American and English Pressed Glass in the Corning Museum of Glass.* The Corning Museum of Glass. Corning, New York. 1981.

Spillman, Jane and Estelle Ferrar. *The Cut and Engraved Glass of Corning: 1868–1940.* The Corning Museum of Glass. Corning, New York. 1977.

Tait, Hugh. *The Golden Age of Venetian Glass.* Published for The Trustees of The British Museum. British Museum Publications, Ltd. London. 1979.

Verriers Français Contemporaries Art et Industrie. Musée des Arts Décoratifs. Paris. 1982. A36.

The Virginia Museum of Fine Arts. Richmond, Virginia. 1979. *Loïe Fuller: Magician of Light.* A loan exhibition organized by Margaret Hail Harris.

Warmus, William. *Emile Gallé: Dreams into Glass.* The Corning Museum of Glass. Corning, New York. 1984.

Watkins, Lura W. *Cambridge Glass 1818 to 1888: The Story of the New England Glass Company.* Marshall Jones Company. Boston. 1930.

Watkins, Lura W. "Pressed Glass of the New England Glass Company." *Journal of Glass Studies.* Vol. XIII. The Corning Museum of Glass. Corning, New York. 1970.

Weatherman, Hazel Marie. *Colored Glassware of the Depression Era 2.* Weatherman Glassbooks. Springfield, Missouri. Second Printing, 1977.

Weinberg, Gladys Davidson. "Mold-Blown Beakers with Mythological Scenes." *Journal of Glass Studies.* Vol. XIV. The Corning Museum of Glass. Corning, New York. 1972.

Wilson, Kenneth M. A book review of *Pittsburgh Glass* by Lowell Innes; cover photograph also. *National Early American Glass Club Bulletin.* No. 119. March 1977. Boston, Massachusetts. p. 93.

Wilson, Kenneth. *New England Glass and Glassmaking.* Thomas Y. Crowell Company. New York City, New York. 1972.